Famous American Statesmen

Sarah Knowles Bolton

Famous American Statesmen

The present edition is a reproduction of previous publication of this classic work. Minor typographical errors may have been corrected without note, however, for an authentic reading experience the spelling, punctuation, and capitalization have been retained from the original text.

ISBN: 978-1-64799-244-6

PREFACE

"With the great, one's thoughts and manners easily become great; ... what this country longs for is personalities, grand persons, to counteract its materialities," says Emerson. Such lives as are sketched in this book are a constant inspiration, both to young and old. They teach Garfield's oft-repeated maxim, that "the genius of success is still the genius of labor." They teach patriotism—a deeper love for and devotion to America. They teach that life, with some definite and noble purpose, is worth living.

I have written of Abraham Lincoln, one of our greatest and best statesmen, in "Poor Boys Who Became Famous," which will explain its omission from this volume.

S. K. B.

CONTENTS

GEORGE WASHINGTON

The "purest figure in history," wrote William E. Gladstone of George Washington.

When Frederick the Great sent his portrait to Washington, he sent with it these remarkable words: "From the oldest general in Europe to the greatest general in the world."

Lord Brougham said: "It will be the duty of the historian, and the sage of all nations, to let no occasion pass of commemorating this illustrious man; and until time shall be no more will a test of the progress which our race has made in wisdom and virtue be derived from the veneration paid to the immortal name of Washington."

At Bridge's Creek, Maryland, in a substantial home, overlooking the Potomac, George Washington was born, February 22, 1732. His father, Augustine, was descended from a distinguished family in England—William de Hertburn, a knight who owned the village of Wessyngton (Washington). He married, at the age of twenty-one, Jane Butler, who died thirteen years afterward. Two years after her death he married Mary Ball, a beautiful girl, of decided character and sterling common-sense. She became a good mother to his two motherless children; two having died in early childhood.

Six children were born to them, George being the eldest. The opportunities for education in the new world, especially on a plantation, were limited. From one of his father's tenants, the sexton of the parish, George learned to read, write, and cipher. He was fond of military things, and organized among the scholars sham-fights and parades; taking the position usually of commander-in-chief, by common consent. This love of war might have come through the influence of his half-brother Lawrence, who had been in battles in the West Indies.

When George was twelve, his father died suddenly, leaving Mary Ball, at thirty-seven, to care for her own five children, one having died in infancy, and two boys by the first marriage. Fortunately, a large estate was left them, which she was to control till they became of age.

While she loved her children tenderly, she exacted the most complete obedience. She was dignified and firm, yet cheerful, and possessed an unusually sweet voice. To his mother's intelligence and moral training George attributed his success in life. She would

1

gather her children about her daily, and read to them from Matthew Hale's "Contemplations, Divine and Moral." The book had been loved by the first wife, who wrote in it, "Jane Washington." Under this George's mother wrote, "and Mary Washington." This book was always preserved with tender care at Mount Vernon, in later years. Such teaching the boy never forgot. When he was thirteen, he wrote "Rules of courtesy and decent behavior in company and conversation," one hundred and ten maxims, which seemed to have great influence over him.

At fourteen, he desired to enter the navy, and a midshipman's warrant was procured by his brother Lawrence. Now he could see the world, and was happy at the prospect. All winter long, the mother's heart ached as she thought of the separation, and finally, when his clothing had been taken on board of a British man-of-war, her affection triumphed, and the lad was kept in his Virginia home; kept for a great work. However disappointed he may have been, his mother's word was law. Those who learn to obey in youth learn also how to govern in later life. George went back to school to study arithmetic and land-surveying. He was thorough in his work, and his record books, still preserved, are neat and exact.

It is never strange that a boy who idolizes his mother should think other women lovable. At fifteen, the bashful, manly boy had given his heart to a girl about his own age, and it was long before he could conquer the affection. A year later he wrote to a friend, "I might, was my heart disengaged, pass my time very pleasantly, as there's a very agreeable young lady lives in the same house; but as that's only adding fuel to fire, it makes me the more uneasy, for by often and unavoidably being in company with her revives my former passion for your Lowland Beauty; whereas, was I to live more retired from young women, I might in some measure alleviate my sorrows, by burying that chaste and troublesome passion in the grave of oblivion."

Years afterwards, the son of this "Lowland Beauty," General Henry Lee, became a favorite with Washington in the Revolutionary War; possibly all the more loved from tender recollections of the mother. General Lee was the father of General Robert E. Lee of the Confederate Army, in the Civil War.

At sixteen, the real work of Washington's life began. Lord Fairfax of Virginia desired his large estates beyond the Blue Ridge to be surveyed, and he knew that the youth had the courage to meet the Indians in the wilderness, and would do his work well.

Washington and a friend set out on horseback for the valley called by the Indians Shenandoah, "the daughter of the stars." He made a record daily of the beauty of the trees—every refined soul

2

loves trees almost as though they were human—and the richness of the soil, and selected the best sites for townships. In his diary he says, "A blowing, rainy night, our straw upon which we were lying took fire, but I was luckily preserved by one of our men awaking when it was in a flame." For three years he lived this exposed life, sleeping out-of-doors, gaining self-reliance, and a knowledge of the Indians, which knowledge he was soon to need.

Trouble had begun already in the Ohio valley, between the French and English, in their claims to the territory. No wonder a sachem asked, "The French claim all the land on one side of the Ohio, the English claim all the land on the other side—now, where does the Indians' land lie?"

Virginia began to make herself ready for a war which seemed inevitable. She divided her province into military districts, and placed one in charge of the young surveyor, only nineteen, who was made adjutant general with the rank of major. Thus early did the sincere, self-poised young man take upon himself great responsibilities. Washington at once began to make himself ready for his duties, by studying military tactics; taking lessons in field-work from his brother Lawrence, and sword exercise from a soldier. This drill was broken in upon for a time by the illness and death of Lawrence, of whom he was very fond, and whom he accompanied to the Barbadoes. Here George took small-pox, from which he was slightly marked through life. The only child of Lawrence soon died, and Mount Vernon came to George by will. He was now a person of wealth, but riches did not spoil him. He did not seek ease; he sought work and honor.

Matters were growing worse in the Ohio valley. The Virginians had erected forts at what is now Pittsburg; and the French, about fifteen miles south of Lake Erie. Governor Dinwiddie determined to make a last remonstrance with the French who should thus presume to come upon English territory. The way to their forts lay through an unsettled wilderness, a distance of from five hundred to six hundred miles. Some Indian tribes favored one nation; some the other. The governor offered this dangerous commission—a visit to the French—to several persons, who hastened to decline with thanks the proffered honor.

Young Washington, with his brave heart, was willing to undertake the journey, and started September 30, 1753, with horses, tents, and other necessary equipments. They found the rivers swollen, so that the horses had to swim. The swamps, in the snow and rain, were almost impassable. At last they arrived at the forts, early in December. Washington delivered his letter to the French, and an answer was written to the governor.

3

On December 25, Washington and his little party started homeward. The horses were well-nigh exhausted, and the men dismounted, put on Indian hunting-dress, and toiled on through the deepening snow. Washington, in haste to reach the governor, strapped his pack on his shoulders, and, gun in hand, with one companion, Mr. Gist, struck through the woods, hoping thus to reach the Alleghany River sooner, and cross on the ice. At night they lit their camp-fire, but at two in the morning they pursued their journey, guided by the north star.

Some Indians now approached, and offered their services as guides. One was chosen, but Washington soon suspected that they were being guided in the wrong direction. They halted, and said they would camp for the night, but the Indian demurred, and offered to carry Washington's gun, as he was fatigued. This was declined, when the Indian grew sullen, hurried forward, and, when fifteen paces ahead, levelled his gun and fired at Washington. Gist at once seized the savage, took his gun from him, and would have killed him on the spot had not the humane Washington prevented. He was sent home to his cabin with a loaf of bread, and told to come to them in the morning with meat. Probably he expected to return before morning, and, with some other braves, scalp the two Americans; but Washington and Gist travelled all night, and reached the Alleghany River opposite the site of Pittsburg.

Unfortunately, the river was not frozen as they had hoped, but was full of broken ice. All day long they worked to construct a raft, with but one hatchet between them. After reaching the middle of the river the men on the raft were hurled into ten feet of water by the floating ice, and Washington was saved from drowning only by clinging to a log. They lay till morning on an island in the river, their clothes stiff with frost, and the hands and feet of poor Gist frozen by the intense cold. The agony of that night Washington never forgot, even in the horrors of Valley Forge.

Happily, the river had grown passable in the night, and they were able to cross to a place of safety. He came home as speedily as possible and delivered the letter to Governor Dinwiddie. His journal was sent to London and published, because of the knowledge it gave of the position of the French. The young soldier of twenty-one had escaped death from the burning straw in surveying, from the Indian's gun, and from drowning. He had shown prudence, self-devotion, and heroism. "From that moment," says Irving, in his delightful life of Washington, "he was the rising hope of Virginia." And he was the rising hope of the new world as well.

The polite letter brought by Washington to the governor had declared that no Englishmen should remain in the Ohio valley!

4

Dinwiddie at once determined to send three hundred troops against the French, and offered the command to Washington. He shrunk from the charge, and it was given to Colonel Fry, while he was made second in command. Fry soon died, and Washington was obliged to assume control. He was equal to the occasion. He said, "I have a constitution hardy enough to encounter and undergo the most severe trials, and, I flatter myself, resolution enough to face what any man dares, as shall be proved when it comes to the test."

The test soon came. In the conflict which followed he was in the thickest of the fight, one man being killed at his side. He wrote to his brother, "I heard the bullets whistle, and, believe me, there is something charming in the sound." Years afterward, he said, when he had long known the sorrows of war, "If I said that, it was when I was young."

At Great Meadows, below Pittsburg, he was defeated by superior numbers, and obliged to evacuate the fort, but the Virginia House of Burgesses thanked him for his bravery.

The next year, England sent out General Braddock, who had been over forty years in the service, a fearless but self-willed officer, to take command of the American forces. Washington gladly joined him as an aide-de-camp. They set out with two thousand soldiers, toward Fort du Quesne (Pittsburg). The amount of baggage astonished Washington, who well knew the swamps and mountains that must be crossed, but Braddock could not be influenced. He remarked to Benjamin Franklin, "These savages may indeed be a formidable enemy to raw militia, but upon the king's regular and disciplined troops, sir, it is impossible they should make an impression." How great an "impression" savages could make upon the "king's regular and disciplined troops" was soon to be shown.

The march was exceedingly difficult. Sometimes a whole day was spent in cutting a passage of two miles over the mountains. Washington urged that the Virginia Rangers be put to the front, as they understood Indian warfare. The general haughtily opposed it, and the regulars in brilliant uniforms, bayonets fixed, colors flying, and drums beating, swept over the open plain to battle, July 9, 1755.

Suddenly there was a cry, "The French and Indians!" The Indian yell struck terror to the hearts of the regulars. They fired in all directions, killing their own men. A panic ensued. Braddock tried to rally his men; even striking them with the flat of his sword. Five horses were killed under him. At last a bullet entered his lungs, and he fell, mortally wounded. Then the men fled precipitately, falling over their dead comrades. Out of eighty-six officers, twenty-six were killed and thirty-six wounded. Nearly half of the whole army were dead or disabled. The Virginia Rangers covered the retreat of the flying regulars, and thus saved a remnant. Braddock, bequeathing his horse and servant, Bishop, to Washington, died broken-hearted, moaning, "Who would have thought it!... We shall better know how to deal with them another time." Washington tenderly read the funeral service, and Braddock was buried in the new and wild country he had come to save.

Washington escaped as by a miracle. He wrote his brother, "By the all-powerful dispensations of Providence, I have been protected beyond all human probability or expectation; for I had four bullets through my coat, and two horses shot under me, yet escaped unhurt, though death was levelling my companions on every side of me." Through life, this man, great in all that mankind prize, loved and believed in the Christian religion. Agnosticism had no charms for him.

Washington returned to Mount Vernon temporarily broken in health, and his fond mother, who was living at the old homestead, wrote begging that he would not again enter the service. In reply he said, "Honored Madam," for thus he always addressed her, "if it is in my power to avoid going to the Ohio again, I shall; but if the command is pressed upon me by the general voice of the country, and offered upon such terms as cannot be objected against, it would reflect dishonor on me to refuse it; and that, I am sure, must and ought to give you greater uneasiness than my going in an honorable command."

Braddock's defeat electrified the colonies. Governor Dinwiddie at once called for troops, and Washington was made "commander-in-chief of all the forces raised or to be raised in Virginia." For two years he protected the people in the attacks of the Indians; his heart so full of pity that he wrote the governor, "I solemnly declare, if I know my own mind, I could offer myself a willing sacrifice to the butchering enemy, provided that would contribute to the people's ease." No wonder that such self-sacrifice and unselfishness won the homage of the State, and later of the nation.

In May, 1758, the condition of the army was such, the men so poorly clad and paid, that the young commander decided to go to Williamsburg to lay the matter before the council. In crossing the Pamunkey, a branch of the York River, he met a Mr. Chamberlayne, who pressed him to dine, more especially as a charming lady was visiting at his house. He accepted the invitation, and there met Martha Custis, a widow of twenty-six, two months younger than himself; a bright, frank, agreeable woman, with dark eyes and hair, below the middle size, a contrast indeed to his striking physique, six feet two inches tall, blue eyes, and grave demeanor.

Martha Dandridge, with amiable disposition and winning manners, had been married at seventeen to Daniel Parke Custis, thirty-eight, a kind-hearted and wealthy land-owner. For seven years they lived at "The White House," on the Pamunkey River, where he died, leaving two children, John Parke and Martha Parke Custis. Mrs. Custis had come to visit the Chamberlaynes, and now was to meet the most popular officer in Virginia.

The dinner passed pleasantly, and then Bishop, the servant, brought Colonel Washington's horse and his own to the gate at the appointed hour. But Colonel Washington did not appear. The afternoon seemed like a dream, for love takes no account of time. The sun was setting when he rose to go, but Major Chamberlayne urged his guest to pass the night. Probably he did not need to be urged, for the most sublime and beautiful force in all the world now controlled the fearless Washington. The next morning he hastened to Williamsburg, transacted his business, returned to the home of Martha Custis, where he spent a day and a night, and left her his betrothed.

The commander went back to camp with a new joy in living. The army was now ordered against Fort du Quesne, under Brigadier-General Forbes of Great Britain; Washington leading the Virginia troops. He seized a moment before leaving to write to Mrs. Custis, which letter Lossing gives in his interesting lives of Mary and Martha Washington:—

"A courier is starting for Williamsburg, and I embrace the opportunity to send a few words to one whose life is now inseparable from mine. Since that happy hour when we made our pledges to each other, my thoughts have been continually going to you as to another self. That an all-powerful Providence may keep us both in safety is the prayer of your ever faithful and

"Ever affectionate friend,"
G. Washington."

The army marched again over the field where the bones of Braddock's men were bleaching in the sun, and approached the fort, only to find that the French had deserted it after setting it on fire, and retreated down the river. Washington, who led the advance, planted the British flag over the smoking ruin of what is now Pittsburg, so called from the illustrious William Pitt. With the French driven out of the Ohio valley, Washington, having served five years in the army, resigned, and married Martha Custis, January 6, 1759. Every inch a soldier he must have looked in his suit of blue cloth lined with red silk, and ornamented with silver trimmings; while his bride wore white satin, with pearl necklace and ear-rings, and pearls in her hair. She rode home in a coach drawn by six horses, while Colonel Washington, on a fine chestnut horse, attended by a brilliant cortége, rode beside her carriage.

The year previous, 1758, Washington had been elected a member of the Virginia Assembly. When he took his seat, the House gave him an address of welcome. He rose to reply, trembled, and could not say a word. "Sit down, Mr. Washington," said the speaker; "your modesty equals your valor, and that surpasses the power of any language I possess." Beautiful attributes of character, not always found in conjunction; valor and modesty!

For three months Washington remained at the home of his wife, to attend to the business of the colony; becoming also guardian of her two pretty children, four and six years of age, whom he seemed to love as his own. When he took his bride to Mount Vernon to live, he wrote to a relative, "I am now, I believe, fixed in this spot with an agreeable partner for life; and I hope to find more happiness in retirement than I ever experienced in the wide and bustling world."

For seventeen years he lived on his estate of eight thousand acres, delighting in agriculture, and enjoying the development of the two children. The years passed quickly, for affection, the holiest thing on earth, brought rest and contentment. He or she is rich who possesses it. To have millions, and yet live in a home where there is no affection, is to be poor indeed.

He was an early riser; in winter often lighting his own fire, and reading by candle-light; retiring always at nine o'clock. He was vestryman in the Episcopal Church, and judge of the county court, as well as a member of the House of Burgesses. So honest was he that a barrel of flour marked with his name was exempted from the usual inspection in West India ports.

Into this busy and happy life came sorrow, as it comes into other lives. Martha Parke Custis, a gentle and lovely girl, died of consumption at seventeen, Washington kneeling by her bedside in prayer as her life went out. The love of both parents now centred in the boy of nineteen, John Parke Custis, who, the following year, left Columbia College to marry a girl of sixteen, Eleanor Calvert. While Washington attended the wedding, Mrs. Washington could not go, in her mourning robes, but sent an affectionate letter to her new daughter.

The quiet life at Mount Vernon was now to be wholly changed. The Stamp Act and the oppressive taxes had stirred America. When the taxes were repealed, save that on tea, and Lord North was urged to include tea also, he said: "To temporize is to yield; and the authority of the mother country, if it is not now supported, will be relinquished forever; a total repeal cannot be thought of till America is prostrate at our feet." Mrs. Washington, like other lovers of liberty, at once ceased to use tea at her table.

When the First Continental Congress met at Philadelphia, September 5, 1774, Washington was among the delegates chosen by Virginia. He rode thither on horseback, with his brilliant friends Patrick Henry and Edmund Pendleton. When they departed from Mount Vernon, the patriotic Martha Washington said: "I hope you will all stand firm. I know George will.... God be with you, gentlemen."

To a relative, who wrote deprecating Colonel Washington's "folly," his wife answered: "Yes; I foresee consequences—dark days, and darker nights; domestic happiness suspended; social enjoyments abandoned; property of every kind put in jeopardy by war, perhaps; neighbors and friends at variance, and eternal separations on earth possible. But what are all these evils when compared with the fate of which the Port Bill may be only a threat? My mind is made up, my heart is in the cause. George is right; he is always right. God has promised to protect the righteous, and I will trust him." Blessings on the woman who, in the darkest hour, knows how to be as the sunlight in her hope and trust, and to be well-nigh a divine embodiment of courage and fortitude! Truly said Schiller: "Honor to women! they twine and weave the roses of heaven into the life of man."

Congress remained in session fifty-one days. When the results of its labors were put before the House of Lords, the great Chatham said: "When your lordships look at the papers transmitted to us from America; when you consider their decency, firmness, and wisdom, you cannot but respect their cause, and wish to make it your own. For myself, I must declare and avow that, in the master states of the world, I know not the people, or senate, who, in such a complication of difficult circumstances, can stand in preference to the delegates of America assembled in General Congress at Philadelphia."

When Patrick Henry was asked, on his return home, who was the greatest man in Congress, he replied: "If you speak of eloquence, Mr. Rutledge of South Carolina is by far the greatest orator; but if you speak of solid information and sound judgment, Colonel Washington is unquestionably the greatest man on that floor." Wise reading in all these years had given Washington "solid information," and "sound judgment" was partly an inheritance from noble Mary Washington.

People all through New England were arming themselves. General Gage, who had been sent to Boston with British troops, said: "It is surprising that so many of the other provinces interest themselves so much in this. They have some warm friends in New York, and I learn that the people of Charleston, South Carolina, are as mad as they are here." He was soon to possess a more thorough knowledge of the American character.

The Boston troops, under Gage, numbered about four thousand. He determined to destroy the military stores at Concord, on the night of April 18, 1775. It was to be done secretly, but as soon as the British regiment started, under Colonel Smith and Major Pitcairn, for Concord, the bells of Boston rang out, cannon were fired, and Paul Revere, with Prescott and Davis, rode at full speed in the bright moonlight to Lexington, to alarm the neighboring country. When cautioned against making so much noise, Revere replied: "You'll have noise enough here before long—the regulars are coming out."

Long before morning, nearly two-score of the villagers, under Captain Parker, gathered on the green, near the church, waiting for the red-coats, who came at double-quick, Major Pitcairn exclaiming, "Disperse, ye villains! Lay down your arms, ye rebels, and disperse!" Unmoved, Captain Parker said to his men, "Don't fire unless you are fired on; but if they want a war, let it begin here." The Revolutionary War began there, to end only when America should be free. Seven Americans were killed, nine wounded, and the rest were put to flight; but the blood shed on Lexington Green made liberty dear to every heart.

The British now marched to Concord, where, in the early morning, they found four hundred and fifty men gathered to receive them. Captain Isaac Davis, who said, when his company led the force, "I haven't a man that is afraid to go," was killed at the first shot, at the North Bridge.

The British troops destroyed all the stores they could find, though most had been removed, and then started toward Boston. All along the road the indignant Americans fired upon them from behind stone fences and clumps of bushes. Tired by their night march, having lost three hundred in killed and wounded, over three times as many as the Americans, they were glad to meet Lord Percy coming to their rescue with one thousand men. He formed a hollow square, and, faint and exhausted, the soldiers threw themselves on the ground within it, and rested.

The whole country seemed to rise to arms. Men came pouring into Boston with such weapons as they could find. Noble Israel Putnam of Connecticut left his plough in the field and hastened to the war.

May 10, Congress again met at Philadelphia. They sent a

second petition to King George, which John Adams called an "imbecile measure." They made plans for the support of the army already gathered at Cambridge from the different States. Who should be the commander of this growing army? Then John Adams spoke of the gentleman from Virginia, "whose skill and experience as an officer, whose independent fortune, great talents, and excellent universal character, would command the approbation of all America, and unite the cordial exertions of all the colonies better than any other person in the Union." June 5, Washington was unanimously elected commander-in-chief.

Rising in his seat, and thanking Congress, he modestly said: "I beg it may be remembered by every gentleman in the room that I this day declare, with the utmost sincerity, I do not think myself equal to the command I am honored with. As to pay, I beg leave to assure the Congress that, as no pecuniary consideration could have tempted me to accept this arduous employment, at the expense of my domestic ease and happiness, I do not wish to make any profit of it. I will keep an exact account of my expenses. Those, I doubt not, they will discharge, and that is all I desire." He wrote to his wife: "I should enjoy more real happiness in one month with you at home than I have the most distant prospect of finding abroad if my stay were to be seven times seven years. But as it has been a kind of destiny that has thrown me upon this service, I shall hope that my undertaking it is designed to answer some good purpose.... I shall feel no pain from the toil or danger of the campaign; my unhappiness will flow from the uneasiness I know you will feel from being left alone." No wonder Martha Washington loved him; so brave that he could meet any danger without fear, yet so tender that the thought of leaving her brought intense pain.

He was now forty-three; the ideal of manly dignity. He at once started for Boston. Soon a courier met him, telling him of the battle of Bunker Hill—how for two hours raw militia had withstood British regulars, killing and wounding twice as many as they lost, and retreating only when their ammunition was exhausted. When Washington heard how bravely they had fought, he exclaimed: "The liberties of the country are safe." Under the great elm (still standing) at Cambridge, Washington took command of the army, July 3, 1775, amid the shouts of the multitude and the roar of artillery. His headquarters were established at Craigie House, afterward the home of the poet Longfellow. Here Mrs. Washington came later, and helped to lessen his cares by her cheerful presence.

The soldiers were brave but undisciplined; the terms of enlistment were short, thus preventing the best work. To provide powder was well-nigh an impossibility. For months Washington drilled his army, and waited for the right moment to rescue Boston from the hands of the British. Generals Howe, Clinton, and Burgoyne had been sent over from England. Howe had strengthened Bunker Hill, and, with little respect for the feelings of the Americans, had removed the pulpit and pews from the Old South Church, covered the floor with earth, and converted it into a riding-school for Burgoyne's light dragoons. They did not consider the place sacred, because it was a "meeting-house where sedition had often been preached."

The "right moment" came at last. In a single night the soldiers fortified Dorchester Heights, cannonading the enemy's batteries in the opposite direction, so that their attention was diverted from the real work. When the morning dawned of March 5, 1776, General Howe saw, through the lifting fog, the new fortress, with the guns turned upon Boston. "I know not what to do," he said. "The rebels have done more work in one night than my whole army would have done in one month."

He resolved to attack the "rebels" by night, and for this attack twenty-five hundred men were embarked in boats. But a violent storm set in, and they could not land. The next day the rain poured in torrents, and when the second night came Dorchester Heights were too strong to be attacked. The proud General Howe was compelled to evacuate Boston with all possible dispatch, March 17, the navy going to Halifax and the army to New York. The Americans at once occupied the city, and planted the flag above the forts. Congress moved a vote of thanks to Washington, and ordered a gold medal, bearing his face, as the deliverer of Boston from British rule.

The English considered this a humiliating defeat. The Duke of Manchester, in the House of Lords, said: "British generals, whose name never met with a blot of dishonor, are forced to quit that town, which was the first object of the war, the immediate cause of hostilities, the place of arms, which has cost this nation more than a million to defend."

The Continental Army soon repaired to New York. Washington spared no pains to keep a high moral standard among his men. He said, in one of his orders: "The general is sorry to be informed that the foolish and wicked practice of profane cursing and swearing—a vice heretofore little known in an American army—is growing into fashion. He hopes the officers will, by example as well as influence, endeavor to check it, and that both they and the men will reflect that we can have little hope of the blessing of Heaven on our arms if we insult it by our impiety and folly. Added to this, it is a vice so mean and low, without any temptation, that

12

every man of sense and character detests and despises it." Noble words!

Great Britain now realized that the fight must be in earnest, and hired twenty thousand Hessians to help subjugate the colonies. When Admiral Howe came over from England, he tried to talk about peace with "Mr." Washington, or "George Washington, Esq.," as it was deemed beneath his dignity to acknowledge that the "rebels" had a general. The Americans could not talk about peace, with such treatment.

Soon the first desperate battle was fought, on Long Island, August 27, 1776, partly on the ground now occupied by Greenwood Cemetery, between eight thousand Americans and more than twice their number of trained Hessians. Washington, from an eminence, watched the terrible conflict, wringing his hands, and exclaiming, "What brave fellows I must this day lose!"

The Americans were defeated, with great loss. Washington could no longer hold New York with his inadequate forces. With great energy and promptness he gathered all the boats possible, and then, so secretly that even his aides did not know his intention, nine thousand men, horses, and provisions, were ferried over the East River. A heavy fog hung over the Brooklyn side, as though provided by Providence, while it was clear on the New York side, so that the men could form in line. Washington crossed in the last boat, having been for forty-eight hours without sleep.

In the morning, the astonished Englishmen learned that the prize had escaped. A Tory woman, the night before, seeing that the Americans were crossing the river, sent her colored servant to notify the British. A Hessian sentinel, not understanding the servant, locked him up till morning, when, upon the arrival of an officer, his errand was known; but the knowledge came too late!

On October 28, the Americans were again defeated, at White Plains, Howe beginning the engagement. The condition of the Continental Army was disheartening. They were half-fed and half-clothed; the "ragged rebels," the British called them. There was sickness in the camp, and many were deserting. Washington said, "Men just dragged from the tender scenes of domestic life, unaccustomed to the din of arms, totally unacquainted with every kind of military skill, are timid, and ready to fly from their own shadows. Besides, the sudden change in their manner of living brings on an unconquerable desire to return to their homes." So great-hearted was the commander-in-chief, though on the field of battle he had no leniency toward cowards.

Washington retreated across New Jersey to Trenton. When he reached the Delaware River, filled with floating ice, he collected all

13

the boats within seventy miles, and transported the troops, crossing last himself. Lord Cornwallis, of Howe's army, came in full pursuit, reached the river just as the last boat crossed, and looked in vain for means of transportation. There was nothing to be done but to wait till the river was frozen, so that the troops could cross on the ice.

Washington, December 20, 1776, told John Hancock, President of Congress, "Ten days more will put an end to the existence of our army." Yet, on the night of December 25, Christmas, with almost superhuman courage, he determined to recross the Delaware, and attack the Hessians at Trenton. The weather was intensely cold. The boats, in crossing, were forced out of their course by the drifting ice. Two men were frozen to death. At four in the morning, the heroic troops took up the line of march, the snow and sleet beating in their faces. Many of the muskets were wet and useless. "What is to be done?" asked the men. "Push on, and use the bayonet," was the answer.

At eight in the morning, the Americans rushed into the town. "The enemy! the enemy!" cried the Hessians. Their leader, Colonel Rahl, fell, mortally wounded. A thousand men laid down their arms and begged for quarter. Washington recrossed the Delaware with his whole body of captives, and the American nation took heart once more. That fearful crossing of the Delaware, in the blinding storm, and the sudden yet marvellous victory which followed, will always live among the most pathetic and stirring scenes of the Revolution. A few days later, January 3, 1777, with five thousand men, Washington defeated Cornwallis at Princeton, exposing himself so constantly to danger that his officers begged him to seek a place of safety.

The third year of the Revolutionary War had opened. France, hating England, sympathizing with America in her struggle for liberty, and being encouraged in this sympathy by the honored Benjamin Franklin, loaned us money, supplied muskets and powder, and many troops under such brave leaders as Lafayette and De Kalb. The year 1777, although our forces were defeated at Brandywine and Germantown, witnessed the defeat of a part of Burgoyne's army at Bennington, Vermont, and, on the 17th of October, the remaining part at Saratoga; over five thousand men, seven thousand muskets, and a great quantity of military stores. Two months later, France made a treaty of alliance with the United States, to the joy of the whole country.

On December 11, Washington went into winter-quarters at Valley Forge, on the west side of the Schuylkill, about twenty miles from Philadelphia. Trees were felled to build huts, the men toiling with scanty food, often barefoot, the snow showing the marks of their bleeding feet. Continental money had so depreciated that forty dollars were scarcely equal in value to one silver dollar. Sickness was decreasing the forces. Washington wrote to Congress: "No less than two thousand eight hundred and ninety-eight men are now in camp unfit for duty, because they are barefoot and otherwise naked." From lack of blankets, he said, "numbers have been obliged, and still are, to sit up all night by fires, instead of taking comfortable rest in a natural and common way." A man less great would have been discouraged, but he trusted in a power higher than himself, and waited in sublime dignity and patience for the progress of events. Martha Washington had come to Valley Forge to share in its privations, and to minister to the sick and the dying.

The years 1778 and 1779 dragged on with their victories and defeats. The next year, 1780, the country was shocked by the treason of Benedict Arnold, who, having obtained command at West Point, had agreed to surrender it to the British for fifty thousand dollars in money and the position of brigadier-general in their army. On September 21, Sir Henry Clinton sent Major John André, an adjutant-general, to meet Arnold. He went ashore from the ship Vulture, met Arnold in a wood, and completed the plan. When he went back to the boat, he found that a battery had driven her down the river, and he must return by land. At Tarrytown, on the Hudson, he was met by three militiamen, John Paulding, David Williams, and Isaac Van Wart, who at once arrested him, and found the treasonable papers in his boots. He offered to buy his release, but Paulding assured him that fifty thousand dollars would be no temptation.

André was at once taken to prison. While there he won all hearts by his intelligence and his cheerful, manly nature. He had entered the British army by reason of a disappointment in love. The father of the young lady had interfered, and she had become the second wife of the father of Maria Edgeworth. André always wore above his heart a miniature of Honora Sneyd, painted by herself. Just before his execution as a spy, he wrote to Washington, asking to be shot. When he was led to the gallows, October 2, 1780, and saw that he was to be hanged, for a moment he seemed startled, and exclaimed, "How hard is my fate!" but added, "It will soon be over." He put the noose about his own neck, tied the handkerchief over his eyes, and, when asked if he wished to speak, said only: "I pray you to bear witness that I meet my fate like a brave man." His death was universally lamented. In 1821, his body was removed to London by the British consul, and buried in Westminster Abbey.

Every effort was made to capture Arnold, but without success. He once asked an American, who had been taken prisoner by the

British, what his countrymen would have done with him had he been captured. The immediate reply was: "They would cut off the leg wounded in the service of your country, and bury it with the honors of war. The rest of you they would hang."

In 1781, the condition of affairs was still gloomy. Some troops mutinied for lack of pay, but when approached by Sir Henry Clinton, through two agents, offering them food and money if they would desert the American cause, the agents were promptly hanged as spies. Such was the patriotism of the half-starved and half-clothed soldiers.

In May of this year, Cornwallis took command of the English forces in Virginia, destroying about fifteen million dollars worth of property. Early in October, Washington with his troops, and Lafayette and De Rochambeau with their French troops, gathered at Yorktown, on the south bank of the York River. For ten days the siege was carried on. The French troops rendered heroic service. Washington was so in earnest that one of his aids, seeing that he was in danger, ventured to suggest that their situation was much exposed. "If you think so, you are at liberty to step back," was the grave response of the general. Shortly afterwards a musket-ball fell at Washington's feet. One of his generals grasped his arm, exclaiming, "We can't spare you yet." When the victory was finally won, Washington drew a long breath and said, "The work is done and well done." Cornwallis surrendered his whole army, over seven thousand soldiers, October 19, 1781.

The American nation was thrilled with joy and gratitude. Washington ordered divine service to be performed in the several divisions, saying, "The commander-in-chief earnestly recommends that the troops not on duty should universally attend, with that seriousness of deportment and gratitude of heart which the recognition of such reiterated and astonishing interpositions of Providence demands of us." Congress appointed a day of thanksgiving and prayer, and voted two stands of colors to Washington and two pieces of field-ordnance to the brave French commanders. When Lord North, Prime Minister of England, heard of the defeat of the British, he exclaimed, "Oh, God! it is all over!"

The nearly seven long years of war were ended, and America had become a free nation.

The articles of peace between Great Britain and the United States were not signed till September 3, 1783. On November 4 the army was disbanded, with a touching address from their idolized commander. On December 4, in the city of New York, in a building on the corner of Pearl and Broad Streets, Washington said good-bye to his officers, losing for a time his wonderful self-command. "I

16

cannot come to each of you to take my leave," he said, "but shall be obliged if each of you will come and take me by the hand." Tears filled the eyes of all, as, silently, one by one, they clasped his hand in farewell, and passed out of his sight.

Then Washington repaired to Annapolis, where Congress was assembled, and at twelve o'clock on the 23d of December, before a crowded house, offered his resignation. "Having now finished the work assigned me, I retire from the great theatre of action; and bidding an affectionate farewell to this august body, under whose orders I have long acted, I here offer my commission, and take my leave of all the employments of public life." "Few tragedies ever drew so many tears from so many beautiful eyes," said one who was present.

The beloved general returned to Mount Vernon, to enjoy the peace and rest which he needed, and the honor of his country which he so well deserved. John Parke Custis, Mrs. Washington's only remaining child, had died, leaving four children, two of whom— Eleanor, two years old, and George Washington, six months old— the general adopted as his own. These brought additional "sweetness and light" into the beautiful home.

The following year the Marquis de Lafayette was a guest at Mount Vernon, and went to Fredericksburg to bid adieu to Washington's mother. When he spoke in high praise of the man whom he so loved and honored, Mary Washington replied quietly, "I am not surprised at what George has done, for he was always a good boy." Blessed mother-heart, that, in training her child, could look into the future, and know, for a certainty, the result of her love and progress! She died August 25, 1789.

Three years later—May 25, 1787—a convention met at Philadelphia to form a more perfect union of the States, and frame a Constitution. Washington was made President of this convention. He had long been reading carefully the history and principles of ancient and modern confederacies, and he was intelligently prepared for the honor accorded him. When the Constitution was finished, and ready for his signature, he said: "Should the United States reject this excellent Constitution, the probability is that an opportunity will never again be offered to cancel another in peace; the next will be drawn in blood."

When the various States, after long debate, had accepted the Constitution, a President must be chosen, and that man very naturally was the man who had saved the country in the perils of war. On the way to New York, then the seat of government, Washington received a perfect ovation. The bells were rung, cannon fired, and men, women, and children thronged the way. Over the bridge crossing the Delaware the women of Trenton had erected an arch of evergreen and laurel, with the words, "The defender of the mothers will be the protector of the daughters." As he passed, young girls scattered flowers before him, singing grateful songs. How different from that crossing years before, with his worn and foot-sore army, amid the floating ice!

The streets of New York were thronged with eager, thankful people, who wept as they cheered the hero, now fifty-seven, who had given nearly his whole life to his country's service. On April 30, 1789, the inauguration took place. At nine o'clock in the morning, religious services were held in all the churches. At twelve, in the old City Hall, in Wall Street, Chancellor Livingston administered the oath of office, Washington stooping down and kissing the open Bible, on which he laid his hand; "the man," says T. W. Higginson, "whose generalship, whose patience, whose self-denial, had achieved and then preserved the liberties of the nation; the man who, greater than Cæsar, had held a kingly crown within reach, and had refused it." Washington had previously been addressed by some who believed that the Colonies needed a monarchy for strong government. Astonished and indignant, he replied: "I am much at a loss to conceive what part of my conduct could have given encouragement to an address which to me seems big with the greatest mischiefs that can befall my country." After taking the oath, all proceeded on foot to St. Paul's Church, where prayers were read.

The next four years were years of perplexity and care in the building of the nation. The great war debt, of nearly one hundred millions, must be provided for by an impoverished nation; commerce and manufactures must be developed; literature and education encouraged, and Indian outbreaks quelled. With a love of country that was above party-spirit, with a magnanimity that knew no self-aggrandizement, he led the States out of their difficulties. When his term of office expired, he would have retired gladly to Mount Vernon for life, but he could not be spared. Thomas Jefferson wrote him: "The confidence of the whole Union is centred in you.... North and South will hang together, if they have you to hang on."

Again he accepted the office of President. Affairs called more than ever for wisdom. He continually counselled "mutual forbearances and temporizing yieldings on all sides." France, who had helped us so nobly, was passing through the horrors of the Revolution. The blood of kings and people was flowing. The French Republic having sent M. Genet as her minister to the United States, he attempted to fit out privateers against Great Britain. Washington knew that America could not be again plunged into a war with

England without probable self-destruction; therefore he held to neutrality, and demanded the recall of Genet. The people earnestly sympathized with France, and, but for the strong man at the head of the nation, would have been led into untold calamities. The country finally came to the verge of war with France, but when Napoleon overthrew the Directory, and made himself First Consul, he wisely made peace with the United States.

Washington declined a third term of office, and sent his beautiful farewell address to Congress, containing the never-to-be-forgotten words: "Of all the dispositions and habits which lead to political prosperity, religion and morality are indispensable supports.... Observe good faith and justice towards all nations. Cultivate peace and harmony with all."

He now returned to Mount Vernon to enjoy the rest he had so long desired. Three years later the great man lay dying, after a day's illness, from affection of the throat. From difficulty of breathing, his position was often changed. With his usual consideration for others, he said to his secretary, "I am afraid I fatigue you too much." "I feel I am going," he said to his physicians. "I thank you for your attentions, but I pray you to take no more trouble about me." The man who could face death on the battle-field had no fears in the quiet home by the Potomac. In the midst of his agony, he could remember to thank those who aided him, and regret that he was a source of care or anxiety. Great indeed is that soul which has learned that nothing in God's universe is a little thing.

At ten in the evening he gave a few directions about burial. "Do you understand me?" he asked. Upon being answered in the affirmative, he replied, "'Tis well!" when he expired without a struggle, December 14, 1799. Mrs. Washington, who was seated at the foot of the bed, said: "'Tis well. All is now over. I shall soon follow him. I have no more trials to pass through."

On December 18, 1799, the funeral procession took its way to the vault on the Mount Vernon estate. The general's horse, with his saddle and pistols, led by his groom in black, preceded the body of his dead master. A deep sorrow settled upon the nation. The British ships lowered their flags to half-mast. The French draped their standards with crape.

Martha Washington died three years later, May 22, 1802, and was buried beside her husband. In 1837, the caskets were enclosed in white marble coffins, now seen by visitors to Mount Vernon. In 1885 a grand marble monument, five hundred and fifty-five feet high, was completed on the banks of the Potomac, at the capital, to the immortal Washington.

Truly wrote Jefferson: "His integrity was most pure; his

justice the most inflexible I have ever known; no motives of interest or consanguinity, of friendship or hatred, being able to bias his decision. He was, indeed, in every sense of the word, a wise, a good, and a great man."

The life of George Washington will ever be an example to young men. He had the earnest heart and manner—never trivial—which women love, and men respect. He had the courage which the world honors, and the gentleness which made little children cling to him. He controlled an army and a nation, because he understood the secret of power—self-control. Well does Mr. Gladstone call him the "purest figure in history;" unselfish, fair, patient, heroic, true.

BENJAMIN FRANKLIN

"To say that his life is the most interesting, the most uniformly successful, yet lived by any American, is bold. But it is, nevertheless, strictly true." Thus writes John Bach McMaster, in his life of the great statesman.

In the year 1706, January 6 (old style), in the small house of a tallow-chandler and soap-boiler, on Milk Street, opposite the Old South Church, Boston, was born Benjamin Franklin. Already fourteen children had come into the home of Josiah Franklin, the father, by his two wives, and now this youngest son was added to the struggling family circle. Two daughters were born later.

The home was a busy one, and a merry one withal; for the father, after the day's work, would sing to his large flock the songs he had learned in his boyhood in England, accompanying the words on his violin.

From the mother, the daughter of Peter Folger of Nantucket, "a learned and godly Englishman," Benjamin inherited an attractive face, and much of his hunger for books, which never lessened through his long and eventful life. At eight years of age, he was placed in the Boston Latin School, and in less than a year rose to the head of his class. The father had hoped to educate the boy for the ministry, but probably money was lacking, for at ten his school-life was ended, and he was in his father's shop filling candle-moulds and running on errands.

For two years he worked there, but how he hated it! not all labor, for he was always industrious, but soap and candle-making were utterly distasteful to him. So strongly was he inclined to run away to sea, as an older brother had done, that his father obtained a situation for him with a maker of knives, and later he was apprenticed to his brother James as a printer.

Now every spare moment was used in reading. The first book which he owned was Bunyan's "Pilgrim's Progress," and after reading this over and over, he sold it, and bought Burton's "Historical Collections," forty tiny books of travel, history, biography, and adventure. In his father's small library, there was nothing very soul-stirring to be found. Defoe's "Essays upon Projects," containing hints on banking, friendly societies for the relief of members, colleges for girls, and asylums for idiots, would not be very interesting to most boys of twelve, but Benjamin read every essay, and, strange to say, carried out nearly every "project" in later life. Cotton Mather's "Essays to do Good," with several leaves torn out, was so eagerly read, and so productive of good, that Franklin wrote, when he was eighty, that this volume "gave me such a turn of thinking as to have an influence on my conduct through life; for I have always set a greater value on the character of a doer of good than on any other kind of reputation; and, if I have been a useful citizen, the public owe the advantage of it to that book."

As the boy rarely had any money to buy books, he would often borrow from the booksellers' clerks, and read in his little bedroom nearly all night, being obliged to return the books before the shop was opened in the morning. Finally, a Boston merchant, who came to the printing-office, noticed the lad's thirst for knowledge, took him home to see his library, and loaned him some volumes. Blessings on those people who are willing to lend knowledge to help the world upward, despite the fact that book-borrowers proverbially have short memories, and do not always take the most tender care of what they borrow.

When Benjamin was fifteen, he wrote a few ballads, and his brother James sent him about the streets to sell them. This the father wisely checked by telling his son that poets usually are beggars, a statement not literally true, but sufficiently near the truth to produce a wholesome effect upon the young verse-maker.

The boy now devised a novel way to earn money to buy books. He had read somewhere that vegetable food was sufficient for health, and persuaded James, who paid the board of his apprentice, that for half the amount paid he could board himself.

Benjamin therefore attempted living on potatoes, hasty pudding, and rice; doing his own cooking,—not the life most boys of sixteen would choose. His dinner at the printing-office usually consisted of a biscuit, a handful of raisins, and a glass of water; a meal quickly eaten, and then, O precious thought! there was nearly a whole hour for books.

He now read Locke on "Human Understanding," and Xenophon's "Memorable Things of Socrates." In this, as he said in later years, he learned one of the great secrets of success; "never using, when I advanced anything that may possibly be disputed, the words certainly, undoubtedly, or any others that give the air of positiveness to an opinion; but rather say, I conceive or apprehend a thing to be so and so; it appears to me, or I should think it so or so, for such and such reasons; or, it is so, if I am not mistaken.... I wish well-meaning, sensible men would not lessen their power of doing good by a positive, assuming manner, that seldom fails to disgust, tends to create opposition, and to defeat every one of those purposes for which speech was given to us, to wit, giving or receiving information or pleasure.... To this habit I think it principally owing that I had early so much weight with my fellow-citizens, when I proposed new institutions or alterations in the old, and so much influence in public councils when I became a member; for I was but a bad speaker, never eloquent, subject to much hesitation in my choice of words, and yet I generally carried my points." A most valuable lesson to be learned early in life.

Coming across an odd volume of the "Spectator," Benjamin was captivated by the style, and resolved to become master of the production, by rewriting the essays from memory, and increasing his fulness of expression by turning them into verse, and then back again into prose.

James Franklin was now printing the fifth newspaper in America. It was intended to issue the first—Publick Occurrences—monthly, or oftener, "if any glut of occurrences happens." When the first number appeared, September 25, 1690, a very important "occurrence happened," which was the immediate suspension of the paper for expressions concerning those in official position. The next newspaper,—the Boston News-Letter,—a weekly, was published April 24, 1704; the third was the Boston Gazette, which James was engaged to print, but, being disappointed, started one of his own, August 17, 1721, called the New England Courant. The American Weekly Mercury was printed in Philadelphia six months before the Courant.

Benjamin's work was hard and constant. He not only set type, but distributed the paper to customers. "Why," thought he, "can I not write something for the new sheet?" Accordingly, he prepared a manuscript, slipped it under the door of the office, and the next week saw it in print before his eyes. This was joy indeed, and he wrote again and again.

The Courant at last gave offence by its plain speaking, and it ostensibly passed into Benjamin's hands, to save his brother from punishment. The position, however, soon became irksome, for the passionate brother often beat Benjamin, till at last he determined to run away. As soon as this became known, James went to every office, told his side of the story, and thus prevented Benjamin from obtaining work. Not discouraged, the boy sold a portion of his precious books, said good-bye to his beloved Boston, and went out into the world to more poverty and struggle.

Three days after this, he stood in New York, asking for work at the only printing-office in the city, owned by William Bradford. Alas! there was no work to be had, and he was advised to go to Philadelphia, nearly one hundred miles away, where Andrew Bradford, a son of the former, had established a paper. The boy could not have been very light-hearted as he started on the journey.

After thirty hours by boat, he reached Amboy, and then travelled fifty miles on foot across New Jersey. It rained hard all day, but he plodded on, tired and hungry, buying some gingerbread of a poor woman, and wishing that he had never left Boston. His money was fast disappearing.

Finally he reached Philadelphia.

"I was," he says in his autobiography, "in my working dress, my best clothes being to come round by sea. I was dirty from my journey; my pockets were stuffed out with shirts and stockings, and I knew no soul nor where to look for lodging. I was fatigued with travelling, rowing, and want of rest. I was very hungry, and my whole stock of cash consisted of a Dutch dollar and about a shilling in copper. The latter I gave the people of the boat for my passage, who at first refused it, on account of my rowing, but I insisted on their taking it; a man being sometimes more generous when he has but a little money than when he has plenty, perhaps through fear of being thought to have but little.

"Then I walked up the street, gazing about, till near the Market-house I met a boy with bread. I had made many a meal on bread, and, inquiring where he got it, I went immediately to the baker's he directed me to, in Second Street, and asked for biscuit, intending such as we had in Boston; but they, it seems, were not made in Philadelphia. Then I asked for a threepenny loaf, and was told they had none such. So, not considering or knowing the difference of money, and the greater cheapness, nor the names of bread, I bade him give me threepenny-worth of any sort. He gave me, accordingly, three great puffy rolls. I was surprised at the quantity, but took it, and, having no room in my pockets, walked off with a roll under each arm, and eating the other.

"Thus I went up Market Street as far as Fourth Street, passing by the door of Mr. Read, my future wife's father; when she, standing at the door, saw me, and thought I made, as I certainly did, a most awkward, ridiculous figure. Then I turned and went down Chestnut Street and part of Walnut Street, eating my roll all the way, and, coming round, found myself again at Market Street wharf, near the boat I came in, to which I went for a draught of the river water; and, being filled with one of my rolls, gave the other two to a woman and her child that came down the river in the boat with us, and were waiting to go farther."

After this, he joined some Quakers who were on their way to the meeting-house, which he too entered, and, tired and homeless, soon fell asleep. And this was the penniless, runaway lad who was eventually to stand before five kings, to become one of the greatest philosophers, scientists, and statesmen of his time, the admiration of Europe and the idol of America. Surely, truth is stranger than fiction.

The youth hastened to the office of Andrew Bradford, but there was no opening for him. However, Bradford kindly offered him a home till he could find work. This was obtained with Keimer, a printer, who happened to find lodging for the young man in the house of Mr. Read. As the months went by, and the hopeful and earnest lad of eighteen had visions of becoming a master printer, he confided to Mrs. Read that he was in love with, and wished to marry, the pretty daughter, who had first seen him as he walked up Market Street, eating his roll. Mr. Read had died, and the prudent mother advised that these children, both under nineteen, should wait till the printer proved his ability to support a wife.

And now a strange thing happened. Sir William Keith, governor of the province, who knew young Franklin's brother-in-law, offered to establish him in the printing business in Philadelphia, and, better still, to send him to England with a letter of credit with which to buy the necessary outfit.

A mine of gold seemed to open before him. He made ready for the journey, and set sail, disappointed, however, that the letter of credit did not come before he left. When he reached England, he ascertained that Sir William Keith was without credit, a vain man and devoid of principle. Franklin found himself alone in a strange country, doubly unhappy because he had used for himself and some impecunious friends one hundred and seventy-five dollars, collected from a business man. This he paid years afterward, ever considering the use of it one of the serious mistakes of his life.

He and a boy companion found lodgings at eighty-seven cents per week; very inferior lodgings they must have been. There was of course no money to buy type, no money to take passage back to America. He wrote a letter to Miss Read, telling her that he was not likely to return, dropped the correspondence, and found work in a printing-office.

After a year or two, a merchant offered him a position as clerk in America, at five dollars a week. He accepted, and, after a three-months voyage, reached Philadelphia, "the cords of love," he said, drawing him back. Alas! Deborah Read, persuaded by her mother and other relatives; had married, but was far from happy. The merchant for whom Franklin had engaged to work soon died, and the printer was again looking for a situation, which he found with Keimer. He was now twenty-one, and life had been anything but cheerful or encouraging.

Still, he determined to keep his mind cheerful and active, and so organized a club of eleven young men, the "Junto," composed mostly of mechanics. They came together once a month to discuss questions of morals, politics, and science. As most of these were unable to buy books—a book in those days often costing several dollars—Franklin conceived the idea of a subscription library, raised the funds, and became the librarian. Every day he set apart an hour or two for study, and for twenty years, in the midst of poverty and hard work, the habit was maintained. If Franklin himself did not know that such a young man would succeed, the world around him must have guessed it. Out of this collection of books—the mother of all the subscription libraries of this country—has grown a great library in the city of Philadelphia.

Keimer proved a business failure; but kindness to a fellow-workman, Meredith, a youth of intemperate habits, led Franklin to another open door. The father of Meredith, hoping to save his son, started the young men in business by loaning them five hundred dollars. It was a modest beginning, in a building whose rent was but one hundred and twenty dollars a year. Their first job of printing brought them one dollar and twenty-five cents. As Meredith was seldom in a condition for labor, Franklin did most of the work, he having started a paper—the Pennsylvania Gazette. Some prophesied failure for the new firm, but one prominent man remarked: "The industry of that Franklin is superior to anything I ever saw of the kind. I see him still at work when I go home from the club, and he is at work again before his neighbors are out of bed."

But starting in business had cost five hundred more than the five hundred loaned them. The young men were sued for debt, and ruin stared them in the face. Was Franklin discouraged? If so at heart, he wisely kept a cheerful face and manner, knowing what poor policy it is to tell our troubles, and made all the friends he could. Several members of the Assembly, who came to have printing done, became fast friends of the intelligent and courteous printer.

In this pecuniary distress, two men offered to loan the necessary funds, and two hundred and fifty dollars were gratefully accepted from each. These two persons Franklin remembered to his dying day. Meredith was finally bought out by his own wish, and Franklin combined with his printing a small stationer's shop, with ink, paper, and a few books. Often he wheeled his paper on a barrow along the streets. Who supposed then that he would some day be President of the Commonwealth of Pennsylvania?

Franklin was twenty-four. Deborah Read's husband had proved worthless, had run away from his creditors, and was said to have died in the West Indies. She was lonely and desolate, and Franklin rightly felt that he could brighten her heart. They were married September 1, 1730, and for forty years they lived a happy life. He wrote, long afterward, "We are grown old together, and if she has any faults, I am so used to them that I don't perceive them." Beautiful testimony! He used to say to young married people, in later years, "Treat your wife always with respect; it will procure respect to you, not only from her, but from all that observe it."

The young wife attended the little shop, folded newspapers, and made Franklin's home a resting-place from toil. He says: "Our table was plain and simple, our furniture of the cheapest. My breakfast was, for a long time, bread and milk (no tea), and I ate it out of a twopenny earthen porringer, with a pewter spoon: but mark how luxury will enter families, and make a progress in spite of principle. Being called one morning to breakfast, I found it in a china bowl, with a spoon of silver. They had been bought for me without my knowledge by my wife, and had cost her the enormous sum of three and twenty shillings! for which she had no other excuse or apology to make, but that she thought her husband deserved a silver spoon and china bowl as well as any of his neighbors."

The years went by swiftly, with their hard work and slow but sure accumulation of property. At twenty-seven, having read much and written considerable, he determined to bring out an almanac, after the fashion of the day, "for conveying instruction among the common people, who bought scarcely any other book." "Poor Richard" appeared in December, 1732; price, ten cents. It was full of wit and wisdom, gathered from every source. Three editions were sold in a month. The average annual sale for twenty-five years was ten thousand copies. Who can ever forget the maxims which have become a part of our every-day speech?—"Early to bed and early to rise, makes a man healthy, wealthy, and wise."—"He that hath a trade, hath an estate."—"One to-day is worth two to-morrows."— "Never leave that till to-morrow which you can do to-day."— "Employ thy time well if thou meanest to gain leisure; and since thou art not sure of a minute, throw not away an hour."—"Three removes are as bad as a fire."—"What maintains one vice would bring up two children."—"Many a little makes a mickle."—"Beware of little expenses; a small leak will sink a great ship."—"If you would know the value of money, go and try to borrow some; for he that goes a-borrowing goes a-sorrowing."—"Rather go to bed supperless than rise in debt."—"Experience keeps a dear school, but fools will learn in no other."

An interesting story is told concerning the proverb, "If you would have your business done, go; if not, send." John Paul Jones, one of the bravest men in the Revolutionary War, had become the terror of Britain, by the great number of vessels he had captured. In one cruise he is said to have taken sixteen prizes; burned eight and sent home eight. With the Ranger, on the coast of Scotland, he captured the Drake, a large sloop-of-war, and two hundred prisoners. At one time, Captain Jones waited for many months for a vessel which had been promised him. Eager for action, he chanced to see "Poor Richard's Almanac," and read, "If you would have your business done, go; if not, send." He went at once to Paris, sought the ministers, and was given command of a vessel, which, in honor of Franklin, he called Bon Homme Richard.

The battle between this ship and the Serapis, when, for three hours and a half, they were lashed together by Jones' own hand, and fought one of the most terrific naval battles ever seen, is well known to all who read history. The Bon Homme Richard sunk after her victory, while her captain received a gold medal from Congress and an appreciative letter from General Washington.

So bravely did Captain Pearson, the opponent, fight, that the King of England made him a knight. "He deserved it," said Jones, "and, should I have the good-fortune to fall in with him again, I will make a lord of him."

No wonder that Franklin's proverbs were copied all over the continent, and translated into French, German, Spanish, Italian, Russian, Bohemian, Greek, and Portuguese. In all these very busy years, Franklin did not forget to study. When he was twenty-seven, he began French, then Italian, then Spanish, and then to review the Latin of his boyhood. He learned also to play on the harp, guitar, violin, and violoncello.

Into the home of the printer had come two sons, William and Francis. The second was an uncommonly beautiful child, the idol of his father. Small-pox was raging in the city, but Franklin could not bear to put his precious one in the slightest peril by inoculation. The dread disease came into the home, and Francis Folger, named for his grandmother—at the age of four years—went suddenly out of it. "I long regretted him bitterly," Franklin wrote years afterwards to his sister Jane. "My grandson often brings afresh to my mind the idea of my son Franky, though now dead thirty-six years; whom I have seldom since seen equalled in every respect, and whom to this day I cannot think of without a sigh." On a little stone in Christ Church burying-ground, Philadelphia, are the boy's name and age, with the words, "The delight of all that knew him."

This same year, when Franklin was thirty, he was chosen clerk of the General Assembly, his first promotion. If, as Disraeli said, "the secret of success in life is for a man to be ready for his opportunity when it comes," Franklin had prepared himself, by study, for his opportunity.

28

The year later, he was made deputy postmaster, and soon became especially helpful in city affairs. He obtained better watch or police regulations, organized the first fire-company, and invented the Franklin stove, which was used far and wide.

At thirty-seven, so interested was he in education that he set on foot a subscription for an academy, which resulted in the noble University of Pennsylvania, of which Franklin was a trustee for over forty years. The following year his only daughter, Sarah, was born, who helped to fill the vacant chair of the lovely boy. The father, Josiah, now died at eighty-seven, already proud of his son Benjamin, for whom in his poverty he had done the best he could.

About this time, the Leyden jar was discovered in Europe by Musschenbroeck, and became the talk of the scientific world. Franklin, always eager for knowledge, began to study electricity, with all the books at his command. Dr. Spence, a gentleman from Great Britain, having come to America to lecture on the subject, Franklin bought all his instruments. So much did he desire to give his entire time to this fascinating subject that he sold his printing-house, paper, and almanac, for ninety thousand dollars, and retired from business. This at forty-two; and at fifteen selling ballads about the streets! Industry, temperance, and economy had paid good wages. He used to say that these virtues, with "sincerity and justice," had won for him "the confidence of his country." And yet Franklin, with all his saving, was generous. The great preacher Whitefield came to Philadelphia to obtain money for an orphan-house in Georgia. Franklin thought the scheme unwise, and silently resolved not to give when the collection should be taken. Then, as his heart warmed under the preaching, he concluded to give the copper coins in his pocket; then all the silver, several dollars; and finally all his five gold pistoles, so that he emptied his pocket into the collector's plate.

Franklin now constructed electrical batteries, introduced the terms "positive" and "negative" electricity, and published articles on the subject, which his friend in London, Peter Collinson, laid before the Royal Society. When he declared his belief that lightning and electricity were identical, and gave his reasons, and that points would draw off electricity, and therefore lightning-rods be of benefit, learned people ridiculed the ideas. Still, his pamphlets were eagerly read, and Count de Buffon had them translated into French. They soon appeared in German, Latin, and Italian. Louis XV. was so deeply interested that he ordered all Franklin's experiments to be performed in his presence, and caused a letter to be written to the Royal Society of London, expressing his admiration of Franklin's learning and skill. Strange indeed that such a scientist should arise

29

in the new world, be a man self-taught, and one so busy in public life.

In 1752, when he was forty-six, he determined to test for himself whether lightning and electricity were one. He made a kite from a large silk handkerchief, attached a hempen cord to it, with a silk string in his hand, and, with his son, hastened to an old shed in the fields, as the thunder-storm approached.

As the kite flew upward, and a cloud passed over, there was no manifestation of electricity. When he was almost despairing, lo! the fibres of the cord began to loosen; then he applied his knuckle to a key on the cord, and a strong spark passed. How his heart must have throbbed as he realized his immortal discovery!

A Leyden jar was charged, and Franklin went home from the old shed to be made a member of the Royal Society of London, to receive the Copley gold medal, degrees from Harvard and Yale Colleges, and honors from all parts of the world. Ah! if Josiah Franklin could have lived to see his son come to such renown! And Abiah, his mother, had been dead just a month! But she knew he was coming into greatness, for she wrote him near the last: "I am glad to hear you are so well respected in your town for them to choose you an alderman, although I don't know what it means, or what the better you will be of it besides the honor of it. I hope you will look up to God, and thank him for all his good providences towards you." Sweetest of all things is the motherhood that never lets go the hand of the child, and always points Godward!

Lightning-rods became the fashion, though there was great opposition, because many believed that lightning was one of the means of punishing the sins of mankind, and it was wrong to attempt to prevent the Almighty from doing his will. Some learned men urged that a ball instead of a point be used at the end of the rod, and George III. insisted that the president of the Royal Society should favor balls. "But, sire," said Sir John Pringle, "I cannot reverse the laws and operations of nature."

"Then, Sir John, you had perhaps better resign," was the reply, and the obstinate monarch put knobs on his conductors.

Through all the scientific discord, Franklin had the rare good-sense to remain quiet, instead of rushing into print. He said, "I have never entered into any controversy in defence of my philosophical opinions; I leave them to take their chance in the world. If they are right, truth and experience will support them; if wrong, they ought to be refuted and rejected. Disputes are apt to sour one's temper and disturb one's quiet."

Franklin was not long permitted to enjoy his life of study. This same year, 1752, he was elected a member of the Pennsylvania

Assembly, and reëlected every year for ten years, "without," as he says, "ever asking any elector for his vote, or signifying, either directly or indirectly, any desire of being chosen." He was also, with Mr. William Hunter of Virginia, appointed postmaster-general for the colonies, having been the postmaster in Philadelphia for nearly sixteen years. So excellent was his judgment, and so conciliatory his manner, that he rarely made enemies, and accomplished much for his constituents. He cut down the rates of postage, advertised unclaimed letters, and showed his rare executive ability and tireless energy.

For many years the French and English had been quarrelling over their claims in the New World, till finally the "French and Indian War," or "Seven Years' War," as it was named in Europe, began. Delegates from the various colonies were sent to Albany to confer with the chiefs of the Six Nations about the defence of the country. Naturally, Franklin was one of the delegates. Before starting, he drew up a plan of union for the struggling Americans, and printed it in the Gazette, with the now well known wood-cut at the bottom; a snake cut into as many pieces as there were colonies, each piece having upon it the first letter of the name of a colony, and underneath the words, "Join or Die." He presented his plan of union to the delegates, who, after a long debate, unanimously adopted it, but it was rejected by some of the colonies because they thought it gave too much power to England, and the king rejected it because he said, "The Americans are trying to make a government of their own."

Franklin joined earnestly in the war, and commanded the forces in his own State, but was soon sent abroad by Pennsylvania, as her agent to bring some troublesome matters before royalty. He reached London, July 27, 1757, with his son William, no longer the friendless lad looking for a position in a printing-house, but the noted scientist, and representative of a rising nation. Members of the Royal Society hastened to congratulate him; the universities at Oxford and Edinburgh conferred degrees upon him. While he attended to matters of business in connection with his mission, he entertained his friends with his brilliant electrical experiments, and wrote for several magazines on politics and science.

After five years of successful labor, Doctor Franklin went back to Philadelphia to receive the public thanks of the Assembly, and a gift of fifteen thousand dollars for his services. His son was also appointed governor of New Jersey, by the Crown. Franklin was now fifty-seven, and had earned rest and the enjoyment of his honors. But he was to find little rest in the next twenty-five years.

The "Seven Years' War" had been terminated by the Treaty of

Paris, February 10, 1763. Of course, great expenses had been incurred. The following year, Mr. Grenville, Prime Minister of England, proposed that a portion of the enormous debt be paid by America through the Stamp Act. The colonies had submitted already to much taxation without any representation in Parliament, and had many grievances. The manufacture of iron and steel had been forbidden. Heavy duties had been laid upon rum, sugar, and molasses, and constables had been authorized to search any place suspected of avoiding the duties.

When the Stamp Act was suggested, the colonies, already heavily in debt by the war, remonstrated in public meetings, and sent their protests to the king. Franklin, having been reappointed agent for Pennsylvania, used all possible effort to prevent its passage, but to no avail. The bill passed in March, 1765. By this act, deeds and conveyances were taxed from thirty-seven cents to one dollar and twenty-five cents apiece; college degrees, ten dollars; advertisements, fifty cents each, and other printed matter in proportion.

At once, the American heart rebelled. Bells were tolled, and flags hung at half-mast. In New York, the Stamp Act was carried about the streets, with a placard, "The folly of England and the ruin of America." The people resolved to wear no cloth of English manufacture. Agents appointed to collect the hated tax were in peril of their lives. Patrick Henry electrified his country by the well known words, "Cæsar had his Brutus, Charles I. had his Cromwell, and George III."—and when the loyalists shouted, "Treason!" he continued, "may profit by their example. If that be treason, make the most of it."

Grenville saw, too late, the storm he had aroused. Franklin was now, as he wrote to a friend, "extremely busy, attending members of both houses, informing, explaining, consulting, disputing, in a continual hurry from morning till night." His examination before the House of Commons filled England with amazement and America with joy. When asked, "If the Stamp Act should be repealed, would it induce the Assemblies of America to acknowledge the rights of Parliament to tax them, and would they erase their resolutions?" he replied, "No, never!"

"What used to be the pride of the Americans?"

"To indulge in the fashions and manufactures of Great Britain."

"What is now their pride?"

"To wear their old clothes over again, till they can make new ones," said the fearless Franklin.

The great commoners William Pitt and Edmund Burke were

our stanch friends. A cry of distress went up from the manufacturers of England, who needed American markets for their goods, and in 1766 the Stamp Act was repealed.

America was overjoyed, but her joy was of short duration; for in the very next year a duty was placed on glass, tea, and other articles. Then riots ensued. The duty was repealed on all save tea. When the tea arrived in Boston Harbor, the indignant citizens threw three hundred and forty chests overboard; in Charlestown, the people stored it in cellars till it mildewed; and from New York and Philadelphia they sent it home again to Old England.

In 1774, the Boston Port Bill, which declared that no merchandise should be landed or shipped at the wharves of Boston, was received by the colonists with public mourning. September 5 of this year, the First Continental Congress met at Philadelphia, and again a manly protest was sent to George III. Again the great Pitt, Earl of Chatham, poured out his eloquence against what he saw was close at hand—"a most accursed, wicked, barbarous, cruel, unjust, and diabolical war." But George III. was immovable.

The days for Franklin were now bitter in the extreme. Ten thousand more troops had been sent to General Gage in Boston, to compel obedience. Franklin's wife was dying in Philadelphia, longing to see her husband, who had now been absent ten years, each year expecting to return, and each year detained by the necessities of the colonies. At last he started homeward, landing May 5, 1775. His daughter had been happily married to Mr. Richard Bache, a merchant, but his wife was dead, and buried beside Franky. The battles of Lexington and Concord had been fought; the War for Freedom was indeed begun.

Franklin was now almost seventy, but ready for the great work before him. He loved peace. He said: "All wars are follies, very expensive and very mischievous ones. When will mankind be convinced of this, and agree to settle their differences by arbitration? Were they to do it, even by the cast of a die, it would be better than by fighting and destroying each other." But now war was inevitable. With the eagerness of a boy he wrote to Edmund Burke: "General Gage's troops made a most vigorous retreat,—twenty miles in three hours,—scarce to be paralleled in history; the feeble Americans, who pelted them all the way, could scarce keep up with them."

He was at once made a member of the Continental Congress, called to meet May 10, at Philadelphia. George Washington and Patrick Henry, John and Samuel Adams, were in the noted assemblage. They came with brave hearts and an earnest purpose. Franklin served upon ten committees: to engrave and print

Continental money, to negotiate with the Indians, to send another but useless petition to George III., to find out the source of saltpetre, and other matters. He was made postmaster-general of the United States, and was also full of work for Pennsylvania.

England had voted a million dollars to conquer the colonies, and had hired nearly twenty thousand Hessians to fight against them, besides her own skilled troops. The army under Washington had no proper shelter, little food, little money, and no winter clothing. Franklin was Washington's friend and helper in these early days of discouragement. At first the people had hoped to keep united to the mother country; now the time had arrived for the Declaration of Independence, by which America was to become a great nation. Thomas Jefferson, John Adams, Benjamin Franklin, Roger Sherman of Connecticut, and Robert R. Livingston of New York were appointed to draw up the document. Jefferson wrote the Declaration, and Franklin and Adams made a few verbal changes. And then, with the feeling so well expressed by Franklin, "We must hang together, or else, most assuredly, we shall all hang separately," the delegates fearlessly signed their names to what Daniel Webster well called the "title-deed of our liberties."

And now another important work devolved upon Franklin. The colonies believed that the French were friendly and would assist. He was unanimously chosen commissioner to France, to represent and plead the cause of his country. Again the white-haired statesman said good-bye to America, and sailed to Europe. As soon as he arrived, he was welcomed with all possible honor. The learned called upon him; his pictures were hung in the shop-windows, and his bust placed in the Royal Library. When he appeared on the street a crowd gathered about the great American. He was applauded in every public resort.

"Franklin's reputation," said John Adams, "was more universal than that of Leibnitz or Newton, Frederick or Voltaire; and his character more beloved and esteemed than any or all of them. His name was familiar to government and people, to kings, courtiers, nobility, clergy, and philosophers, as well as plebeians, to such a decree that there was scarcely a peasant or a citizen, a valet de chambre, coachman or footman, a lady's chamber-maid or a scullion in a kitchen, who was not familiar with it, and who did not consider him a friend to humankind. When they spoke of him they seemed to think he was to restore the golden age." Royalty made him welcome at court, and Marie Antoinette treated him with the graciousness which had at first won the hearts of the French to the beautiful Austrian. France made a treaty of alliance with America, and recognized her independence, February 6, 1778, which gave joy and hope to the struggling colonies. Franklin was now made minister plenipotentiary. What a change from the hated work of moulding tallow candles!

The great need of the colonies was money to carry on the war, and, pressed as was France in the days preceding her own revolution, when M. Necker was continually opposing the grants, she loaned our country—part of it a gift—over five million dollars, says James Parton, in his admirable life of Franklin. For this reason, as well as for the noble men like Lafayette who came to our aid, the interests of France should always be dear to America. When the Revolutionary War was over, Franklin helped negotiate the peace, and returned to America at his own request in the fall of 1785, receiving among his farewell presents a portrait of Louis XVI., set with four hundred and eight diamonds. Thomas Jefferson became minister in his stead. When asked if he had replaced Dr. Franklin, he replied, "I succeed; no one can ever replace him."

He was now seventy-nine years old. He had been absent for nine years. When he landed, cannon were fired, church-bells rung, and crowds greeted him with shouts of welcome. He was at once made President of the Commonwealth of Pennsylvania, and at eighty-one a delegate to the convention that framed our Constitution, where he sat regularly five hours a day for four months. To him is due the happy suggestion, after a heated discussion, of equal representation for every State in the Senate, and representation in proportion to population in the House.

At eighty-four, in reply to a letter to Washington, he received these tender words:—

"If to be venerated for benevolence, if to be admired for talents, if to be esteemed for patriotism, if to be beloved for philanthropy, can gratify the human mind, you must have the pleasing consolation to know that you have not lived in vain. And I flatter myself that it will not be ranked among the least grateful occurrences of your life to be assured that, so long as I retain my memory, you will be recollected with respect, veneration, and affection, by your sincere friend,

"George Washington."

The time for the final farewell came, April 17, 1790, near midnight, when the gentle and great statesman, doubly great because so gentle, slept quietly in death. Twenty thousand persons gathered to do honor to the celebrated dead. Not only in this country was there universal mourning, but across the ocean as well. The National Assembly of France paid its highest eulogies.

By his own request, Franklin was buried beside his wife and

Franky, under a plain marble slab, in Christ Church Cemetery, Philadelphia, with the words,—

Benjamin }   Franklin.
And   }   1790
Deborah }

He was opposed to ostentation. He used to quote the words of Cotton Mather to him when he was a boy. On leaving the minister's house, he hit his head against a beam. "'Stoop,' said Mather; 'you are young, and have the world before you; stoop as you go through it, and you will miss many hard thumps!' This advice, thus beat into my head, has frequently been of use to me, and I often think of it when I see pride mortified, and misfortunes brought upon people by their carrying their heads too high."

Tolerant with all religions, sweet-tempered, with remarkable tact and genuine kindness, honest, and above jealousy, he adopted this as his rule, which we may well follow: "To go straight forward in doing what appears to me to be right, leaving the consequences to Providence."

THOMAS JEFFERSON

Five miles east of Charlottesville, Virginia, near where the River Rivanna enters the James, Thomas Jefferson was born, April 13, 1743, the third in a family of eight children.

Peter Jefferson, his father, descended from a Welsh ancestry, was a self-made man. The son of a farmer, with little chance for schooling, he improved every opportunity to read, became, like George Washington, a surveyor, and endured cheerfully all the perils of that pioneer life. Often, in making his survey across the Blue Ridge Mountains, he was obliged to defend himself against the attacks of wild beasts, and to sleep in hollow trees. When the provisions gave out, and his companions fell fainting beside him, he subsisted on raw flesh, and stayed on until his work was completed.

So strong was he physically that when two hogsheads of tobacco, each weighing a thousand pounds, were lying on their sides, he could raise them both upright at once. Besides this great strength of body, he developed great strength of mind. Shakespeare and Addison were his favorites. It was not strange that by and by he became a member of the Virginia House of Burgesses.

When Peter Jefferson was thirty-one, he married into a family much above his own socially—Jane, the daughter of Isham Randolph, a rich and cultured gentleman. She was but nineteen, of a most cheerful and hopeful temperament, with a passionate love of nature in every flower and tree.

From these two the boy Thomas inherited the two elements that make a man's character beautiful, not less than a woman's—strength and sweetness. With his mother's nature, he found delight in every varying cloud, every rich sunset or sunrise, and in that ever new and ever wonderful change from new moon to full and from full to new again. How tender and responsive such a soul becomes! How it warms toward human nature from its love for the material world!

When Thomas was five years old, he was sent to a school where English only was taught. The hours of confinement doubtless seemed long to a child used to wander at will over the fields, for one day, becoming impatient for school to be dismissed, he went out-of-doors, knelt behind the house, and repeated the Lord's Prayer, thus hoping to expedite matters!

At nine he entered the family of Rev. William Douglas, a Scotch clergyman, where he learned Greek, Latin, and French. So fond did he become of the classics that he said, years later, if he were obliged to decide between the pleasure derived from them and the estate left him by his father, he would have greatly preferred poverty and education.

All these early years at "Shadwell," the Jefferson home,—so named after his mother's home in England, where she was born,—Thomas had an especially dear companion in his oldest sister, Jane. Her mind was like his own, quick and comprehensive, and her especial delight, like his, was in music. Three things, he said, became a passion with him, "Mathematics, music, and architecture." Jane had a charming voice, and her brother became a skilled performer on the violin, often practising three hours a day in his busy student life.

Peter Jefferson, the strong, athletic Assemblyman, died suddenly when Thomas was but fourteen, urging, as his dying request, that this boy be well educated. There was but one other son, and he an infant. The sweet-tempered Mrs. Jefferson, under forty, was left with eight children to care for; but she kept her sunny, hopeful heart.

When Thomas was a little more than sixteen, he entered the college of William and Mary, at Williamsburg. He was a somewhat shy, tall, slight boy, eager for information, and warm-hearted. It was not surprising that he made friends with those superior to himself in mental acquirements. He says, in his Memoirs: "It was my great good-fortune, and what, perhaps, fixed the destinies of my life, that Dr. William Small of Scotland was the professor of mathematics, a man profound in most of the useful branches of science, with a happy talent of communication, correct and gentlemanly manners, and an enlarged and liberal mind. He, most happily for me, became soon attached to me, and made me his daily companion when not engaged in the school; and from his conversation I got my first views of the expansion of science and of the system of things in which we are placed. Fortunately, the philosophical chair became vacant soon after my arrival at college, and he was appointed to fill it per interim; and he was the first who ever gave in that college regular lectures in ethics, rhetoric, and belles-lettres. He returned to Europe in 1762, having previously filled up the measure of his goodness to me by procuring for me, from his most intimate friend, George Wythe, a reception as a student of law under his direction, and introduced me to the acquaintance and familiar table of Governor Fauquier, the ablest man who had ever filled that office."

The governor, though an accomplished scholar and great patron of learning, was very fond of card-playing, and of betting in the play. In this direction his influence became most pernicious to

Virginia. Strangely enough, young Jefferson never knew one card from another, and never allowed them to be played in his house.

He devoted himself untiringly to his books. He worked fifteen hours a day, allowing himself only time to run out of town for a mile in the twilight, before lighting the candles, as necessary exercise. Though, from the high social position of his mother, he had many acquaintances at Williamsburg, Thomas went little in society, save to dine with the prominent men above mentioned. These were a constant stimulant to him. A great man, or the written life of a great man, becomes the maker of other great men. The boy had learned early in life one secret of success; to ally one's self to superior men and women.

Years afterward, he wrote to his eldest grandson, "I had the good-fortune to become acquainted very early with some characters of very high standing, and to feel the incessant wish that I could ever become what they were. Under temptations and difficulties, I would ask myself, what would Dr. Small, Mr. Wythe, Peyton Randolph do in this situation? What course in it will insure me their approbation? I am certain that this mode of deciding on my conduct tended more to correctness than any reasoning powers I possessed. Knowing the even and dignified lives they pursued, I could never doubt for a moment which of two courses would be in character for them. From the circumstances of my position, I was often thrown into the society of horse-racers, card-players, fox-hunters, scientific and professional men, and of dignified men; and many a time have I asked myself in the enthusiastic moment of the death of a fox, the victory of a favorite horse, the issue of a question eloquently argued at the bar or in the great council of the nation, well, which of these kinds of reputation should I prefer—that of a horse-jockey, a fox-hunter, an orator, or the honest advocate of my country's rights?"

The very fact that Jefferson thus early in life valued character and patriotism above everything else was a sure indication of a grand and successful manhood. We usually build for ourselves the kind of house we start to build in early years. If it is an abode of pleasure, we live in the satiety and littleness of soul which such a life brings. If it is an abode of worship of all that is pure and exalted, we walk among high ideals, with the angels for ministering spirits, and become a blessing to ourselves and to mankind.

In these college-days, Jefferson became acquainted with the fun-loving, brilliant Patrick Henry, forming a friendship that became of great value to both. After two years in college, where he had obtained a fair knowledge of French, Spanish, and Italian, besides his Latin and Greek, he went home to spend the winter in reading law. But other thoughts continually mingled with Coke. On every page he read the name of a beautiful girl of whom he had become very fond. She had given him a watch-paper, which having become spoiled accidentally, the law-student wrote to his friend John Page, afterward governor of Virginia, "I would fain ask the favor of Miss Becca Burwell to give me another watch-paper of her own cutting, which I should esteem much more, though it were a plain round one, than the nicest in the world, cut by other hands." He asked advice of Page as to whether he had better go to her home and tell her what was in his heart. "Inclination tells me to go, receive my sentence, and be no longer in suspense; but reason says, 'If you go, and your attempt proves unsuccessful, you will be ten times more wretched than ever.'"

He battled with Coke all winter and all the next summer,—a young man in love who can thus bend himself to his work shows a strong will,—going to Williamsburg in October to attend the General Court, and to meet and ask Miss Burwell for her heart and hand. Alas! he found her engaged to another. Possibly, he was "ten times more wretched than ever," but it was wise to know the worst.

A young man of twenty-one usually makes the best of an unfortunate matter, remembering that life is all before him, and he must expect difficulties. The following year, a sister married one of his dearest friends, Dabney Carr; and the same year, 1765, his pet sister, Jane, died. To the end of his life, he never forgot this sorrow; and, even in his extreme old age, said "that often in church some sacred air, which her sweet voice had made familiar to him in youth, recalled to him sweet visions of this sister, whom he had loved so well and buried so young."

After five years spent in law studies, rising at five, even in winter, for his work, he began to practise, with remarkable success. He was not a gifted speaker, but, having been a close student, his knowledge was highly valued. Years afterward, an old gentleman who knew Jefferson, when asked, "What was his power in the court-room?" answered, "He always took the right side."

Parton says, in his valuable life of Jefferson, "He had most of the requisites of a great lawyer; industry, so quiet, methodical, and sustained that it amounted to a gift; learning, multifarious and exact; skill and rapidity in handling books; the instinct of research, that leads him who has it to the fact he wants, as surely as the hound scents the game; a serenity of temper, which neither the inaptitude of witnesses nor the badgering of counsel could ever disturb; a habit of getting everything upon paper in such a way that all his stores of knowledge could be marshalled and brought into action; a ready sympathy with a client's mind; an intuitive sense of what is due to the opinions, prejudices, and errors of others; a knowledge of the few avenues by which alone unwelcome truth can find access to a human mind; and the power to state a case with the clearness and brevity that often make argument superfluous."

In 1768, when he was only twenty-five years old, he offered himself as a candidate for the Virginia Legislature, and was elected. He entered upon his public life, which lasted for forty years, with the resolution "never to engage, while in public office, in any kind of enterprise for the improvement of my fortune;" and he kept his resolution.

Two years after he began to practise law, the house at "Shadwell" was burned. He was absent from home, and greatly concerned about his library. When a colored man came to tell him of his loss, Jefferson inquired eagerly for his books. "Oh," replied the servant, carelessly, "they were all burnt, but ah! we saved your fiddle!"

A new house was now begun, two miles from the Shadwell home, on a hill five hundred and eighty feet high, which he called afterwards "Monticello," the Italian for "Little Mountain." This had long been a favorite retreat for Jefferson. He and Dabney Carr had come here day after day, in the summer-time, and made for themselves a rustic seat under a great oak, where they read law together, and planned the rose-colored plans of youth. Sweet, indeed, is it that we have such plans in early years. Those get most out of life who live much in the ideal; who see roses along every pathway, and hear Nature's music in every terrific storm.

Jefferson was building the Monticello home with bright visions for its future. Another face had come into his heart, this time to remain forever. It was a beautiful face; a woman, with a slight, delicate form, a mind remarkably trained for the times, and a soul devoted to music. She had been married, and was a widow at nineteen. Her father was a wealthy lawyer; her own portion was about forty thousand acres of land and one hundred and thirty-five slaves. Although Jefferson had less land, his annual income was about five thousand dollars, from this and his profession.

Martha Skelton was now twenty-three, and Jefferson nearly twenty-nine. So attractive a woman had many suitors. The story is told that two interested gentlemen came one evening to her father's house, with the purpose of having their future definitely settled. When they arrived, they heard singing in the drawing-room. They listened, and the voices were unmistakably those of Jefferson and Martha Skelton. Making up their minds that "their future was definitely settled," as far as she was concerned, they took their hats and withdrew.

Jefferson was married to the lady January 1, 1772, and after

41

the wedding started for Monticello. The snow had fallen lightly, but soon became so deep that they were obliged to quit the carriage and proceed on horseback. Arriving late at night, the fires were out and the servants in bed; but love keeps hearts warm, and darkness and cold were forgotten in the satisfaction of having won each other. This satisfaction was never clouded. For years, the home life deepened with its joys and sorrows. A little girl, Martha, was first born into the home; then Jane, who died when eighteen months old, and then an only son, who died in seventeen days. Monticello took on new beauty. Trees were set out and flower-beds planted. The man who so loved nature made this a restful and beautiful place for his little group.

The year after Jefferson's marriage, Dabney Carr, the brilliant young member of the Virginia Assembly, a favorite in every household, eloquent and lovable, died in his thirtieth year. His wife, for a time, lost her reason in consequence. Carr was buried at "Shadwell," as Jefferson was away from home; but, upon his return, the boyish promise was kept, and the friend was interred under the old oak at Monticello, with these words on the stone, written by Jefferson:—

"To his Virtue, Good-Sense, Learning, and Friendship,
this stone is dedicated by Thomas Jefferson, who,
of all men living, loved him most."

At once, Mrs. Carr, with her six little children, came to Jefferson's home, and lived there ever after, he educating the three sons and three daughters of his widowed sister as though they were his own. Thus true and tender was he to those whom he loved.

For some years past, Jefferson had been developing under that British teaching which led America to freedom. When a student of law, he had listened to Patrick Henry's immortal speech in the debate on the Stamp Act. "I attended the debate," said Jefferson in his Memoir, "and heard the splendid display of Mr. Henry's talents as a popular orator. They were indeed great; such as I have never heard from any other man. He appeared to me to speak as Homer wrote.... I never heard anything that deserved to be called by the same name with what flowed from him; and where he got that torrent of language from is inconceivable. I have frequently shut my eyes while he spoke, and, when he was done, asked myself what he had said, without being able to recollect a word of it. He was no logician. He was truly a great man, however,—one of enlarged views."

The whole country had become aflame over the burning of the

Gaspee, in March, 1772,—a royal schooner anchored at Providence, R. I. The schooner came there to watch the commerce of the colonies, and to search vessels. She made herself generally obnoxious. Having run aground in her chase of an American packet, a few Rhode Islanders determined to visit her and burn her. The little company set out in eight boats, muffling their oars, reaching her after midnight. The Gaspee was taken unawares, the hands of the crew tied behind them, and the vessel burned.

At once a reward of five thousand dollars was offered for the detection of any person concerned; but, though everybody knew, nobody would tell. Word came from England "that the persons concerned in the burning of the Gaspee schooner, and in the other violences which attended that daring insult, should be brought to England to be tried." This fired the hearts of the colonists. The Virginia House of Burgesses appointed a committee to correspond with other Legislatures on topics which concerned the common welfare. The royal governor of Virginia had no liking for such free thought and free speech as this, and dissolved the House, which at once repaired to a tavern and continued its deliberations.

Soon a convention was called, before which Jefferson's "Summary View of the Rights of British America" was laid. It was worded as a skilful lawyer and polished writer knew how to word it; and it stated the case so plainly that, when it was published, and sent to Great Britain, Jefferson, to use his own words, "had the honor of having his name inserted in a long list of proscriptions enrolled in a bill of attainder commenced in one of the Houses of Parliament, but suppressed by the hasty step of events." Remoteness from England doubtless saved his life.

Jefferson went up to the Continental Congress at Philadelphia, which opened May 10, 1775, taking his "Summary View" with him. The delegates were waiting to see what Virginia had to say in these important days. She had instructed her men to offer a resolution that "the United Colonies be free and independent States," which was done by Richard Henry Lee, on June 7. Four days later, Congress appointed a committee of five to prepare a Declaration of Independence. Thomas Jefferson, only thirty-two, one of the youngest members of Congress, was made chairman. How well he had become fitted to write this immortal document! It was but a condensation of the "Summary View." He was also, says John T. Morse, in his life of Jefferson, "a man without an enemy. His abstinence from any active share in debate had saved him from giving irritation."

The Declaration still exists in Jefferson's clear handwriting. For three days the paper was hotly debated, "John Adams being the colossus of the debate." Jefferson did not speak a word, though Franklin cheered him as he saw him "writhing under the acrimonious criticism of some of its parts."

When it was adopted, the country was wild with joy. It was publicly read from a platform in Independence Square. Military companies gathered to listen to its words, fired salutes, and lighted bonfires in the evenings. The step, dreaded, yet for years longed for, had been taken—separation and freedom, or union and slavery. Jefferson came to that Congress an educated, true-hearted lover of his country; he went back to Martha Jefferson famous as long as America shall endure. He was reëlected to Congress, but declined to serve, as he wished to do important work in his own State, in the changing of her laws.

But now, October 8, 1776, came a most tempting offer; that of joint commissioner with Benjamin Franklin and Silas Deane to represent America at the court of France. He had always longed for European travel; he was a fine French scholar, and could make himself most useful to his new country, but his wife was too frail to undertake the long journey. She was more to him than the French mission, and he stayed at home.

Born with a belief in human brotherhood and a love for human freedom, he turned his attention in the Virginia Legislature to the repeal of the laws of entail and primogeniture, derived from England. He believed the repeal of these, and the adoption of his bill "for establishing religious freedom," would, as he said, form a system by which every fibre would be eradicated of ancient or future aristocracy. "The repeal of the laws of entail would prevent the accumulation and perpetuation of wealth in select families.... The abolition of primogeniture, and equal partition of inheritances, removed the feudal and unnatural distinctions which made one member of every family rich and all the rest poor.... The restoration of the rights of conscience relieved the people from taxation for the support of a religion not theirs."

There was much persecution of Dissenters by the Established Church. Baptists were often thrown into prison for preaching, as Patrick Henry declared, "the Gospel of the Saviour to Adam's fallen race." For nine years the matter of freedom of conscience was wrestled with, before Virginia could concede to her people the right to worship God as they pleased.

Jefferson was averse to slavery, worked for the colonization of the slaves, and in 1778 carried through a bill against their further importation. He wrote later, in his "Notes on Virginia": "The whole commerce between master and slave is a perpetual exercise of the most boisterous passions, the most unremitting despotism, on the

44

one part, and degrading submissions on the other.... I tremble for my country when I reflect that God is just; that his justice cannot sleep forever; that, considering numbers, nature, and natural means only, a revolution of the wheel of fortune, an exchange of situations, is among possible events; that it may become probable by supernatural interference! The Almighty has no attribute which can take side with us in such a contest." When his State could not bring itself to adopt his plan of freeing the slaves, he wrote in his autobiography, in 1821, "The day is not distant when it must bear and adopt it, or worse will follow. Nothing is more certainly written in the book of fate than that these people are to be free." How great indeed was the man who could look beyond his own personal interests for the well-being of the race!

He worked earnestly for common schools and the establishment of a university in his native State, believing that it is the right and duty of a nation to make its people intelligent and capable of self-government.

In June, 1779, Jefferson was made governor of Virginia, to succeed Patrick Henry, her first governor. The Revolutionary War had been going forward, with some victories and some defeats. Virginia had given generously of men, money, and provisions. The war was being transferred to the South, as its battle-ground. British fleets had laid waste the Atlantic coast. Benedict Arnold and Cornwallis had ravaged Virginia. When General Tarlton was ordered to Charlottesville, in 1781, and it seemed probable that Monticello would fall into his hands, Jefferson moved his family to a place of safety.

When the British arrived, and found that the governor was not to be captured, they retired without committing the slightest injury to the place. This was in return for kindness shown by Jefferson to four thousand English prisoners, who had been sent from near New York, to be in camp at Charlottesville, where it seemed cheaper to provide for them. Jefferson rightly said: "It is for the benefit of mankind to mitigate the horrors of war as much as possible. The practice, therefore, of modern nations, of treating captive enemies with politeness and generosity, is not only delightful in contemplation, but really interesting to all the world—friends, foes, and neutrals."

Two faithful servants at Monticello, fearful that the silver might be stolen by the red-coats, concealed it under a floor a few feet from the ground; Cæsar, removing a plank, and slipping through the cavity, received it from the hands of Martin. The soldiers came just as the last piece was handed to Cæsar; the plank was immediately restored to its place, and for nearly three days and nights the poor colored man remained in the dark, without food, guarding his master's treasures. When a soldier put his gun to the breast of Martin and threatened to fire unless Jefferson's whereabouts was disclosed, the brave fellow answered, "Fire away, then!" A man or woman who wins and holds such loyalty from dependents is no ordinary character.

After holding the office of governor for two years, Jefferson resigned, feeling that a military man would give greater satisfaction. Such a one followed him, but with no better success among the half-despairing patriots, destitute of money and supplies. Jefferson, with his sensitive spirit, felt keenly the criticisms of some of the people, saying, "They have inflicted a wound on my spirit which will only be cured by the all-healing grave." He refused to return to public life, and looked forward to happy years of quiet study at Monticello.

How little we know the way which lies before us. We long for sunlight, and perchance have only storms. We love to be as children who must be carried over the swamps and rough places, not knowing that strength of manhood and womanhood comes generally through struggling. The "happy years" at Monticello were already numbered. Another little girl had come to gladden the heart of the man who so loved children, and had quickly taken her departure. And now Martha Jefferson, at thirty-four, the sweet, gentle woman who had lived with him only ten short years, was also going away. She talked with him calmly about the journey; she said she could not die content if she thought their children would have a stepmother. The young governor, without a moment's thought as to his future happiness, taking her hand, solemnly promised that he would never marry again, and he kept his word. It is not known that any person ever entered the place left vacant in his heart by Martha Jefferson's death.

For four months he had watched by her bedside, or had his books so near her that he could work without being separated from her. When she died he fainted, and remained so long insensible that the attendants thought he could never be restored to consciousness. For three weeks he kept his room, ministered to by his little daughter Martha, who wound her arms about his neck, with that inexpressible consolation that only a pure, sweet child-nature can give. She said years later, "I was never a moment from his side. He walked almost incessantly, night and day, only lying down occasionally, when nature was completely exhausted.... When, at last, he left his room, he rode out, and from that time he was on horseback rambling about the mountain, in the least frequented roads, and just as often through the woods. In those melancholy rambles I was his constant companion, a solitary witness to many a burst of grief."

He longed now for a change of scene; Monticello was no more a place of peace and rest. Being elected to Congress, he took his seat in November, 1783. To him we owe, after much heated discussion, the adoption of the present system of dollars and cents, instead of pounds and shillings. In May, 1784, he was appointed minister to France, to join Dr. Franklin and John Adams in negotiating commercial treaties. He sailed in July, taking with him his eldest child, Martha, leaving Mary and an infant daughter with an aunt.

The educated governor and congressman of course found a cordial welcome in Parisian society, for was he not the author of the Declaration of Independence, endeared to all lovers of liberty, in whatever country. He was charmed with French courtesy, thrift, and neatness, but he was always an American in sentiment and affection. He wrote to his young friend, James Monroe, afterwards President: "The pleasure of the trip to Europe will be less than you expect, but the utility greater. It will make you adore your own country,—its soil, its climate, its equality, liberty, laws, people, and manners. How little do my countrymen know what precious blessings they are in possession of, and which no other people on earth enjoy!" More and more he loved, and believed in, a republic. He wrote to a friend: "If all the evils which can arise among us from the republican form of government, from this day to the day of judgment, could be put into scale against what this country suffers from its monarchical form in a week, or England in a month, the latter would preponderate. No race of kings has ever presented above one man of common-sense in twenty generations. The best they can do is to leave things to their ministers; and what are their ministers but a committee badly chosen?"

Jefferson spent much time in looking up the manufacturing and agricultural interests of the country, and kept four colleges—Harvard, Yale, William and Mary, and the College of Philadelphia—advised of new inventions, new books, and new phases of the approaching Revolution.

He had placed his daughter Martha in a leading school. His letters to her in the midst of his busy life show the beautiful spirit of the man, who was too great ever to rise above his affectional nature. "The more you learn the more I love you," he wrote her; "and I rest the happiness of my life on seeing you beloved by all the world, which you will be sure to be if to a good heart you join those accomplishments so peculiarly pleasing in your sex. Adieu, my dear child; lose no moment in improving your head, nor any opportunity of exercising your heart in benevolence."

47

His baby-girl, Lucy, died two years after her mother, and now only little Mary was left in America. He could not rest until this child was with him in France. She came, with a breaking heart on leaving the old Virginia home and her aunt. On board the vessel she became so attached to the captain that it was almost impossible to take her from him. She spent some weeks with Mrs. John Adams in London, who wrote: "A finer child I never saw. I grew so fond of her, and she was so much attached to me, that, when Mr. Jefferson sent for her, they were obliged to force the little creature away."

Once in Paris, the affectionate child was placed at school with her sister Martha, to whom Jefferson wrote: "She will become a precious charge upon your hands.... Teach her, above all things, to be good, because without that we can neither be valued by others nor set any value on ourselves. Teach her to be always true; no vice is so mean as the want of truth, and at the same time so useless. Teach her never to be angry; anger only serves to torment ourselves, to divert others, and alienate their esteem."

The love of truth was a strong characteristic of Jefferson's nature, one of the most beautiful characteristics of any life. There is no other foundation-stone so strong and enduring on which to build a granite character as the granite rock of truth. Jefferson wrote to his children and nephews: "If you ever find yourself in any difficulty, and doubt how to extricate yourself, do what is right, and you will find it the easiest way of getting out of the difficulty.... Give up money, give up fame, give up science, give the earth itself, and all it contains, rather than do an immoral act. And never suppose that, in any possible situation or any circumstances, it is best for you to do a dishonorable thing." Again he wrote: "Determine never to be idle. No person will have occasion to complain of the want of time, who never loses any. It is wonderful how much may be done if we are always doing."

After five years spent in France, most of which time he was minister plenipotentiary, Dr. Franklin having returned home, and John Adams having gone to England, Jefferson set sail for America, with his two beloved children, Martha, seventeen, and Mary, eleven. He had done his work well, and been honored for his wisdom and his peace-loving nature. Daniel Webster said of him: "No court in Europe had at that time a representative in Paris commanding or enjoying higher regard, for political knowledge or for general attainments, than the minister of this then infant republic."

Even before Jefferson reached home he had been appointed Secretary of State by President Washington. He accepted with a sense of dread, and his subsequent difficulties with Alexander

Hamilton, Secretary of the Treasury, realized his worst fears. The one believed in centralization of power—a stronger national government; the other believed in a pure democracy—the will of the people, with the least possible governing power. The two men were opposite in character, opposite in financial plans, opposite in views of national polity. Jefferson took sides with the French, and Hamilton with the English in the French Revolution. The press grew bitter over these differences, and the noble heart of George Washington was troubled. Finally Jefferson resigned, and retired to Monticello. "I return to farming," he said, "with an ardor which I scarcely knew in my youth."

Three years later, he was again called into public life. As Washington declined a reëlection, John Adams and Thomas Jefferson became the two Presidential candidates. The one receiving the most votes of the electors became President, and the second on the list, Vice-President. John Adams received three more votes than Jefferson, and was made President.

On March 4, 1797, Jefferson, as Vice-President, became the leader of the Senate, delivering a short but able address. Much of the next four years he spent at Monticello, watching closely the progress of events. Matters with the French republic grew more complicated. She demanded an alliance with the United States against England, which was refused, and war became imminent. At the last moment, John Adams rose above the tempest of the hour, went quite half-way in bringing about a reconciliation, and the country was saved from a useless and disastrous war.

The Federalists had passed some unwise measures, such as the "Alien Law," whereby the President was authorized to send foreigners out of the country; and the "Sedition Law," which punished with fine and imprisonment freedom of speech and of the press. Therefore, at the next presidential election, when Adams and Jefferson were again candidates, the latter was made President of the United States, the Federalists having lost their power, and the Republicans—afterwards called Democrats—having gained the ascendancy.

The contest had been bitter. Jefferson's religious belief had been strongly assailed. Through it all he had the common-sense to know that the cool-headed, good-natured man, who has only words of kindness, and who rarely or never makes an enemy, is the man who wins in the end. He controlled himself, and therefore his party, in a manner almost unexampled.

March 4, 1801, at the age of fifty-eight, in a plain suit of clothes, the great leader of Democracy rode to the Capitol, hitched his horse to the fence, entered the Senate Chamber, and delivered his inaugural address. Thus simple was the man, who wished ever to be known as "the friend of the people." Alas! that sweet Martha Jefferson could not have lived to see this glad day! To what a proud height had come the hard-working college boy and the tender-hearted, tolerant man!

As President, he was the idol of his party, and, in the main, a wise leader. He made few removals from office, chiefly those appointed by John Adams just as he was leaving the Presidency. Jefferson said removals "must be as few as possible, done gradually, and bottomed on some malversation or inherent disqualification." One of the chief acts was the purchase from France of a great tract of land, called the Territory of Louisiana, for fifteen million dollars.

During his second four years in office, there were more perplexities. Aaron Burr, Vice-President during Jefferson's first term, was tried on the charge of raising an army to place himself on the throne of Mexico, or at the head of a South-western confederacy. England, usually at war with France, had issued orders prohibiting all trade with that country and her allies; Napoleon had retorted by a like measure. Both nations claimed the right to take seamen out of United States vessels. The British frigate Leopard took four seamen by force from the American frigate Chesapeake. The nation seemed on the verge of war, but it was postponed, only to come later, in 1812, under James Madison.

Congress passed the Embargo Act, by which all American vessels were detained in our own ports. It had strong advocates and strong opponents, but was repealed as soon as Jefferson retired from office. Owing to these measures our commerce was well-nigh destroyed.

At the age of sixty-five years, Jefferson retired to Monticello, "with a reputation and popularity," says Mr. Morse, "hardly inferior to that of Washington." He had had the wisdom never to assume the bearing of a leader. He had been careful to avoid disputes. Once, when riding, he met a stranger, with whom engaging in conversation, he found him bitterly opposed to the President. Upon being asked if he knew Mr. Jefferson personally, he replied, "No, nor do I wish to."

"But do you think it fair to repeat such stories about a man, and condemn one whom you do not dare to face?"

"I shall never shrink from meeting him if he ever comes in my way."

"Will you, then, go to his house to-morrow, and be introduced to him, if I promise to meet you there?"

50

"Yes, I will."

The stranger came, to his astonishment found that the man he had talked with was the President himself, dined with him, and became his firm friend and supporter ever afterward.

For the next seventeen years, Jefferson lived at Monticello, honored and visited by celebrities from all the world. Sometimes as many as fifty persons stayed at his home over night. One family of six came from abroad, and remained with him for ten months. His daughter Martha, married to Thomas Mann Randolph, presided over his hospitable home, and with her eleven children made the place a delight, for she had "the Jefferson temperament—all music and sunshine." The beautiful Mary, who married her cousin, John W. Eppes, had died at twenty-six, leaving two small children, who, like all the rest, found a home with Jefferson.

In the midst of this loving company, the great man led a busy life, carrying on an immense correspondence, by means of which he exerted a commanding influence on the questions of the day as well as on all social matters. To a child named for him, he wrote a letter which the boy might read after the statesman's death. In it are these helpful words: "Adore God. Reverence and cherish your parents. Love your neighbor as yourself. Be just. Be true. Murmur not at the ways of Providence."

To his daughter Mary he wrote these lines, which well might be hung up in every household:—

"Harmony in the married state is the very first object to be aimed at. Nothing can preserve affections uninterrupted but a firm resolution never to differ in will, and a determination in each to consider the love of the other as of more value than any object whatever on which a wish had been fixed. How light, in fact, is the sacrifice of any other wish when weighed against the affections of one with whom we are to pass our whole life. And though opposition in a single instance will hardly of itself produce alienation, yet every one has his pouch into which all these little oppositions are put. While that is filling, the alienation is insensibly going on, and when filled it is complete. It would puzzle either to say why, because no one difference of opinion has been marked enough to produce a serious effect by itself. But he finds his affections wearied out by a constant stream of little checks and obstacles.

"Other sources of discontent, very common indeed, are the little cross-purposes of husband and wife, in common conversation; a disposition in either to criticise and question whatever the other says; a desire always to demonstrate and make him feel himself in the wrong, and especially in company. Nothing is so goading. Much better, therefore, if our companion views a thing in a light different from what we do, to leave him in quiet possession of his view. What is the use of rectifying him, if the thing be unimportant, and, if important, let it pass for the present, and wait a softer moment and more conciliatory occasion of revising the subject together. It is wonderful how many persons are rendered unhappy by inattention to these little rules of prudence."

Jefferson rose early; the sun, he said, had not for fifty years caught him in bed. But he bore great heart-sorrow in these declining years, and bore it bravely. His estate had diminished in value, and he had lost heavily by indorsements for others. His household expenses were necessarily great. Finally, debts pressed so heavily that he sold to Congress the dearly prized library, which he had been gathering for fifty years. He received nearly twenty-four thousand dollars for it, about half its original value. But this amount brought only temporary relief.

Then he attempted to dispose of some of his land by lottery, as was somewhat the fashion of the times. The Legislature reluctantly gave permission, but as soon as his friends in New York, Philadelphia, and Baltimore heard of his pecuniary condition, they raised about eighteen thousand dollars for him, and the lottery plan was abandoned. He was touched by this proof of esteem, and said: "No cent of this is wrung from the tax-payer; it is the pure and unsolicited offering of love."

Jefferson was now, as he said, "like an old watch, with a pinion worn out here and a wheel there, until it can go no longer." On July 3, 1826, after a brief illness, he seemed near the end. He desired to live till the next day, and frequently asked if it were the Fourth. He lingered till forty minutes past the noon of July 4, and then slept in death. That same day, John Adams, at ninety-one, was dying at Quincy, Mass. His last words were, as he went out at sunset, the booming of cannon sounding pleasant to his patriotic heart, "Thomas Jefferson still lives." He did not know that his great co-laborer had gone home at midday. "The two aged men," says T. W. Higginson, "floated on, like two ships becalmed at nightfall, that drift together into port, and cast anchor side by side." Beautiful words!

The death of two Presidents at this memorable time has given an additional sacredness to our national Independence Day.

Among Jefferson's papers were found, carefully laid away, "some of my dear, dear wife's handwriting," and locks of hair of herself and children. Also a sketch of the granite stone he desired for his monument, with these words to be inscribed upon it.

Here was buried
Thomas Jefferson,
Author of the Declaration of Independence,
Of the Statute of Virginia for Religious Freedom,
And Father of the University of Virginia.

He was buried by his family and servants, on the spot selected by himself and Dabney Carr in boyhood, his wife on one side and his loving Mary on the other.

The beloved Monticello passed into other hands. Martha Jefferson and her children would have been left penniless had not the Legislatures of South Carolina and Louisiana each voted her ten thousand dollars. Thomas Jefferson Randolph, the grandson, with the assistance of his daughters, who established a noted school, paid all the remaining debts, many thousand dollars, to save the honor of their famous ancestor.

To the last, Jefferson kept his sublime faith in human nature and in the eternal justice of republican principles, saying it is "my conviction that should things go wrong at any time, the people will set them to rights by the peaceable exercise of their elective rights." Whatever his religious belief in its details of creed, he said, "I am a Christian in the only sense in which Jesus wished any one to be— sincerely attached to his doctrines in preference to all others." He compiled a little book of the words of Christ, saying, "A more precious morsel of ethics was never seen."

In his public life he was honest, in his domestic life lovable, and he died, as he had lived, tolerant of the opinions of others, even-tempered, believing in the grandeur and beauty of human nature. What though we occasionally trust too much! Far better that than to go through life doubting and murmuring! That he believed too broadly in States' Rights for the perpetuity of the Union, our late Civil War plainly showed, and his views on Free Trade are, of course, shared by a portion only of our citizens. However, he gave grandly of the affection of his heart and the power of his intellect, and he received, as he deserved, the love and honor of thousands, the world over.

ALEXANDER HAMILTON

To the quiet and picturesque island of Nevis, one of the West Indies, many years ago, a Scotch merchant came to build for himself a home. He was of a proud and wealthy family, allied centuries before to William the Conqueror.

On this island lived also a Huguenot family, who had settled there after the revocation of the Edict of Nantes, which drove so many Protestants out of the country. In this family was a beautiful and very intellectual girl, with refined tastes and gentle, cultured manners. Through the ambition of her mother she had contracted a marriage with a Dane of large wealth, followed by the usual unhappiness of marrying simply for money. A divorce resulted, and the attractive young woman married the Scotch merchant, James Hamilton. A son, Alexander, was born to them, January 11, 1757.

But he was born into privation rather than joy and plenty. The generous and kindly father failed in business; the beautiful mother died in his childhood, and he was thrown upon the bounty of her relations.

The opportunities for education on the island were limited. The child read all the books he could lay his hands upon, becoming especially fond of Plutarch's Lives and Pope's works. He was fortunate also in having the friendship of a superior man, Dr. Knox, a Presbyterian clergyman, who delighted in the boy's quick and comprehensive mind.

At twelve years of age he was obliged to earn money, and was placed in the counting-house of Nicholas Cruger. Probably, like other boys, he wished he were rich, but found later in life that success is usually born of effort and economy. He early chose "Perseverando" for his motto, and it helped to carry him to the summit of power.

That the counting-house was not congenial to him, a letter to a school-fellow in New York plainly shows. "To confess my weakness, Ned, my ambition is prevalent, so that I contemn the grovelling condition of a clerk, or the like, to which my fortune condemns me, and would willingly risk my life, though not my character, to exalt my station. I am confident, Ned, that my youth excludes me from any hopes of immediate preferment, nor do I desire it, but I mean to prepare the way for futurity. I'm no philosopher, you see, and may be justly said to build castles in the air; my folly makes me ashamed, and beg you'll conceal it; yet,

Neddy, we have seen such schemes successful, when the projector is constant. I shall conclude by saying, I wish there was a war."

The "projector was constant," and the "schemes became successful." He was indeed "preparing the way for futurity," this lad not yet fourteen. At this time, Mr. Cruger made a visit to New York, and left the precocious boy in charge of his business. Such reliance upon him increased his self-reliance, and helped to fit him to advise and uphold a nation in later years.

In these early days he began to write both prose and poetry. When he was fifteen, the Leeward Islands were visited by a terrific hurricane. In one town five hundred houses were blown down. So interested was Alexander in this novel occurrence that he wrote a description of it for a newspaper. When the authorship was discovered, it was decided by the relatives that such a boy ought to be educated. The money was raised for this purpose, and he sailed for New York, taking with him some valuable letters of introduction from Dr. Knox.

He was soon attending a grammar-school at Elizabeth, New Jersey. The principal, Francis Barber, was a fine classical scholar, patriotic, entering the Revolutionary War later; the right man to impress his pupils for good. Alexander, with his accustomed energy and ambition, set himself to work. In winter, wrapt in a blanket, he studied till midnight, and in summer, at dawn, resorted to a cemetery near by, where he found the quiet he desired. In a year he was ready to enter college.

Attracted to Princeton, he asked Dr. Witherspoon, the president of the college, the privilege of taking the course in about half the usual time. The good days of election in study had not yet dawned. The dull and the bright must have the same routine; the one urged to his duties, the other tired by the delay. The doctor could not establish so peculiar a precedent, and Princeton missed the honor of educating the great statesman.

He entered Columbia College, and made an excellent record for himself. In the debating club, say his classmates, "he gave extraordinary displays of richness of genius and energy of mind." He won strong friendships to himself by his generous and unselfish nature, and his ardent love for others. It is only another proof of the old rule, that "Like begets like." Those who give love in this world usually receive it. Selfishness wins nothing—self-sacrifice, all things.

The college-boy was often seen walking under the large trees on what is now Dey Street, New York, talking to himself in an undertone, and apparently in deep thought. The neighbors knew the slight, dark-eyed lad, as the "young West Indian," and wondered concerning his future. When he was seventeen, a "great meeting in

55

the fields" was held in New York, July 6, 1774. While Hamilton was studying, the colonies of America had been looking over into the promised land of freedom, driven thither by some unwise task-masters. Boston had seasoned the waters of the Atlantic with British tea. New York, well filled with Tories, yet had some Patriots, who felt that the hour was approaching when all must stand together in the demand for liberty. Accordingly, the "great meeting" was called, to teach the people the lessons of the past and the duties of the future.

Hamilton had recently returned from a visit to Boston, and was urged to be present and speak at the meeting. He at first refused, being a stranger in the country and unknown. He attended, however; and when several speakers had addressed the eager crowds, thoughts flowed into the youth's mind and pleaded for utterance. He mounted the platform. The audience stared at the stripling. Then, as he depicted the long endured oppression from England, urged the wisdom of resistance, and painted in glowing colors the sure success of the colonies, the hearts of the multitude took fire with courage and hope. When he closed, they shouted, "It is a collegian! it is a collegian!"

Hamilton was no longer a West Indian; he was, heart and soul, an American. Liberty now grew more exciting than college books. Dr. Seabury, afterwards Bishop of Connecticut, wrote two tracts entitled "Free Thoughts on the Proceedings of the Continental Congress," and "Congress Canvassed by a Westchester Farmer." These pamphlets attempted to show the foolishness of opposing a monarchy like England. They were scattered broadcast.

Then tracts appeared in answer; clear, terse, sound, and able. These said, "No reason can be assigned why one man should exercise any power or preëminence over his fellow-creatures more than another, unless they have voluntarily vested him with it. Since, then, Americans have not, by any act of theirs, empowered the British Parliament to make laws for them, it follows they can have no just authority to do it.... If, by the necessity of the thing, manufactures should once be established, and take root among us, they will pave the way still more to the future grandeur and glory of America; and, by lessening its need of external commerce, will render it still securer against the encroachments of tyranny."

This was rank heterodoxy toward a power which had crippled the manufactures of America in all possible ways, and wished to keep her a great agricultural country. "The sacred rights of mankind," said the writer, "are not to be rummaged for among old parchments or musty records; they are written, as with a sunbeam, in the whole volume of human nature, by the hand of the Divinity

56

itself, and can never be erased or obscured by mortal power." The wonder grew as to the authorship of these pamphlets. Some said John Jay wrote them; some said Governor Livingstone. When it was learned that Hamilton, only eighteen, had composed them, the Tories stood aghast, and the Patriots saw that a new star had risen in the heavens.

Hamilton knew that the war was inevitable; that the time must soon come for which he longed when he wrote to his friend Ned, "I wish there was a war." He immediately began to study military affairs. There are always places to be filled by those who make themselves ready. He was learning none too early. His corps, called the "Hearts of Oak" in green uniforms and leathern caps, drilled each morning. While engaged in removing cannon from the battery, a boat from the Asia, a British ship-of-war, fired into the men, killing the person who stood next to Hamilton. At once the drums were beaten, and the people rushed to arms. The king's store-houses were pillaged, and the "Liberty Boys" marched through the streets, threatening revenge on every Tory.

Young Hamilton, fearless before the Asia, could also be fearless in defence of his friends. Dr. Cooper, the President of Columbia College, was a pronounced Tory. When the mob approached the steps of the institution, Hamilton, nothing daunted, appeared before them, and urged coolness, lest they bring "disgrace on the cause of liberty." Dr. Cooper imagined that his liberal pupil was assisting the mob, and cried out from an upper window, "Don't listen to him, gentlemen! he is crazy, he is crazy!" But the mob did listen, and the president was saved from harm.

The Revolutionary War had begun. Lexington and Bunker Hill were as beacon-fires to the new nation. In 1776, the New York Convention ordered a company of artillery to be raised, and Hamilton applied for the command of it. Only nineteen, and very boyish in looks, his fitness for the position was doubted, till his excellent examination proved his knowledge, and he was appointed captain. He used the last money sent him by his relatives in the West Indies, to equip his company.

College days were now over, and the busy life of the soldier had commenced. For most young men, the stirring events of the times would have filled every moment and every thought. Not so the man born to have a controlling and permanent influence in the republic. He found time to study about money circulation, rates of exchange, commerce, taxes, increase of population, and the like, because he knew that a great work must be done by somebody after the war. How true it is that if we fit ourselves for a great work, the work will find us.

Meantime, Captain Hamilton drilled his troops so well that General Greene observed it, made the acquaintance of the captain, invited him to his headquarters, and spoke of him to Washington. Had not the work been well done, it would not have commanded attention, but this attention was an important stepping-stone to fame and honor. Hamilton was ever after a most loyal friend to General Greene.

The company was soon called into active service. At the disastrous battle of Long Island, Hamilton was in the thickest of the fight, and brought up the rear, losing his baggage and a field-piece. After the retreat up the Hudson, at Harlem Heights, Washington observed the skill used in the construction of some earthworks, and, finding that the engineer was the young man introduced to him by General Greene, invited him to his tent. This was the beginning of a life-long and most devoted friendship between the great commander and the boyish captain.

Later, at the battles of Trenton and Princeton, Hamilton was fearless and heroic. "Well do I recollect the day," said a friend, "when Hamilton's company marched into Princeton. It was a model of discipline; at their head was a boy, and I wondered at his youth; but what was my surprise when, struck with his slight figure, he was pointed out to me as that Hamilton of whom we had already heard so much.... A mere stripling, small, slender, almost delicate in frame, marching beside a piece of artillery, with a cocked hat pulled down over his eyes, apparently lost in thought, with his hand resting on a cannon, and every now and then patting it, as if it were a favorite horse or a pet plaything."

He had so won the esteem and approbation of Washington that he was offered a position upon his staff, which he accepted March 1, 1777, with the rank of lieutenant-colonel. His work now was constant and absorbing. The correspondence was immense, but all was done with that clearness and elegance of diction which had marked the young collegian. He was popular with old and young, being called the "Little Lion," as a term of endearment, in appreciation of bravery and nobility of character.

When the skies looked darkest, as at Valley Forge, Hamilton was habitually cheerful, seeing always a rainbow among the clouds. His enthusiasm was contagious. He carried men with him by a belief in his own powers, and by deep sympathy with others. Lafayette loved him as a brother. He wrote Hamilton, "Before this campaign I was your friend and very intimate friend, agreeably to the ideas of the world. Since my second voyage, my sentiment has increased to such a point the world knows nothing about. To show

58

both, from want and from scorn of expression, I shall only tell you—Adieu!"

Baron Steuben used to say, in later days, "The Secretary of the Treasury is my banker; my Hamilton takes care of me when he cannot take care of himself."

Hamilton wrote to his dear friend Laurens, "Cold in my professions—warm in my friendships—I wish it were in my power, by actions rather than words, to convince you that I love you.... You know the opinion I entertain of mankind, and how much it is my desire to preserve myself free from particular attachments, and to keep my happiness independent of the caprices of others. You should not have taken advantage of my sensibility to steal into my affections without my consent."

Best of all, Washington confided in him, and loved him, and we usually love those in whom we have confided. When he wanted a calcitrant general, like Gates, brought to terms, he sent the tactful, clear-headed Hamilton on the mission. When he wanted decisive action, he sent the same fearless young officer, who knew no such word as failure. Sometimes he broke down physically, but the power of youth triumphed, and he was soon at work again.

On his expedition to General Gates, in November, 1777, with all his desire to keep himself "free from particular attachments," he laid the foundation for the one lasting attachment of his life. At the house of the wealthy and distinguished General Philip Schuyler, he met and liked the second daughter, Elizabeth. Three years later, in the spring of 1780, when the officers brought their families to Morristown, the acquaintance ripened into love, and December 14, 1780, when Hamilton was twenty-three, he was married to Miss Schuyler. The father of the young lady was proud and happy in her choice. He wrote Hamilton, "You cannot, my dear sir, be more happy at the connection you have made with my family than I am. Until the child of a parent has made a judicious choice, his heart is in continual anxiety; but this anxiety was removed the moment I discovered it was you on whom she placed her affections."

In this year, 1780, the country was shocked by the treason of Benedict Arnold. Hamilton was sent in pursuit, only to find that he had escaped to the British. He ministered to the heart-broken wife of Arnold, as best he could. He wrote to a friend, "Her sufferings were so eloquent that I wished myself her brother, to have a right to become her defender."

For Major André he had the deepest sympathy, and admiration of his manly qualities. He wrote to Miss Schuyler, afterward his wife, "Poor André suffers to-day. Everything that is amiable in virtue, in fortitude, in delicate sentiment and accomplished manners, pleads for him; but hard-hearted policy calls for a sacrifice. I urged a compliance with André's request to be shot, and I do not think it would have had an ill effect."

A month after his marriage, his only difficulty with General Washington occurred. The commander-in-chief had sent for Hamilton to confer with him, who, meeting Lafayette, was stopped by him for a few moments' conversation on business. When he reached Washington, the general said, "Colonel Hamilton, you have kept me waiting at the head of the stairs these ten minutes. I must tell you, sir, you treat me with disrespect." The proud young aid answered, "I am not conscious of it, sir; but since you have thought it necessary to tell me so, we part." He therefore resigned his position, glad to be free to take a more active part in the war. Washington, with his usual magnanimity, made overtures of reconciliation, and they became ever after trusted co-workers.

All these years, Hamilton had shown himself brave and untiring in the interests of his adopted country. At the battle of Monmouth, his horse was shot under him. At Yorktown, at his own earnest request, he led the perilous assault upon the enemy's works, and carried them. When Hamilton saw that the enemy was driven back, he humanely ordered that not a British soldier should be killed after the attack. He says in his report, "Incapable of imitating examples of barbarity, and forgetting recent provocations, the soldiers spared every man who ceased to resist."

Washington appreciated his heroism, and said, "Few cases have exhibited greater proof of intrepidity, coolness, and firmness than were shown on this occasion."

Letters home to his wife show the warm heart of Hamilton. "I am unhappy—I am unhappy beyond expression. I am unhappy because I am to be so remote from you; because I am to hear from you less frequently than I am accustomed to do. I am miserable, because I know you will be so.... Constantly uppermost in my thoughts and affections, I am happy only when my moments are devoted to some office that respects you. I would give the world to be able to tell you all I feel and all I wish; but consult your own heart, and you will know mine.... Every day confirms me in the intention of renouncing public life, and devoting myself wholly to you. Let others waste their time and their tranquillity in a vain pursuit of power and glory; be it my object to be happy in a quiet retreat, with my better angel."

At the close of the Revolutionary War, he repaired to Albany, spending the winter at the home of General Schuyler, his wife's father. He had but little money, and his dues in the service of an impoverished country were unpaid; but he had what was far better, ability. He determined to study law. For four months, he bent himself unreservedly to his work, and was admitted to the bar. He steadily refused offers of pecuniary aid from General Schuyler, preferring to support his wife and infant son by his own exertions. Such a man, of proud spirit and unwavering purpose, would, of course, succeed.

Friends who appreciated the service he had rendered to his country now interceded in his behalf, and he was appointed Continental receiver of taxes for New York. To accept a position meant, to him, persistent labor, and success in it if possible. He at once repaired to Poughkeepsie, where the Legislature was in session; presented his plans of taxation, and prevailed upon that body to pass a resolution asking for a convention of the States that a Union might be effected, stronger than the existing Confederation.

The position as receiver of taxes was sometimes a disagreeable one, but it was another round in the ladder which carried him to fame. He had increased the number of his acquaintances. His energy and his knowledge of public questions had been revealed to the people; and the result was his election to Congress, at the age of twenty-five. Thus rapidly the ambitious, energetic, and intelligent young man had risen in influence.

That his voice would be heard in Congress was a foregone conclusion. General Schuyler wrote his daughter soon after Congress met: "Participate afresh in the satisfaction I experience from the connection you have made with my beloved Hamilton. He affords me happiness too exquisite for expression. I daily experience the pleasure of hearing encomiums on his virtue and abilities, from those who are capable of distinguishing between real and pretended merit. He is considered, as he certainly is, the ornament of his country, and capable of rendering it the most essential services, if his advice and suggestions are attended to."

The country was deeply in debt from the Revolutionary War. It had no money with which to pay its soldiers; its paper currency was nearly worthless; dissatisfaction was apparent on every hand. There was little unity of interest among the States. Hamilton's plans for raising money, and for a more centralized government, were unheeded; and, after a year in Congress, he returned to the practice of law, saying, "The more I see, the more I find reason for those who love this country to weep over its blindness."

As soon as the war was over, the people began to grow more bitter than ever toward the Tories, or loyalists. Harsh legislative measures were passed. The "Trespass Act" declared that any person who had left his abode in consequence of invasion could collect damages of those who had occupied the premises during his absence. A widow, reduced to poverty by the war, brought suit against a rich Tory merchant, who had lived in her house while the Tories held the city. Hamilton, feeling that a principle of justice was involved, took the part of the merchant, and by a brilliant speech, in which he contended that "the fruits of immovables belong to the captor so long as he remains in actual possession of them," he gained the case. Of course, he brought upon himself much obloquy; was declared to be a "Britisher," and lover of monarchy, a charge to which he must have grown accustomed in later years.

Hamilton's pen was not idle in this controversy. He wrote a pamphlet, advocating respect for law and justice, which was called "Phocion," from its signature. It was read widely, both in England and America. Among the many replies was one signed "Mentor," which drew from Hamilton a "Second letter of Phocion." So inflamed did public opinion become that in one of the clubs it was decided that one person after another should challenge Hamilton, till he should fall in a duel. This came to the knowledge of "Mentor" and the abhorrent plan was stopped by his timely interference. There are too few men and women great enough to be tolerant of ideas in opposition to their own, or to persons holding those ideas. Tolerance belongs to great souls only.

Matters in the States had so grown from bad to worse, and Congress, with its limited powers, was so helpless, that a convention was finally called at Philadelphia, May 25, 1787, to provide for a more complete and efficient Union. Nine States sent delegates: Massachusetts, New York, New Jersey, Pennsylvania, Delaware, Virginia, North Carolina, South Carolina, and Georgia. General Washington was made president of the convention. A plan of government was submitted, called the "Virginia plan," which provided for a Congress of two branches, one to be elected by the people, the other from names suggested by the State Legislatures. There was to be a President, not eligible for a second term. Then the "New Jersey plan" was submitted; which was simply a revision of the Articles of Confederation.

The debates were earnest, but most intelligent; for men in those times had studied the existing governments of the world, and the fate of previous republics. Hamilton was present as a delegate, and, early in the convention, gave his plan for a new government, in a powerful speech, six hours long. He reviewed the whole domain of history, the present condition of the States, and the reasons for it, and then developed his plan. Those only could vote for President and Senators who owned a certain amount of real estate. These officials were to hold office for life or during good behavior. The President should appoint the Governors of the various States.

Of course, the believers in "States' Rights" could not for a moment concede such power to one man, at the head of a nation. When Hamilton affirmed that the "British government was the best model in existence," he awoke the antagonism of the American heart. He probably knew that his plan could not be adopted, but it strengthened the advocates of a central government. Many delegates went home under protest; but the Constitution, brought into its present form largely by James Madison, was finally adopted, and sent to the different States for ratification.

The opposition to its adoption was very great. Hamilton, with praiseworthy spirit, accepted it as the best thing attainable under the circumstances, and worked for it night and day with all the vigor and power of his masterly intellect. To the Federalist he contributed fifty-one papers in defence of the Constitution, and did more than any other man to secure its ultimate adoption.

Henry Cabot Lodge, in his clear and admirable "Life of Hamilton," says: "As an exposition of the meaning and purposes of the Constitution, the Federalist is now, and always will be cited, on the bench and at the bar, by American commentators, and by all writers on constitutional law. As a treatise on the principles of federal government it still stands at the head, and has been turned to as an authority by the leading minds of Germany, intent on the formation of the German Empire."

Party feeling ran high. When a State enrolled herself in favor of the Constitution, bonfires, feasts, and public processions testified to the joy of a portion of the people; while the burning in effigy of prominent Federalists, mobs and riots, testified to the anger of the opponents. In the State of New York the contest was extremely bitter. Hamilton used all his logic, his eloquence, his fire, and his boundless activity to carry the State in favor of the Constitution. Said Chancellor Kent: "He urged every motive and consideration that ought to sway the human mind in such a crisis. He touched, with exquisite skill, every chord of sympathy that could be made to vibrate in the human breast. Our country, our honor, our liberties, our firesides, our posterity were placed in vivid colors before us."

When told by a friend, who was just starting on a journey, that he would be questioned in relation to the adoption of the Constitution, Hamilton replied: "God only knows! Several votes have been taken, by which it appears that there are two to one against us." But suddenly his face brightened, as he said, "Tell them that the convention shall never rise until the Constitution is adopted."

The excitement in New York city became intense. Crowds collected on the street-corners, and whispered, "Hamilton is speaking yet!" Late in the evening of July 28, 1788, it was announced that the Constitution had been adopted by New York, the vote standing thirty to twenty-seven. At once the bells were rung and guns were fired. A great procession was formed of professional men and artisans, bearing pictures of Washington and Hamilton, and banners, with the words "Federalist," "Liberty of the Press," and "The Epoch of Liberty." The federal frigate Hamilton was fully manned, and received the plaudits of the crowds.

When the Constitution was adopted, at last, Washington was made President, April 30, 1789. It was not strange that he chose for his Secretary of the Treasury the man who had studied finance by the camp-fires of the Revolution. At thirty-two Hamilton was in the Cabinet of his country. At once Congress asked him to prepare a report on the public credit, stating his plan of providing for the public debt. In about three months the report was ready. It advocated the funding of all the debts of the United States incurred through the war. As to the foreign and domestic debts, all persons seemed agreed that these should be paid; but the assumption of the debts of the different States met with the most violent opposition. Those who owed a few million dollars were unwilling to help those who owed many millions.

Hamilton advocated a foreign loan, not to exceed twelve millions, and a revenue derived from taxes on imports; such a revenue as would not only provide funds for the new nation, but protect manufactures from the competition of the old world. The believers in protection have had no more earnest or able advocate than Hamilton.

His next report was an elaborate one upon national banks, and the establishment of a United States bank, which should give a uniform system of bank-notes, instead of the unreliable and uneven values of the notes of the State banks. His financial policy, while it aroused the bitterest enmity in some quarters, raised the United States from bankruptcy to the respect of her creditors, abroad and at home. When the old cry of "unconstitutional!" was heard, as it has been heard ever since when any great matter is suggested, Hamilton taught the people to feel that the implied powers of the Constitution were great enough for all needs, and that the document must be interpreted by the spirit as well as the letter of the law. Capitalists were his strong advocates, as they well knew that a firm and safe financial policy was at the root of success and progress.

Very soon after his report on banks, he transmitted to Congress a report on the establishment of a mint, showing wide research on the subject of coinage. Besides these papers, he reported on the purchase of West Point, on public lands, navigation laws, on the post-office, and other matters, always showing careful study, good judgment, and patriotism.

That he was accused of being a monarchist signified little, as there were hundreds of people at that time who feared that the republic would go down, as had others in past centuries. He so deprecated the lack of central power in the government that he exaggerated the dangers of the people's rule. This lack of trust in the masses and in the power of the Constitution, and Thomas Jefferson's trust in self-government and belief in States' rights, led, at last, to the bitter and public disagreement of these two great men, the Secretary of the Treasury and the Secretary of State. Each was honest in his belief; each was tolerant of most men, but intolerant of the other to the end of life.

Hamilton naturally became the leader of the Federalists, as Jefferson the leader of the Republicans, or Democrats, as they are now called. One party saw in Hamilton the great thinker, the safe guardian of the destinies of the people; the other party thought it saw a bold and unscrupulous man, who would sit on a throne if that were possible. Hamilton's character was assailed, sometimes with truth, but oftener without truth. He was not perfect, but he was great, and in most respects noble.

The French Revolution was now interesting all minds. Genet had been sent to America by the French Republic, as her minister. Hamilton urged neutrality, and looked with horror upon the growing excesses in France. Jefferson, with his hatred of monarchy, was lenient, and, in the early part of the Revolution, sympathetic. The United States became divided into two great factions, for and against France. Genet fanned the flames till the patient Washington could endure it no longer; the unwise minister was recalled, and neutrality was proclaimed April 22, 1793.

Through all this matter, Hamilton had the complete love and confidence of Washington. When it was deemed wise to send a special commissioner to effect a treaty with England, that proper commercial relations be maintained, Hamilton was at once suggested. Party feeling opposed, and John Jay was appointed. When he returned from his mission, Great Britain having consented to pay us ten million dollars for illegal seizure of vessels, we agreeing to pay all debts owed to her before the Revolutionary War, the people rose in wrath against the treaty, and burned Jay in effigy. When Hamilton was speaking for its adoption at a public meeting in New York, he was assaulted by stones. "Gentlemen," he said, coolly, "if you use such strong arguments, I must retire." After this he wrote essays, signed "Camillus," in defence of the treaty, and helped largely to secure its acceptance.

Meantime, the Excise Law, whereby distilled spirits were taxed, caused the "Whiskey Insurrection" in Pennsylvania. Hamilton, who believed in the prompt execution of law, urged Washington to take decisive measures. The President called out thirteen thousand troops, and the refusal to pay the taxes was no more heard of.

Hamilton, like Jefferson, had become weary of his six years of public life; his increasing family needed more than his limited salary, and he resigned, returning to his law practice in the city of New York.

When a new President was chosen to succeed Washington, it was not the real leader of the party, Hamilton, but one who had elicited less opposition by strong measures—John Adams, a man of long and distinguished service, both in England and America. Hamilton seems to have preferred Thomas Pinckney of South Carolina, and thus to have gained the ill-will of Adams, which helped at last to split the Federal party.

When Adams and Jefferson became the Presidential nominees in 1800, Hamilton threw himself heartily into the contest in the State of New York. Here he found himself pitted against a rare antagonist, the most famous lawyer in the State except himself, Aaron Burr. He was well born, being the son of the president of the college at Princeton, and the grandson of Jonathan Edwards. Like Hamilton, he was precocious; being ready to enter Princeton when he was eleven years old. He was short in stature, five feet and six inches in height; with fine black eyes, and gentle and winsome manners. Both these men won the most enduring friendships from men and women—homage indeed. Both were intense in nature, though Burr had far greater self-control. Both were brave to rashness; both were untiring students; both loved and always gained authority. Burr had won honors in the Revolutionary War. He had married at twenty-six, a woman ten years older than himself, a widow with two children, with neither wealth nor beauty, whom he idolized for the twelve years she was spared to him, for her rare mind and devoted affection. From her he learned to value intellect in woman. He used to write her before marriage, "Deal less in sentiments, and more in ideas." When she died, he said, "The mother of my Theo was the best woman and finest lady I have ever known." For his only child, his beloved Theodosia, he seemed to have but one wish, that she be a scholar. He said to his wife, "If I could foresee that Theo would become a mere fashionable woman, with all the attendant frivolity and vacuity of mind, adorned with whatever grace and allurement, I would earnestly pray God to take her forthwith hence. But I yet hope by her to convince the world what neither sex appear to believe—that women have souls!"

At ten years of age, she was studying Horace and Terence, learning the Greek grammar, speaking French, and reading Gibbon.

This Theo, the idol of his life, afterward married to Governor Alston of South Carolina, loved him with a devotion that will forever make one gleam of sunshine in a life full of shadows. When the dark days came, she wrote him, "I witness your extraordinary fortitude with new wonder at every new misfortune. Often, after reflecting on this subject, you appear to me so superior, so elevated above all other men; I contemplate you with, such a strange mixture of humility, admiration, reverence, love, and pride, very little superstition would be necessary to make me worship you as a superior being; such enthusiasm does your character excite in me.... I had rather not live than not be the daughter of such a man."

Burr's success in the law had been phenomenal. When he was studying for admission to the bar, he often passed twenty hours out of the twenty-four over his books.

And now, Colonel Burr, at thirty-six, after being in the United States Senate for six years, was the candidate for Vice-President on the Jefferson ticket. Hamilton's eloquence stirred the State of New York in the contest; but Burr's generalship in politics won the votes, and he was elected.

Hamilton went back again to his large law practice. Men sought him with the belief that if he would take their cases, there was no doubt of the result. An aged farmer came to him to recover a farm for which a deed had been obtained from him in exchange for Virginia land. Hamilton heard the case; then wrote to the wealthy speculator to call upon him. When he came, Hamilton said, "You must give me back that deed. I do not say that you knew that the title to these lands is bad; but it is bad. You are a rich—he is a poor man. How can you sleep on your pillow? Would you break up the only support of an aged man and seven children?" He walked the floor rapidly, as he exclaimed, "I will add to my professional services all the weight of my character and powers of my nature; and you ought to know, when I espouse the cause of innocence and of the oppressed, that character and those powers will have their weight."

The property was reconveyed to the farmer, who gratefully asked Hamilton to name the compensation. "Nothing! nothing!" said he. "Hasten home and make your family happy."

Hamilton was clear in his reasoning; a master in constitutional law; persuasive in his manner; sometimes highly impassioned, sometimes solemn and earnest. Says Henry Cabot Lodge: "Force of intellect and force of will were the sources of his success.... Directness was his most distinguishing characteristic, and, whether he appealed to the head or the heart, he went straight to the mark.... He never indulged in rhetorical flourishes, and his style was simple and severe.... That which led him to victory was the passionate energy of his nature, his absorption in his work, his contagious and persuasive enthusiasm."

"There was a fascination in his manner, by which one was led captive unawares," says another writer. "On most occasions, when animated with the subject on which he was engaged, you could see the very workings of his soul, in the expression of his countenance; and so frank was he in manner that he would make you feel that there was not a thought of his heart that he would wish to hide from your view."

"Alexander Hamilton was the greatest man this country ever produced," said Judge Ambrose Spencer.... "He argued cases before me while I sat as judge on the bench. Webster has done the same. In power of reasoning Hamilton was the equal of Webster; and more than this can be said of no man. In creative power Hamilton was infinitely Webster's superior.... He, more than any man, did the thinking of the time."

His chief relaxation from work was at "The Grange," his summer home at Harlem Heights, not far from the spot, it is said, where he first attracted the eye of Washington. Beeches, maples, and many evergreens abounded. The Hudson River added its beauty to the picturesque place. Here he read the classics for pleasure, and the Bible. To a friend he said: "I have examined carefully the evidence of the Christian religion; and, if I was sitting as a juror upon its authenticity, I should unhesitatingly give my verdict in its favor.... I can prove its truth as clearly as any proposition ever submitted to the mind of man."

At "The Grange" he was especially happy with his family. He said, "My health and comfort both require that I should be at home—at that home where I am always sure to find a sweet asylum from care and pain.... It will be more and more my endeavor to abstract myself from all pursuits which interfere with those of affection. 'Tis here only I can find true pleasure."

When Hamilton was forty-four, he endured the great affliction of his life. His eldest son, Philip, nineteen, just graduated from Columbia College, deeply wounded by the political attacks upon his father, challenged to a duel one of the men who had made objectionable remarks. The lad fell at the first fire, a wicked sacrifice to a barbarous "code of honor." After twenty hours of agony, he died, surrounded by the stricken family. Hamilton was especially proud of this son, of whom he said, when he gave his oration at

Columbia College, "I could not have been contented to have been surpassed by any other than my son."

For three years Hamilton worked on with a hope which was never broken, constantly adding to his fame. And then came the fatal error of his life. All along he had opposed Aaron Burr. When named for a foreign mission, Hamilton helped to defeat him. When the tie vote came between Jefferson and Burr in the Presidential returns, Hamilton said, "The appointment of Burr as President will disgrace our country abroad." When Burr was nominated for Governor of New York, Hamilton used every effort to defeat him, and succeeded. Burr, exasperated and disappointed at his failures, sent Hamilton a challenge. He wrote to Hamilton, "Political opposition can never absolve gentlemen from the necessity of a rigid adherence to the laws of honor and the rules of decorum. I neither claim such privilege nor indulge it in others." Alas! that some men in public life, even now, forget the "laws of honor and the rules of decorum" in their treatment of opponents.

Everything in Hamilton's career protested against this suicidal combat. He was only forty-seven, distinguished and beloved, with a wife and seven children dependent upon him.

Before going to the fatal meeting, he wrote his feelings about duelling. "My religious and moral principles are strongly opposed to the practice of duelling, and it would even give me pain to be obliged to shed the blood of a fellow-creature in a private combat forbidden by the laws.... To those who, with me, abhorring the practice of duelling, may think that I ought on no account to have added to the number of bad examples, I answer that my relative situation, as well in public as private, enforcing all the considerations which constitute what men of the world denominate honor, imposed on me (as I thought) a peculiar necessity not to decline the call. The ability to be in future useful, whether in resisting mischief or effecting good, in those crises of our public affairs which seem likely to happen, would probably be inseparable from a conformity with public prejudice in this particular."

He made his will, leaving all, after the payment of his debts, to his "dear and excellent wife." "Should it happen that there is not enough for the payment of my debts, I entreat my dear children, if they, or any of them, should ever be able, to make up the deficiency. I, without hesitation, commit to their delicacy a wish which is dictated by my own. Though conscious that I have too far sacrificed the interests of my family to public avocations, and on this account have the less claim to burden my children, yet I trust in their magnanimity to appreciate as they ought this my request. In so unfavorable an event of things, the support of their dear mother, with the most respectful and tender attention, is a duty, all the sacredness of which they will feel. Probably her own patrimonial resources will preserve her from indigence. But in all situations they are charged to bear in mind that she has been to them the most devoted and best of mothers." And then, the great statesman, after writing two farewell letters to "my darling, darling wife," conformed to "public prejudice" by hastening with his second, at daybreak, to meet Aaron Burr, at Weehawken, two miles and a half above Hoboken. It was a quiet and beautiful spot, one hundred and fifty feet above the level of the Hudson River, shut in by trees and vines, but golden with sunlight on that fatal morning.

At seven o'clock the two distinguished men were ready, ten paces apart, to take into their own hands that most sacred of all things, human life. There was no outward sign of emotion, though the one must have thought of his idol, Theodosia, and the other of his pretty children, still asleep. Hamilton had determined not to fire, and so permitted himself to be sacrificed. The word of readiness was given. Burr raised his pistol and fired, and Hamilton fell headlong on his face, his own weapon discharging in the air. He sank into the arms of his physician, saying faintly, "This is a mortal wound," and was borne home to a family overwhelmed with sorrow. The oldest daughter lost her reason.

For thirty-one hours he lay in agony, talking, when able, with his minister about the coming future, asking that the sacrament be administered, and saying, "I am a sinner. I look to Him for mercy; pray for me."

Once when all his children were gathered around the bed, he gave them one tender look, and closed his eyes till they had left the room. He retained his usual composure to the last, saying to his wife, frenzied with grief, "Remember, my Eliza, you are a Christian." He died at two o'clock on the afternoon of July 12, 1804. The whole nation seemed speechless with sorrow. In New York all business was suspended. At the funeral, a great concourse of people, college societies, political associations, and military companies, joined in the common sorrow. Guns were fired from the British and French ships in the harbor; on a platform in front of Trinity Church, Governor Morris pronounced a eulogy, General Hamilton's four sons, the eldest sixteen and the youngest four, standing beside the speaker. Thus the great life faded from sight in its vigorous manhood, leaving a wonderful record for the aspiring and the patriotic, and a prophecy of what might have been accomplished but for that one fatal mistake.

Aaron Burr hastened to the South, to avoid arrest; but public execration followed him. He became implicated in a scheme for putting himself at the head of Mexico, was arrested and tried for treason, and, though legally acquitted, was obliged to flee to England, and from there to Sweden and Germany. Finally he came home, only to hear that Theodosia's beautiful boy of eleven was dead. Poor and friendless, he longed now for the one person who had never forsaken him, his daughter. She started from Charleston in a pilot-boat, for New York, and was never heard from afterwards. Probably all went down in a storm off Cape Hatteras. When it was reported in the papers that the boat had been captured by pirates, Burr said, "No, no, she is indeed dead. Were she alive, all the prisons in the world could not keep her from her father. When I realized the truth of her death, the world became a blank to me, and life had then lost all its value."

When he was nearly eighty, he married a lady of wealth; but they were unhappy, and soon separated. He died on Staten Island, cared for at the last by the children of an old friend. His courage and fortitude the world will always admire; but it can never forget the fatal duel by which Alexander Hamilton was taken from his country, in the prime of his life and in the midst of his great work.

The name of Hamilton will not be forgotten. The Hon. Chauncey M. Depew of New York, on February 22, 1888, gave the great statesman this well deserved tribute of praise:—

"The political mission of the United States has so far been wrought out by individuals and territorial conditions. Four men of unequal genius have dominated our century, and the growth of the West has revolutionized the republic. The principles which have heretofore controlled the policy of the country have mainly owed their force and acceptance to Hamilton, Jefferson, Webster, and Lincoln.

"The first question which met the young confederacy was the necessity of a central power strong enough to deal with foreign nations and to protect commerce between the States. At this period Alexander Hamilton became the savior of the republic. If Shakespeare is the commanding originating genius of England, and Goethe of Germany, Hamilton must occupy that place among Americans. This superb intelligence, which was at once philosophic and practical, and with unrivalled lucidity could instruct the dullest mind on the bearing of the action of the present on the destiny of the future, so impressed upon his contemporaries the necessity of a central government with large powers that the Constitution, now one hundred and one years old, was adopted, and the United States began their life as a nation."

ANDREW JACKSON

George Bancroft said, "No man in private life so possessed the hearts of all around him; no public man of the country ever returned to private life with such an abiding mastery over the affections of the people.... He was as sincere a man as ever lived. He was wholly, always, and altogether sincere and true. Up to the last he dared do anything that it was right to do. He united personal courage and moral courage beyond any man of whom history keeps the record.... Jackson never was vanquished. He was always fortunate. He conquered the wilderness; he conquered the savage; he conquered the veterans of the battle-field of Europe; he conquered everywhere in statesmanship; and when death came to get the mastery over him, he turned that last enemy aside as tranquilly as he had done the feeblest of his adversaries, and passed from earth in the triumphant consciousness of immortality."

Thus wrote Bancroft of the man who rose from poverty and sorrow to receive the highest gift which the American nation can bestow. The gift did not come through chance; it came because the man was worthy of it, and had earned the love and honor of the people.

In 1765, among many other emigrants, a man, with his wife and two sons, came to the new world from the north of Ireland. They were linen-weavers, poor, but industrious, and members of the Presbyterian Church. They settled at Waxhaw, North Carolina, not far from the South Carolina boundary, and the husband began to build a log house for his dear ones. This man was the father of Andrew Jackson.

Scarcely had the log house been built, and a single crop raised, before the wife was left a widow and the children fatherless. There was a quiet funeral, a half-dozen friends standing around an open grave, and then the little house passed into other hands, and Mrs. Jackson went to live at the home of her brother-in-law.

Not long after the funeral, a third son was born, March 15, 1767, whom the stricken mother named Andrew Jackson, after his father. He was welcomed in tears, and naturally became the idol of her young heart. Three weeks later, she moved to the house of another brother-in-law to assist in his family. She was not afraid to work, and she bent herself to the hard labor of pioneer life. There was no sorrow in the labor, for was she not doing it for her sons, and a noble woman knows no hardship in her self-sacrifice for love.

72

Her ambition seems to have centred in the slight, light-haired, blue-eyed Andrew, who, she hoped, one day might become a Presbyterian minister. How he was to obtain a college education, perhaps, she did not discern, but she trusted, and trust is a divine thing.

The barefooted boy attended a school kept by Dr. Waddell. He made commendable progress in his studies, from his quick and ardent temperament, but he loved fun even better than books. He was impulsive, ambitious, and persevering. He could run foot-races as rapidly as the bigger boys, and loved to wrestle or engage in anything which seemed like a battle. Says an old schoolmate, "I could throw him three times out of four, but he would never stay throwed. He was dead game, even then, and never would give up."

To the younger boys he was a protector, but from the older he would brook no insult, and was sometimes hasty and overbearing. One of the best traits in the boy's character was his love for his mother. His intense nature knew no change, and he was loyal and single of purpose forever. He used to say in later life, "One of the last injunctions given me by my mother was never to institute a suit for assault and battery or for defamation; never to wound the feelings of others nor suffer my own to be outraged: these were her words of admonition to me; I remember them well, and have never failed to respect them; my settled course through life has been to bear them in mind, and never to insult or wantonly to assail the feelings of any one; and yet many conceive me to be a most ferocious animal, insensible to moral duty and regardless of the laws both of God and man."

He did nothing slowly nor indifferently. He bent his will to his work, even at that early age, and knew no such word as failure. When the boy was thirteen, an incident occurred which made a lasting impression. The British General Tarlton, in the Revolutionary War, with three hundred cavalry, came against Waxhaw, surprised the militia, killing one hundred and thirteen and wounding one hundred and fifty. The little settlement was terrorized. The meeting-house became a hospital, and Mrs. Jackson, with her sons, helped to minister to the wants of the suffering soldiers. Andrew learned not only lessons in war, but to dream of future rewards to the British.

When Cornwallis, after the surrender of General Gates, moved his whole army toward Waxhaw, Mrs. Jackson and her sons were obliged to seek a safe retreat with a distant relative. Here Andrew did "chores" for his board. "Never," said one who knew him well at this time, "did Andrew come home from the shops without bringing with him some new weapon with which to kill the enemy. Sometimes it was a rude spear, which he would forge while waiting for the blacksmith to finish his job. Sometimes it was a club or a tomahawk. Once he fastened the blade of a scythe to a pole, and, on reaching home, began to cut down the weeds with it that grew about the house, assailing them with extreme fury, and occasionally uttering words like these, 'Oh, if I were a man, how I would sweep down the British with my grass blade!'"

A year later, when Mrs. Jackson had returned to Waxhaw, the brothers were both taken prisoners in a skirmish. Being commanded to clean the boots of a British officer, Andrew refused, saying, "Sir, I am a prisoner of war, and claim to be treated as such."

The angry Englishman drew his sword, and rushed at the boy, who, attempting to defend himself from the blow, received a deep gash in his left hand, and also on his head, the scars of which he bore through life. Robert, the brother, also refused to clean the boots, and was prostrated by the sword of the brutal officer. Soon after, the boys were taken with other prisoners to Camden, eighty miles distant, a long and agonizing journey for wounded men.

They found the prison a wretched place, with no medical supplies; the food scanty, and small-pox raging among the inmates. The poor mother, hearing of their forlorn condition, hastened to the place. Both her boys were ill of the dreaded small-pox, and both suffering from their sword-wounds. She arranged for the exchange of prisoners, and took her sons home; Robert to die in her arms two days later, and Andrew to be saved at last after a perilous illness of several months. Her oldest son, Hugh, had already given his life to his country in the war.

Almost broken-hearted with the loss of her two sons, yet intensely patriotic, she hastened to the Charleston prison-ships, to care for the wounded, taking with her provisions and medicine sent by loving wives and daughters. The blessed ministrations proved of short duration. Mrs. Jackson was taken ill of ship-fever, died after a brief illness, and was buried in the open plain near by. The grave is unmarked and unknown. When, years later, her illustrious son had become President, he tried to find the burial-place of the woman he idolized, but it was impossible.

Andrew was now an orphan, and poor; but he had what makes any boy or man rich, the memory of a devoted, heroic mother. Such a person has an inspiration that is like martial music on the field of battle; he is urged onward to duty forevermore. The world is richer for all such instances of ideal womanhood; the womanhood that gives rather than receives; that seeks neither admiration nor self-aggrandizement; that, like the flowers, sends out the same fragrance whether in royal gardens or beside the peasant's door; that lives to lighten others' sorrows, to rest tired humanity, to sweeten the bitterness of life by her loveliness of soul; that is to the world around her

"A new and certain sunrise every day."

Fatherless, motherless, brotherless, the boy of fifteen looked about him to see what his life-work should be. In the family of a distant relative he found a home. The son was a saddler. For six months Andrew worked at this trade. But other plans were in his mind. He knew how his mother had desired that he might be educated. But how could a boy win his way without money? For two years or more, little is known of him. It is believed that he taught a small school. When nearly eighteen, he had made up his mind to study law, a somewhat remarkable decision for a boy in his circumstances.

If he studied at all, it should be under the best of teachers; so he rode to Salisbury, seventy-five miles from Waxhaw, and entered the office of Mr. Spruce McCay, an eminent lawyer, and later a judge of distinction.

For nearly two years he studied, enjoying also the sports of the time, and making, as he did all through life, close friends who were devoted to his interests. When in the White House, forty-five years afterward, he said, "I was but a raw lad then, but I did my best." And he did his best through life!

He loved a fine horse almost as though it were human; he enjoyed the society of ladies, and possessed a grace and dignity of manner that surprised those who knew the hardships of his life. His eager intelligence, his quick, direct glance, that bespoke alertness of mind, won him attention, even more than would beauty of person. Over six feet in height, slender to delicacy, he gave the impression of leadership, from his bravery and self-reliance. Emerson well says, "The basis of good manners is self-reliance.... Self-trust is the first secret of success; the belief that, if you are here, the authorities of the universe put you here, and for cause or with some task strictly appointed you in your constitution."

When his two years of law-study were ended, the work was but just begun. There was reputation to be made, and perhaps a fortune, but where and how? For a year he seems not to have found a law opening; the streams of fortune do not always flow toward us—we have to make the journey by persistent and hard rowing

75

against the tide. He probably worked in a store owned by some acquaintances, earning for daily needs.

At twenty-one came his first opportunity; came, as it often comes, through a friend. Mr. John McNairy was appointed a judge of the Superior Court of the Western District of North Carolina (Tennessee), and young Jackson, his friend, public prosecutor of the same district. He moved to Nashville in 1788, to begin his difficult work. He was obliged to ride on horseback over the mountains and through the wilderness, often among hostile Indians, his life almost constantly in danger. Once, while travelling with a party of emigrants, when all slept save the sentinels, he sat against a tree, smoking his corn-cob pipe and keeping an eager watch. Soon he heard the notes of what seemed to be various owls! He quietly roused the whole party and moved them on. An hour later, a company of hunters lay down by the fires which Jackson had left, and before daylight all save one man were killed by the Indians.

Sometimes the young lawyer slept for twenty successive nights in the wilderness. This was no life of ease and luxury. At Nashville he found lodgings in the house of the widow of Colonel John Donelson, a brave pioneer from Virginia, who had been killed by the Indians. And here Jackson met the woman who was to prove his good angel as long as she lived. With Mrs. Donelson lived her dark-haired and dark-eyed daughter Rachel, married to Lewis Robards from Kentucky. Vivacious, kindly, and sympathetic, Rachel had been the idol of her father, and probably would have been of her husband had it not been for his jealous disposition. He became angry at Jackson, as he had been at others, and made her life so unhappy that she separated from him and went to friends in Natchez, with the approval of her mother, and the entire confidence and respect of her husband's relatives.

After a divorce in 1791, Jackson married her, when they were each twenty-four years old. History does not record a happier marriage. To the last, she lived for him alone, but not more fully than he lived for her. With the world he was thought to be domineering and harsh, and was often profane; but with her he was patient, gentle, and deferential. When he won renown, she was happy for his sake, but she did not care for it for herself. Her kindness of heart took her among the sick and the unfortunate, and everywhere she was a welcome comforter. She lived outside of self, and found her reward in the homage of her husband and her friends.

Jackson soon began to prosper financially. Often he would receive his fee in lands, a square mile of six hundred and forty acres

76

or more, so that after a time he was the possessor of several thousand acres. Success came also from other sources. When a convention was called to form a constitution for the new State of Tennessee, Jackson was chosen a delegate. He took an active part in the organization of the State—he was active in whatever he engaged—and bravely espoused her claims against the general government for expenses incurred in Indian conflicts. Tennessee felt that she had a true friend in Jackson, and, when she wanted a man to represent her in Congress, she sent him to the House of Representatives. This honor came at twenty-nine years of age—a strange contrast to the years when he made saddles or did "chores" for his board, and longed to "sweep down the British with his grass blade."

Jackson served his State well by securing compensation for every man who had done service or lost his property in the Indian wars. It was not strange, therefore, that, when a vacancy occurred in the United States Senate, Jackson was chosen to fill the place, in the autumn of 1797. Only thirty years old! Rachel Jackson might well be proud of him.

But the following year he resigned his position, glad to be, as he supposed, out of official life. He was, however, too prominent to be allowed to remain in private life, and was elected to a judgeship of the Supreme Court of Tennessee. As he had made it a rule "never to seek and never to decline public duty," he accepted, on the small salary of six hundred dollars a year. While many other men in the State were more learned in the law than Jackson, yet the people believed in his honesty and integrity, and therefore he was chosen. Quick to decide and slow to change his mind, in fifteen days he had disposed of fifty cases, says James Parton, in his entertaining life of Andrew Jackson.

After six years, longing for a more active life, Jackson resigned, and was made major-general of the militia of the State. This position was given, not without opposition, he receiving only one more vote than his chief competitor. That one vote, perhaps, led to New Orleans and the Presidency. This office was in accordance with his natural tastes. Since boyhood, he had loved the stir and command of battle, and believed he should like to conquer an enemy as he had met and conquered every obstacle that lay athwart his path.

As there was no war in progress, he continued his law practice. But, not satisfied with this alone, he became a merchant, trading with the Indians, selling blankets, hardware, and the like, and receiving in return cotton and other produce of the country. In the panic of 1798, he became financially embarrassed, but, true to his manly nature, he worked steadily on till every dollar was paid. He sold twenty-five thousand acres of his wild land, sold his home, and moved into a log house at the Hermitage, seven miles out from Nashville, and preserved for himself the best thing on earth, a good name. So honest was he believed to be, when a Tennessean went to Boston bankers for a loan, with several leading names on his paper, they said, "Do you know General Jackson? Could you get his endorsement?"

"Yes, but he is not worth a tenth as much as either of these men whose names I offer you," was the response.

"No matter; General Jackson has always protected himself and his paper, and we'll let you have the money on the strength of his name." And the loan was granted.

Honest and just though he was, he permitted his own fiery nature, or a perverted public opinion, to lead him into acts which tarnished his whole subsequent career. Quick to resent a wrong, he was morbidly sensitive about the circumstances of his marriage with Rachel Robards. When they were married, in 1791, they supposed that the divorce, applied for, had been granted, but they learned in 1793, two years afterward, that it was not legally obtained till the latter date. They were at once remarried, but the matter caused much idle talk, and, as General Jackson came into prominence, his enemies were not slow to rehearse the story. The slightest aspersion of his wife's character aroused all the anger of his nature, and, says Parton, "For the man who dared breathe her name except in honor, he kept pistols in perfect condition for thirty-seven years." And, as duelling was the disgraceful fashion of the times, Jackson did not hesitate to use his pistols.

In 1806, when he was thirty-nine, one of those miscalled "affairs of honor" took place. Charles Dickinson, a prominent man of the State, in the course of a long quarrel, had spoken disparagingly of Mrs. Jackson, and he was therefore challenged to mortal combat. Thursday morning, May 29, he kissed his young wife tenderly, telling her he was going to Kentucky, and "would be home, sure, to-morrow night." He met Jackson on the banks of the Red River. The one was tall, erect, and intense; the other young, handsome, an expert marksman, and determined to make no mistake in his fatal work.

Dickinson fired with his supposed unerring aim, and missed! The bullet grazed Jackson's breast, and years later was the true cause of his death. Jackson took deliberate aim, intending to kill his opponent, and succeeded. The ball passed quite through

Dickinson's body. His wife was sent for, being told that he was dangerously wounded. On her way thither she met, in a rough emigrant wagon, the body of her husband. He had "come home, sure, to-morrow night"—but dead! He was deeply mourned by the State, which sympathized with his wife and infant child. General Jackson made bitter enemies by this act. Rachel had been avenged, but at what a fearful cost!

Eighteen years had gone by since Jackson's marriage. He had received distinguished honors; he had been a Representative, a Senator, a Judge of the Supreme Court of the State, a Major-General of the militia, but one joy was wanting. No children had been born in the home. Mrs. Jackson's nephews and nieces were often at the Hermitage, and he made her kindred his own; but both loved children, and this one blessing was denied them. In 1809, twins were born to Mrs. Jackson's brother. One of these, when but a few days old, was taken to the Hermitage, and the general adopted him, giving him his own name, Andrew Jackson.

Ever after, this child was a comfort and a delight. Visitors would often find the general reading, with the boy in the rocking-chair beside him or in his lap. Hon. Thomas H. Benton, in his "Thirty Years' View," tells this story: "I arrived at his house one wet, chilly evening in February, and came upon him in the twilight, sitting alone before the fire, a lamb and a child between his knees. He started a little, called a servant to remove the two innocents to another room, and explained to me how it was. The child had cried because the lamb was out in the cold, and begged him to bring it in, which he had done to please the child, his adopted son, then not two years old. The ferocious man does not do that! and though Jackson had his passions and his violence, they were for men and enemies— those who stood up against him—and not for women and children, or the weak and helpless; for all whom his feelings were those of protection and support."

Jackson was always the friend of young men—a constant inspiration to them to do their best. He knew the possibilities of a barefooted boy like himself. The world owes thanks to those who are its inspiration; whose minds develop ours; whose sweetness of nature makes us grow lovable, as plants grow in the sunshine; whose ideals become our ideals; who lead us up the mountains of faith and trust and hope, but the cord is silken and we never know that we are led; who go through life loving and serving—for love is service; who are our comfort and strength—we lean on those whom we love.

While Jackson was the friend of young men, especially he was loyal to any who were near his heart. He was like another great man, in a great war, the hero of 1812 and the hero of 1861. Jackson and Grant were true to those who had been true to them. Only a man of small soul forgets the ladder by which he climbs.

The second war with Great Britain had come upon the American people, June 19, 1812. Our country had suffered in its commerce through the continued wars of England with France. Vessels had been searched by the English, to find persons suspected of being British subjects; often American seamen were impressed into their service. On the ocean, the contest between English and American ships became almost constant. While a portion of the States were not in favor of the war, one person was surely in favor, and ready for it; one who had not forgotten the deaths of his mother and brothers in the Revolutionary War; who had not forgotten the wounds on his head and hand. That person was General Jackson.

He at once offered to the Governor of Louisiana, for the defence of New Orleans, three thousand soldiers. The offer was accepted, and he started for Natchez, there to await orders. The men were in the best of spirits, kept hopeful and enthusiastic by the ardor of their commander, who said to them: "Perish our friends—perish our wives—perish our children (the dearest pledges of Heaven)—nay, perish all earthly considerations—but let the honor and fame of a volunteer soldier be untarnished and immaculate. We now enjoy liberties, political, civil, and religious, that no other nation on earth possesses. May we never survive them! No, rather let us perish in maintaining them. And if we must yield, where is the man that would not prefer being buried in the ruins of his country than live the ignominious slave of haughty lords and unfeeling tyrants?"

After a time the "orders" came, but what was the astonishment and indignation of both officers and men to hear that their services were not needed, as the British evidently did not intend to attack New Orleans; that they were to disband and return to Tennessee. Without pay or rations, five hundred miles from home!—Jackson felt that it was an insult. He took an oath that they should never disband till they were at their own doors; that he would conduct his brave three thousand through the wilderness and the Indian tribes, and be responsible for expenses. One hundred and fifty of his men were ill. He put those who could ride on horses, and then, walking at their head, led the gallant company toward home.

The soldiers used to say that he was "tough as hickory;" then "Old Hickory" grew to be a term of endearment, which he bore ever afterward. A month later, and the disappointed soldiers were at Nashville. Before they disbanded, they were marched out upon the public square, and received a superb stand of colors. The needle-work was on white satin; eighteen orange stars in a crescent, with two sprigs of laurel, and the words, "Tennessee Volunteers—Independence, in a state of war, is to be maintained on the battle-ground of the Republic. The tented field is the post of honor. Presented by the ladies of East Tennessee." Under these words were all the implements of war; cannons, muskets, drums, swords, and the like. Jackson and his men never forgot this offering of love, and showed themselves worthy of it in after years.

If Jackson was not needed at New Orleans, he was soon needed elsewhere. Tecumseh, the great Indian chief, saw the lands of his fathers passing into the hands of the white men. He had long been uniting the western tribes from Florida to the northern lakes, and, now that we were at war with England, he believed the hour of their delivery was come. He at once incited the Creeks of Alabama to arms.

In the southern portion of that State, forty miles north of Mobile, stood Fort Mims. The whites had become alarmed at the hostile attitude of the Indians, and over five hundred men, women, and children had crowded into the fort for safety. On the 30th of August, 1813, a thousand Creek warriors in their war paint and feathers, uttering their terrible war-whoops, rushed into the fort, tomahawked the men and women, and trampled the children into the dust. The buildings were burned, and the plain was covered with dead bodies. The massacre at Fort Mims blanched every face and embittered every heart. The Tennesseans offered at once to march against the Creeks. The hot-headed General Jackson had been wounded in a quarrel with Thomas H. Benton, and was suffering from the ball in his shoulder, which he carried there for twenty years. But he put his left arm into a sling, and, though emaciated through long weeks of illness, he led his twenty-five hundred men into the Indians' country.

The provisions did not follow them as had been arranged. Jackson wrote home earnestly for money and food. He said, "There is an enemy whom I dread much more than I do the hostile Creeks, and whose power, I am fearful, I shall first be made to feel—I mean the meagre monster, Famine." And yet he encouraged his men with these brave words: "Shall an enemy wholly unacquainted with military evolution, and who rely more for victory on their grim visages and hideous yells than upon their bravery or their weapons—shall such an enemy ever drive before them the well

81

trained youths of our country, whose bosoms pant for glory and a desire to avenge the wrongs they have received? Your general will not live to behold such a spectacle; rather would he rush into the thickest of the enemy, and submit himself to their scalping-knives.... With his soldiers he will face all dangers, and with them participate in the glory of conquest."

The first battle with the Creeks was fought under General John Coffee at Talluschatches, thirteen miles from Jackson's camp, the friendly Creeks leading the way, wearing white feathers and white deer's-tails to distinguish them from the hostile tribes. The whites, maddened by the memory of Fort Mims, fought like tigers; the Indians, sullen and revengeful at the prospect of losing their homes and their hunting-grounds, neither asked nor gave quarter, and fought heroically. Nearly the whole town perished.

On the battle-field was found a dead mother with her arms clasped about a living child. The babe was brought into camp, and Jackson asked some of the Indian women to care for it. "No!" said they, "all his relations are dead; kill him too." The baby was cared for at General Jackson's expense till the campaign was over, and then carried to the Hermitage, where he grew to young manhood as a petted son. The general and his wife gave him the name of Lincoyer. In his seventeenth year he died of consumption, sincerely mourned by his devoted friends.

Following the battle of Talluschatches, General Jackson moved against Talladega, and, after a bloody conflict, rescued one hundred and fifty friendly Creeks. Returning to camp, he found starvation staring him in the face. The men were becoming desperate; yet he kept his cheerfulness, dividing with them the last crust. One morning a gaunt, hungry-looking soldier approached General Jackson as he was sitting under a tree, eating, and asked for some food, saying that he was nearly starving.

"It has been a rule with me," said the general, "never to turn away a hungry man, when it is in my power to relieve him, and I will most cheerfully divide with you what I have." Putting his hand in his pocket, he drew forth a few acorns. "This is the best and only fare I have," he said, and the soldier was comforted.

Many of the men had enlisted for three months only, and were impatient to return home. Finally, the militia determined to return with or without the general's consent. Jackson heard of their intention, and at once ordered the volunteers to detain them, peaceably if they could, forcibly if they must. Then the volunteers, in turn, attempted to go back, but were met by Jackson's firm resolve to shoot the first man who took a step toward home.

"I cannot," he said, "must not believe that the 'Volunteers of Tennessee,' a name ever dear to fame, will disgrace themselves, and a country which they have honored, by abandoning her standard, as mutineers and deserters; but should I be disappointed, and compelled to resign this pleasing hope, one thing I will not resign— my duty. Mutiny and sedition, so long as I possess the power of quelling them, shall be put down; and even when left destitute of this, I will still be found in the last extremity endeavoring to discharge the duty I owe my country and myself." That one word, "duty," was the key-note of Jackson's life. It was his religion—it was his philosophy.

With all Jackson's kindness to his men, they knew that he could be severe. John Woods, a boy not eighteen, the support of aged parents, was shot for refusing to obey a superior officer. That he could have been spared seems probable, but Jackson taught hard lessons to his undisciplined troops, and sometimes in a harsh manner.

In seven months the Creeks had been utterly routed; half their warriors were dead, and the rest were broken in spirit. Weathersford, their most heroic chief, the leader at the Fort Mims massacre, sought General Jackson at his camp.

"How dare you," said Jackson, "ride up to my tent, after having murdered the women and children at Fort Mims?"

"General Jackson, I am not afraid of you," was the reply. "I fear no man, for I am a Creek warrior. I have nothing to request in behalf of myself. You can kill me, if you desire. But I come to beg you to send for the women and children of the war party, who are now starving in the woods. Their fields and cribs have been destroyed by your people, who have driven them to the woods without an ear of corn. I hope that you will send out parties, who will conduct them safely here, in order that they may be fed. I exerted myself in vain to prevent the massacre of the women and children at Fort Mims. I am now done fighting. The Red Sticks are nearly all killed. If I could fight you any longer, I would most heartily do so. Send for the women and children. They never did you any harm. But kill me, if the white people want it done."

"Kill him! kill him!" shouted several voices.

"Silence!" exclaimed Jackson. "Any man who would kill as brave a man as this would rob the dead!"

Weathersford's request was granted, and the women and children of the war party were provided for. The chief died many years afterward, a planter in Alabama, respected by the Americans for his bravery and his honor.

The Creek war over, Jackson went back to Tennessee, a noted, successful soldier. He had not only conquered the Creeks, but he had won for himself the position of major-general in the United States army, having in charge the department of the South. He was now forty-seven, and had indeed reached a high position. Mississippi voted him a sword, and other States sent testimonials of appreciation. All this time he was a constant sufferer in body, and only kept himself from his bed by his indomitable will. The Hermitage could not long keep the ardent, tireless general from the front. He soon established his headquarters at Mobile, and prepared to defend a thousand miles of coast from the British. He had but a small army at his command, and was far from Washington, with scarcely any means of communication. Indeed, the English had captured that city already, and burned most of its public buildings.

The English had attacked Mobile Point, been defeated, and retired to Pensacola, Florida. Spain owned Florida, and was supposed to be neutral, but she was in reality friendly and helpful to England, and allowed her to use the State as a base of operations. Jackson wrote to Washington asking leave to attack Pensacola. The answer did not come back till the war of 1812 was over and Jackson had won renown for himself and his country. He did not wait for an answer, however, but stormed Pensacola, captured it, and then hastened to New Orleans, where he expected the next attack would be made. He used to say to young men, "Always take all the time to reflect that circumstances will permit; but when the time for action has come, stop thinking." And at Pensacola he stopped thinking, and acted. Nothing was ready for his coming, but all eyes turned to the conquerer of the Creeks as the savior of New Orleans. Women gathered around him and looked trustingly toward the erect, self-centred, bronzed soldier. Men flocked willingly to his service, glad to do his bidding. He summoned the engineers of the city and ordered every bayou to be obstructed by earth and sunken logs. The city was put under martial law. No person was permitted to leave the place without a written permit signed by the general or one of his staff. The street lamps were extinguished at nine o'clock, after which hour any person without the necessary permit or not having the countersign was apprehended as a spy and held for examination. All able-bodied men, black and white, were compelled to serve as soldiers or sailors.

He had with him about two thousand troops, and four thousand more within ten or fifteen days' march. Against these, for the most part undisciplined troops, a British force of twenty thousand men was coming, with a fleet of fifty ships, carrying a thousand guns. Much of this army had served under the great Wellington in France; its present leader, General Packenham, was Wellington's brother-in-law. He was only thirty-eight, brave, and the idol of his men. Some of the ships had been with Nelson in the battle of the Nile. The flower of England's army and navy had been sent to conquer the independent and self-reliant Americans.

So certain were the British of conquest that several families were with the fleet, husbands and brothers having been appointed already to civil offices. Another person was also confident of victory—the man who had seen but fourteen months of service, but who from boyhood had never known what it was to be defeated. He inspired others with the same confidence. Says Latour, in his history of the war in West Florida and Louisiana, "The energy manifested by General Jackson spread, as it were, by contagion, and communicated itself to the whole army. There was nothing which those who composed it did not feel themselves capable of performing, if he ordered it to be done. It was enough that he expressed a wish or threw out the slightest intimation, and immediately a crowd of volunteers offered themselves to carry his views into execution."

The English fleet entered Lake Borgne, sixty miles north-east from New Orleans, on December 10, 1814. Twelve days later they had reached the Mississippi River, nine miles below the city. The next day, when Jackson was informed of their approach, he said, bringing his clenched fist down upon the table, "By the Eternal, they shall not sleep on our soil!"

At once, with, as Parton says, that "calm impetuosity and that composed intensity which belonged to him," he sent word to the various regiments to meet him at three o'clock at a specified place. And then he lay down and slept for a short time, his only rest during the next three days and three nights. Few men except General Jackson, with his iron will, could have slept at such a time. A messenger came, sent by some ladies, asking what they should do if the city were attacked.

"Say to them not to be uneasy. No British soldier shall enter the city as an enemy, unless over my dead body," and he kept his word.

At three o'clock the men were hastening on to meet the "red-coats." Twilight came early, and the moon rose dimly over the battle-field. The signal of attack was to be a shot fired from the ship Carolina. At half-past seven, the first gun was heard, then seven others, and the word was given—Forward.

And forward they went, with quick steps and eager hearts. A

tremendous fire opened upon our artillery-men. The horses attached to the cannon became unmanageable, and one of the pieces was turned over into the ditch. Jackson dashed into the midst of the fray, exclaiming, "Save the guns, my boys, at every sacrifice," and the guns were saved. Men fought hand to hand in the smoke and the darkness; the British using their bayonets, and the Americans their long hunting-knives. Prisoners were taken and retaken. Till ten o'clock the battle raged; when our men fell back upon the Roderiguez canal, to wait till the morning sun should show where to begin the deadly work. When the morning came, the battle-field presented a ghastly appearance. Says a British officer concerning the American dead, "Their hair, eyebrows, and lashes were thickly covered with hoar-frost, or rime, their bloodless cheeks vying with its whiteness. Few were dressed in military uniforms, and most of them bore the appearance of farmers or husbandmen. Peace to their ashes! they had nobly died in defending their country."

The Roderiguez canal was now strongly fortified. Spades, crowbars, and wheelbarrows had been sent from the city. The canal was deepened and the earth thrown up on the side. Fences were torn away, and rails driven down to keep the sand from falling back into the canal. The line of defence, a mile long, was four or five feet high in some places. Cotton bales from a neighboring ship were used.

"Here," said Jackson, "we will plant our stakes, and not abandon them until we drive these 'red-coat' rascals into the river or the swamp."

While these busy preparations were going on, food was brought to General Jackson, which he ate in the saddle. Christmas day came. The English Admiral Cochrane had said, "I shall eat my Christmas dinner in New Orleans." General Jackson heard of it, and remarked, "Perhaps so; but I shall have the honor of presiding at that dinner."

The Americans were ready, but the British did not make the expected attack. Every man was at his post. When an officer, the son of one of Jackson's best friends, said to him, "May I go to town to-day?" the reply was, "Of course, Captain Livingston, you may go; but ought you to go?" The young man blushed, bowed, and returned to duty.

Meantime, the British were not idle. They had determined to silence the guns of the American ships, and, with great toil, had brought up into the swampy ground nine field-pieces, two howitzers, one mortar, a furnace for heating balls, and the necessary

86

ammunition. At dawn on the morning of December 27 the firing began. The Carolina, after a terrific bombardment, blew up. The Louisiana fought her way out into a place of safety.

The days went by slowly under the dreadful suspense. On New Year's day, General Packenham cannonaded the Americans and was driven back. On January 8, the final battle began. Early in the morning, the British moved against the Americans. Jackson walked along the lines, cheering the men, "Stand to your guns. Don't waste your ammunition. See that every shot tells. Give it to them, boys! Let us finish the business to-day."

And every shot did tell. The sharpshooters aimed at the officers, and the batteries mowed down the British regulars. Seeing them falter, Packenham rushed among the men, shouting, "For shame! recollect that you are British soldiers!" Taking off his hat, he spurred his horse to the head of the wavering column. A ball splintered his right arm. Then the Highlanders came to the support of their comrades.

"Hurrah! brave Highlanders!" he said, as a mass of grape-shot tore open his thigh and killed his horse. Another shot struck him, and he was borne under a live-oak to die. The great tree is still standing.

At nine o'clock in the morning the battle was virtually over. The English lost seven hundred killed, fourteen hundred wounded, and five hundred taken prisoners; while the Americans lost but eight killed and thirteen wounded. "The field was so thickly strewn with the dead that, from the American ditch, you could have walked a quarter of a mile to the front on the bodies of the killed and disabled.... The course of the column could be distinctly traced in the broad red line of the victims of the terrible batteries and unerring guns of the Americans. They fell in their tracks; in some places, whole platoons lay together, as if killed by the same discharge."

The news of this great victory at New Orleans astonished the North, and made Jackson the hero of his time. The whole country was proud of a man who could win such a battle, losing the lives of so few of his men. Nearly every State passed resolutions in his praise. The Senate and House of Representatives ordered a gold medal to be struck in his honor. Philadelphia enjoyed a general illumination; one of the transparencies representing the general on horseback in pursuit of the enemy, with the words, "This day shall ne'er go by, from this day to the ending of the world, but He in it shall be remembered." Henry Clay said, "Now I can go to England without mortification."

When Jackson and his army returned to New Orleans, men, women, and children came out to meet them. Young ladies strewed flowers along the way; children crowned the general with laurel, and an impressive service was held in his honor in the Cathedral. He replied, "For myself, to have been instrumental in the deliverance of such a country is the greatest blessing that Heaven could confer. That it has been effected with so little loss—that so few tears should cloud the smiles of our triumph, and not a cypress leaf be interwoven in the wreath which you present, is a source of the most exquisite enjoyment."

Mrs. Jackson and little Andrew, now seven years old, came down from the Hermitage, and his cup of joy was indeed full. To have Rachel's commendation was more than to have that of all of the world besides. The ladies of New Orleans gave to her a valuable set of topaz jewelry, and to the general a diamond pin. A month later, they were at home once more. He had shown the good judgment, the calm bravery, the comprehensive outlook, the quick decision, the tender compassion of the great soldier. Perhaps the busy public life was over—who could tell?

Four months later, General Jackson went to Washington, at the request of the Secretary of War, to arrange about the stations of the army in the South. The journey thither was one constant ovation. At a great banquet tendered him at Lynchburg, Virginia, Thomas Jefferson, then seventy-two, gave this toast: "Honor and gratitude to those who have filled the measure of their country's honor." At Washington also he received distinguished attention.

In 1817, the Seminole Indians of Georgia and Alabama had become hostile. General Jackson was the man to conquer them. He immediately marched into their country with eighteen hundred whites and fifteen hundred friendly Indians, and in five months subjugated them.

Florida was purchased in 1819, and two years later Jackson was appointed its governor, with a salary of five thousand dollars. Mrs. Jackson joined him there, but neither was happy, and he soon resigned, and returned with her to the Hermitage. He had built for her a new house, a two-story brick, surrounded by a double piazza. He was at this time frail in health, and did not expect ever to live in the home, but wished it to be made beautiful for her. He hoped now to live a quiet life, enjoying his garden and his farm; but the nation had other plans for him.

In 1823, Jackson was elected to the United States Senate, twenty-six years after his first appearance in that body. He was now prominently mentioned as a candidate for the Presidency. Strange contrast indeed to the days when, bare-footed and orphaned, he struggled for the rudiments of an education.

While he had many ardent friends, he had strong opponents. Daniel Webster said, "If General Jackson is elected, the government of our country will be overthrown; the judiciary will be destroyed;" yet he added, "His manners are more presidential than those of any of the candidates. He is grave, mild, and reserved. My wife is for him decidedly." Jefferson said, "I feel very much alarmed at the prospect of seeing General Jackson President. He is one of the most unfit men I know of for the place. He has had very little respect for laws or constitution, and is, in fact, an able military chief. His passions are terrible.... He has been much tried since I knew him, but he is a dangerous man." But the people knew he had conquered the Indians and the British, and they believed in him.

The candidates for the Presidency in 1824 were Jackson, John Quincy Adams, William H. Crawford, and Henry Clay. While Jackson received the largest popular vote, the House of Representatives, balloting by States, elected John Quincy Adams. It was believed that Clay used his influence for Adams against Jackson, and this caused the election of Adams, a scholarly man, the son of John Adams, and long our representative abroad.

Four years later, in 1828, the people made their voices heard at the ballot-box, and Jackson was elected by a large majority. The contest had been exceedingly personal and annoying. The old stories about his marriage were again dragged through the press. Mrs. Jackson, a victim of heart disease, was unduly troubled, and became broken in health. When he was elected, she said, "Well, for Mr. Jackson's sake, I am glad; for my own part, I never wished it."

Jackson had built for her a small brick church in the Hermitage grounds, and here, where the neighbors and servants gathered, she found her deepest happiness, and sighed for no greater sphere of usefulness. When she urged the general to join her church, he said, "My dear, if I were to do that now, it would be said, all over the country, that I had done it for the sake of political effect. My enemies would all say so. I cannot do it now, but I promise you that, when once more I am clear of politics, I will join the church."

The people of Nashville were of course proud that one from their city had been chosen to so high a position, and tendered him a banquet on December 23, the anniversary of the first battle at New Orleans. A few days before this, Mrs. Jackson was taken ill, but she urged her husband to make himself ready for the banquet. While he had watched by her bedside constantly, on the evening of December 22, she was so much better that he consented to lie down on a sofa in an adjoining room. He had not been there five minutes before a cry was heard from Mrs. Jackson. He hastened to her, but she never breathed again.

He could not believe that she was dead. When they brought a table to lay her body upon it, he said tenderly, in a choking voice, "Spread four blankets upon it. If she does come to, she will lie so hard upon the table."

All night long he sat beside the form of his beloved Rachel, often feeling of her heart and pulse. In the morning he was wholly inconsolable, and, when he found that she was really dead, the body could scarcely be forced from his arms.

At the funeral, the road to the Hermitage was almost impassable. The press said of her, "Her pure and gentle heart, in which a selfish, guileful, or malicious thought, never found entrance, was the throne of benevolence.... To feed the hungry, to clothe the naked, to supply the indigent, to raise the humble, to notice the friendless, and to comfort the unfortunate, were her favorite occupations.... Thus she lived, and when death approached, her patience and resignation were equal to her goodness; not an impatient gesture, not a vexatious look, not a fretful accent escaped her: but her last breath was charged with an expression of tenderness for the man whom she loved more than her life, and honored next to her God." Only such a nature could have held the undivided love of an impetuous, imperious man. Jackson, like so many other unchristian men, had the wisdom to desire and to choose for himself a Christian wife.

He prepared a tomb for her like an open summer-house, and buried her under the white dome supported by marble pillars. On the tablet above her are the words, "Here lie the remains of Mrs. Rachel Jackson, wife of President Jackson.... Her face was fair, her person pleasing, her temper amiable, her heart kind; she delighted in relieving the wants of her fellow-creatures, and cultivated that divine pleasure by the most liberal and unpretending methods; to the poor she was a benefactor; to the rich an example; to the wretched a comforter; to the prosperous an ornament; her piety went hand in hand with her benevolence, and she thanked her Creator for being permitted to do good. A being so gentle and so virtuous, slander might wound, but could not dishonor. Even Death, when he tore her from the arms of her husband, could but transport her to the bosom of her God."

Such a woman need have no fear that she will fade out of a human heart. While Jackson lived, he wore her miniature about his neck, and every night laid it open beside her prayer-book at his bedside. Her face was the last thing upon which his eyes rested before he slept, through those eight years at the White House, and the first thing upon which his eyes opened in the morning. Possibly it is not given to all women to win and hold so complete and beautiful an affection; perchance the fault is sometimes theirs.

Andrew Jackson went to Washington, having grown "twenty years older in a night," his friends said. His nephew, Andrew Jackson Donelson, and his lovely wife accompanied him. Earl, the artist, who had painted her picture ("her" always meant Rachel with General Jackson), for this reason found a home also at the White House.

The inauguration seemed to have drawn the whole country together. Webster said, "I never saw such a crowd here before. Persons have come five hundred miles to see General Jackson, and they really seem to think that the country is rescued from some dreadful danger." After the ceremony, crowds completely filled the White House.

During the first year of the Presidency, the unfortunate maxim which had found favor in New York politics, "To the victors belong the spoils," began to be carried out in the removal, it is believed, of nearly two thousand persons from office, and substituting those of different political opinions. The removals raised a storm of indignation from the opposite party, which did not in the least disturb General Jackson.

In his first message to Congress, after maintaining that a long tenure of office is corrupting, urging that the surplus revenue be apportioned among the several States for works of public utility, he took strong ground against rechartering the United States Bank. This caused much alarm, for the influence of the bank was very great. Its capital was thirty-five million dollars. The parent bank was at Philadelphia, with twenty-five branches in the large cities and towns. Since Alexander Hamilton's time, a government bank had been a matter of contention. When the second was started in 1816, after the war of 1812, business seemed to revive, but many persons believed, with Henry Clay, that such a bank was unconstitutional, and a vast political power that might be, and was, corruptly used. Complaints were constantly heard that officials were favored.

When the bill to recharter the bank passed Congress, Jackson promptly vetoed the bill. He said, "We can, at least, take a stand against all new grants of monopolies and exclusive privileges, against any prostitution of our government to the advancement of the few at the expense of the many." A few years later he determined to put an end to the bank by removing all the surplus funds, amounting to ten millions, and placing them in certain State banks. When Mr. Duane, the Secretary of the Treasury, would not remove the deposits, General Jackson immediately removed him, putting Roger B. Taney in his place. Congress passed a vote of censure on the President, but it was afterward expunged from the records. Speculation resulted from the distribution of the money; the panic of 1836-37 followed, which the Whigs said was caused by the destruction of the bank, and the Democrats by the bank itself.

The United States Bank was not the only disturbing question in these times. The tariff, which was advantageous to the manufacturers of the North, was considered disadvantageous to the agricultural interests of the South. Bitter feeling was engendered by the discussion, till South Carolina, under the leadership of John C. Calhoun, declared that the acts of Congress on the tariff were null and void; therefore, nullification or disunion became the absorbing topic. Then came the great dispute between Robert Y. Hayne and Daniel Webster.

If the nullifiers or believers in extreme States' rights supposed Jackson to be on their side, they were quickly undeceived. When Jefferson's birthday, April 13, was observed in Washington, as it had been for twenty years, Jackson sent the following toast: "Our Federal Union: it must be preserved." He wrote to the citizens of Charleston, "Every enlightened citizen must know that a separation, could it be effected, would begin with civil discord, and end in colonial dependence on a foreign power, and obliteration from the list of nations." He said, "If this thing goes on, our country will be like a bag of meal with both ends open. Pick it up in the middle or endwise, it will run out."

Still, South Carolina was not to be deterred, with the eloquent Calhoun as her leader, and the Nullification Ordinance was passed November 24, 1832. At once the governor was authorized to accept the service of volunteers. Medals were struck bearing the words, "John C. Calhoun, First President of the Southern Confederacy."

By the time South Carolina was ready to break the laws, another person was ready to enforce them. Jackson at once sent General Scott to take command at Charleston, with gun-boats close by, and sent also an earnest and eloquent protest to the seceding State. Public meetings were held in the large cities of the North. The tariff was modified at the next session of Congress, but the disunion doctrines were allowed to grow till thirty years later, when they bore the bitter fruit of civil war.

When Jackson was asked, years afterward, what he would have done with Calhoun and the nullifiers if they had continued, he replied, "Hung them as high as Haman. They should have been a terror to traitors to all time, and posterity would have pronounced it the best act of my life." When difficulties arose about the Cherokees of Georgia, he removed them to the Indian Territory; a harsh measure it seemed, but perhaps not harder for the tribes than to have attempted to live among hostile whites. When the French king neglected to pay the five million dollars agreed upon for injuries done to our shipping, Jackson recommended to make reprisals on French merchantmen, and the money was paid. The national debt was paid under Jackson, who believed rightly that this, as well as every other kind of debt, is a curse. The Eaton affair showed his loyalty to friends. John H. Eaton, Secretary of War, had married the widow of a purser in the Navy, formerly the daughter of a tavern-keeper in Washington. Her conduct had caused criticism, and the ladies of the Cabinet would not associate with her—even though President Jackson tried every means in his power to compel it, as Eaton was his warm friend.

When the eight years of presidential life were over, Jackson sent his farewell address to the people of the country, who had idolized him, and whom he had loved, he said, "with the affection of a son," and retired to the Hermitage. The people of Nashville met him with outstretched arms and tearful faces. He was seventy years old, their President, and he had come home to live and die with them.

He was now through with politics, and wanted to carry out her wishes, to join the little Hermitage church. The night of decision was full of meditation and prayer. One morning in 1843, the church was crowded to see the ex-President make a public confession of the Christian religion. He went home to read his Bible more carefully than ever—he had never read less than three chapters daily for thirty-five years, such is the influence of early education received at a mother's knee.

The following year, 1844, Commodore Elliot offered the sarcophagus which he brought from Palestine, believed to have contained the remains of the Roman Emperor, Alexander Severus, to President Jackson for his final resting-place.

A letter of cordial thanks was returned, with the words, "I cannot consent that my mortal body shall be laid in a repository prepared for an emperor or a king. My republican feelings and principles forbid it; the simplicity of our system of government forbids it.... I have prepared an humble depository for my mortal body beside that wherein lies my beloved wife, where, without any pomp or parade, I have requested, when my God calls me to sleep with my fathers, to be laid."

The May of 1845 found General Jackson feeble and emaciated, but still deeply interested in his country, writing letters to President Polk and other statesmen about Texas, hoping ever to avert war if possible. "If not," he said, "let war come. There will be patriots enough in the land to repel foreign aggression, come whence it may, and to maintain sacredly our just rights and to perpetuate our glorious constitution and liberty, and to preserve our happy Union." He made his will, bequeathing all his property to his adopted son, because, said he, "If she were alive, she would wish him to have it all, and to me her wish is law."

On Sunday, June 8, 1845, the family and servants gathered about the great man, who was dying at the age of seventy-eight, having fought against wounds and disease all his life. "My dear children," he said, "do not grieve for me; it is true I am going to leave you; I am well aware of my situation. I have suffered much bodily pain, but my sufferings are but as nothing compared with that which our blessed Saviour endured upon that accursed cross, that all might be saved who put their trust in him.... I hope and trust to meet you all in Heaven, both white and black—both white and black." Then he kissed each one, his eyes resting last, affectionately, upon his granddaughter Rachel, named for his wife, and closely resembling her in loveliness of character; then death came.

Two days before he died, he said, "Heaven will be no Heaven to me if I do not meet my wife there." Who can picture that meeting? He used to say, "All I have achieved—fame, power, everything—would I exchange, if she could be restored to me for a moment." How blessed must have been the restoration, not "for a moment," but for eternity!

The lawn at the Hermitage was crowded with the thousands who came to attend the funeral. From the portico, the minister spoke from the words, "These are they which came out of great tribulation, and washed their robes white in the blood of the Lamb."

All over the country, public meetings were held in honor of the illustrious dead; the man who had said repeatedly, "I care nothing about clamors; I do precisely what I think just and right."

"He had had honors beyond anything which his own heart had ever coveted," says Prof. William G. Sumner, in his life of Jackson. "His successes had outrun his ambition. He had held more power than any other American had ever possessed. He had been idolized by the great majority of his countrymen, and had been surfeited with adulation."

Politicians sometimes sneered about his "kitchen cabinet" at Washington, the devoted friends who influenced him but did not hold official position, for, self-reliant though he was to a marvellous degree, he was neither afraid nor ashamed to be influenced by those who loved him. He was absolutely sincere and unselfish. He hated intensely, and loved intensely; with an affection as unchanging as his adamantine will. Patriotic, determined, energetic, and heroic, he attained success where others would have failed. He illustrated Emerson's words, "The man who stands by himself, the universe will stand by him also." Francis P. Blair, his devoted friend, used to say, "Of all the men I have known, Andrew Jackson was the one most entirely sufficient for himself." During his presidency, the steamboat which once conveyed him and his party down the Chesapeake was unseaworthy, and one of the men exhibited much alarm. "You are uneasy," said the general; "you never sailed with me before, I see."

As a soldier, he was a brave, wise, skilful leader; as a statesman, honest, earnest, fearless, true—"I do precisely what I think just and right."

Said a friend who knew him well, "There was more of the woman in his nature than in that of any man I ever knew—more of woman's tenderness toward children, and sympathy with them. Often has he been known, though he never had a child of his own, to walk up and down by the hour with an infant in his arms, because by so doing he relieved it from the cause of its crying; more also of woman's patience and uncomplaining, unnoticing submissiveness to trivial causes of irritation. There was in him a womanly modesty and delicacy.... By no man was the homage due to woman, the only true homage she can receive—faith in her—more devoutly rendered.... This peculiar tenderness of nature entered largely, no doubt, into the composition of that manner of his, with which so many have been struck, and which was of the highest available stamp as regards both dignity and grace."

Much of what he was in character he owed to Rachel Jackson. He once said to a prominent man, "My wife was a pious Christian woman. She gave me the best advice, and I have not been unmindful of it. When the people, in their sovereign pleasure, elected me President of the United States, she said to me, 'Don't let your popularity turn your mind away from the duty you owe to God. Before him we are all alike sinners, and to him we must all alike give account. All these things will pass away, and you and I and all of us must stand before God.' I have never forgotten it, and I never shall."

DANIEL WEBSTER

In the little town of Salisbury, New Hampshire, now called Franklin, Daniel Webster was born, January 18, 1782, the ninth in a family of ten children. Ebenezer, the father, descended from a sturdy Puritan ancestry, had fought in the French and Indian Wars; a brave, hardy pioneer. He had cleared the wilderness for his log house, married a wife who bore him five children, after which she died, and then married a second time, Abigail Eastman, a woman of vigorous understanding, yet tender and self-sacrificing. Of the five children of the latter wife, three daughters and two sons, Daniel was the fourth, a slight, delicate child, whose frail body made him especially dear to the mother, who felt that at any time he might be taken out of her arms forever.

"In this hut," said Webster, years later, speaking of his father and mother, "they endured together all sorts of privations and hardships; my mother was constantly visited by Indians, who had never gone to a white man's house but to kill its inhabitants, while my father, perhaps, was gone, as he frequently was, miles away, carrying on his back the corn to be ground, which was to support his family."

The father was absent from home, also, on more important errands. When the news of the battle of Bunker Hill thrilled the colonies, Captain Webster, who had won his title in the earlier wars, raised a company, and at once started for the scene of action. He fought at Bennington under Stark, being the first to scale the Tory breastworks, at White Plains, and was at West Point when Arnold attempted to surrender it to the British. He stood guard before General Washington's headquarters, the night of Arnold's treason. No wonder, when Washington looked upon the robust form nearly six feet high, with black hair and eyes, and firm decisive manner, he said, "Captain Webster, I believe I can trust you."

And so thought the people of New Hampshire, for they made him a member of both Houses of the State Legislature at various times, and a Judge of the Court of Common Pleas in his own county.

The delicate boy Daniel was unable to work on the farm like his brother Ezekiel, two years older, but found his pleasure and pastime in reading, and in studying nature. The home, "Elms Farm," as it was called later, from the elms about it, was in a valley at a bend of the Merrimac. From here the boy gazed upon Mount Kearsarge, and Mount Washington, the king of the White Mountain peaks, and if he did not dream of what the future had in store for him, he grew broad in soul from such surroundings. Great mountains, great reaches of sea or plain, usually bring great thoughts and plans to those who view them with a loving heart.

Daniel had little opportunity for schooling in those early years. He says, in his autobiography, "I do not remember when or by whom I was taught to read, because I cannot, and never could, recollect a time when I could not read the Bible. I suppose I was taught by my mother, or by my elder sisters. My father seemed to have no higher object in the world than to educate his children to the full extent of his very limited ability. No means were within his reach, generally speaking, but the small town-schools. These were kept by teachers, sufficiently indifferent, in the several neighborhoods of the township, each a small part of the year. To these I was sent with the other children.... In these schools nothing was taught but reading and writing; and as to these, the first I generally could perform better than the teacher, and the last a good master could hardly instruct me in; writing was so laborious, irksome, and repulsive an occupation to me always."

Much of the boy's time was spent in rambles along the Merrimac river, formed by the Winnipiseogee and the Pemigewasset, "the beau ideal of a mountain stream; cold, noisy, winding, and with banks of much picturesque beauty." He loved to fish along the streams, having for company an old British soldier and sailor, Robert Wise. "He was," says Webster, "my Isaac Walton. He had a wife but no child. He loved me, because I would read the newspapers to him, containing the accounts of battles in the European wars. When I have read to him the details of the victories of Howe and Jervis, etc., I remember he was excited almost to convulsions, and would relieve his excitement by a gush of exulting tears. He finally picked up a fatherless child, took him home, sent him to school, and took care of him, only, as he said, that he might have some one to read the newspaper to him. He could never read himself. Alas, poor Robert! I have never so attained the narrative art as to hold the attention of others as thou, with thy Yorkshire tongue, hast held mine. Thou hast carried me many a mile on thy back, paddled me over and over and up and down the stream, and given whole days in aid of my boyish sports, and asked no meed but that, at night, I would sit down at thy cottage door, and read to thee some passage of thy country's glory!"

Daniel heard of battles from another source beside Robert Wise. In the long winter evenings, when the family were snow-bound, Captain Webster would tell stories of the Revolutionary War, and the boy grew patriotic, as he heard of the brave soldiers who died to bring freedom to unborn generations. When he was eight years old, with all the money at his command, twenty-five cents, he went into a little shop "and bought," as he says, "a small cotton pocket-handkerchief, with the Constitution of the United States printed on its two sides. From this I learned either that there was a Constitution, or that there were thirteen States. I remember to have read it, and have known more or less of it ever since." Years afterward he said, "that there was not an article, a section, a clause, a phrase, a word, a syllable, or even a comma, of that Constitution, which he had not studied and pondered in every relation and in every construction of which it was susceptible."

How important a part this twenty-five cent handkerchief played in the lives of the two Webster boys! There is no soil so mellow as that of a child's mind; it needs no enriching save love that warms it like sunshine. What is planted there early, grows rank and tall, and mothers do most of the planting.

The lad's reading in these boyish days was confined mostly to the "Spectator," and Pope's "Essay on Man." The whole of the latter he learned to repeat. "We had so few books," he says, "that to read them once or twice was nothing. We thought they were all to be got by heart." The yearly almanac was regarded as "an acquisition." Once when Ezekiel and he had a dispute, after retiring, as to a couplet at the head of the April page, Daniel got up, groped his way to the kitchen, lighted a candle, looked at the quotation, found himself in the wrong, and went back to bed. But he had inadvertently, at two o'clock at night in midwinter, set the house on fire, which was saved by his father's presence of mind. Daniel said, "They were in pursuit of light, but got more than they wanted."

Exceedingly fond of poetry, at twelve he could repeat many of the hymns of Dr. Watts. Later, he found delight in Don Quixote, of which he says, "I began to read it, and it is literally true that I never closed my eyes until I had finished it; nor did I lay it down, so great was the power of that extraordinary book on my imagination." Later still, Milton, Shakespeare, and the Bible became his inspiration.

Years after, he used to say, "I have read through the entire Bible many times. I now make it a practice to go through it once a year. It is the book of all others for lawyers as well as for divines; and I pity the man that cannot find in it a rich supply of thought, and of rules for his conduct. It fits man for life—it prepares him for death!"

Captain Webster had secretly nourished the thought that he should send Daniel to college, but he was not a man to awaken false hopes, so he made no mention of his thoughts. An incident related by Daniel shows his father's heart in the matter. "Of a hot day in

July, it must have been in one of the last years of Washington's administration, I was making hay with my father. About the middle of the forenoon, the Honorable Abiel Foster, who lived in Canterbury, six miles off, called at the house, and came into the field to see my father. He was a worthy man, college-learned, and had been a minister, and was not a person of any considerable natural power. He talked a while in the field and went on his way. When he was gone, my father called me to him, and we sat down beneath the elm, on a haycock. He said, 'My son, that is a worthy man; he is a member of Congress; he goes to Philadelphia, and gets six dollars a day, while I toil here. It is because he had an education, which I never had. If I had had his early education, I should have been in Philadelphia in his place. I came near it as it was. But I missed it, and now I must work here.' 'My dear father,' said I, 'you shall not work. Brother and I shall work for you, and will wear our hands out, and you shall rest.' And I remember to have cried, and I cry now at the recollection. 'My child,' said he, 'it is of no importance to me. I now live but for my children. I could not give your elder brothers the advantages of knowledge, but I can do something for you. Exert yourself, improve your opportunities, learn, learn, and, when I am gone, you will not need to go through the hardships which I have undergone, and which have made me an old man before my time.'"

Daniel never forgot those precious words, "Improve your opportunities, learn, learn." The next year, 1796, he went to Phillips Exeter Academy, where he found ninety boys. He had come with his plain clothes from his plain home, while many of the others had come from rich and aristocratic families. Sometimes the boys ridiculed his country ways and country dress. Little they knew of the future that was to give them some slight renown simply because they happened to be in the same class with this country lad! When will the world learn not to judge a person by his clothes! When the first term at Exeter was near its close, the usher, Nicholas Emery, afterward an eminent lawyer in Portland, Maine, said to Webster, "You may stop a few minutes after school: I wish to speak to you." He then told the lad that he was a better scholar than any in his class, that he learned more readily and easily, and that if he returned to school he should be put into a higher class, and not be hindered by boys who cared more for play and dress than for solid improvement.

"These were the first truly encouraging words," said Mr. Webster, "that I ever received with regard to my studies. I then resolved to return, and pursue them with diligence and so much ability as I possessed." Blessings on thee, Nicholas Emery! Strange that either from indifference, or what we think the world will say, we forget to speak a helpful or an encouraging word. True appreciation is not flattery.

Daniel was at this time extremely diffident—a manner that speaks well for a boy or girl generally—and was helped out of it by a noble young teacher, Joseph Stevens Buckminster, who died at twenty-eight. Mr. Webster says, "I believe I made tolerable progress in most branches which I attended to while in this school; but there was one thing I could not do—I could not make a declamation. I could not speak before the school. The kind and excellent Buckminster sought, especially, to persuade me to perform the exercise of declamation like other boys, but I could not do it. Many a piece did I commit to memory, and recite and rehearse in my own room, over and over again, yet, when the day came, when the school collected to hear declamations, when my name was called, and I saw all eyes turned to my seat, I could not raise myself from it. Sometimes the instructors frowned, sometimes they smiled. Mr. Buckminster always pressed and entreated, most winningly, that I would venture, but I could never command sufficient resolution. When the occasion was over, I went home and wept bitter tears of mortification."

After nine months at Exeter, Daniel began to study with Rev. Samuel Wood, a minister in the adjoining town of Boscawen, six miles from Salisbury. As Captain Webster was driving over with his son, he communicated to him his plan of sending him to college. "I remember," says Daniel Webster, "the very hill which we were ascending, through deep snows, in a New England sleigh, when my father made known this purpose to me. I could not speak. How could he, I thought, with so large a family, and in such narrow circumstances, think of incurring so great an expense for me? A warm glow ran all over me, and I laid my head on my father's shoulder and wept."

All through life, Mr. Webster, greatest of American orators, was never afraid nor ashamed to weep. Children are not, and the nearer we keep to the naturalness of children, with reasonable self-control, the more power we have over others, and the sweeter and purer grow our natures.

While Daniel was at Dr. Wood's, a characteristic incident occurred. He says: "My father sent for me in haying time to help him, and put me into a field to turn hay, and left me. It was pretty lonely there, and, after working some time, I found it very dull; and as I knew my father was gone away, I walked home, and asked my sister Sally if she did not want to go and pick some whortle-berries. She said, yes. So I went and got some horses, and put a side-saddle on one, and we set off. We did not get home until it was pretty late, and I soon went to bed. When my father came home he asked my mother where I was, and what I had been about. She told him. The next morning, when I awoke, I saw all the clothes I had brought from Dr. Wood's tied up in a small bundle again. When I saw my father, he asked me how I liked haying. I told him I found it 'pretty dull and lonesome yesterday.' 'Well,' said he, 'I believe you may as well go back to Dr. Wood's.' So I took my bundle under my arm, and on my way I met Thomas W. Thompson, a lawyer in Salisbury; he laughed very heartily when he saw me. 'So,' said he, 'your farming is over, is it?'"

In August, 1797, when Daniel was fifteen, he entered Dartmouth College; there he proved a genial, affectionate friend, and a devoted student. But for this natural warmth of heart, he probably never would have been an orator, for those only move others whose own hearts are moved. "He had few intimates," says Henry Cabot Lodge, in his admirably written and discriminating "Life of Webster," "but many friends. He was generally liked as well as universally admired, was a leader in the college societies, active and successful in sports, simple, hearty, unaffected, without a touch of priggishness, and with a wealth of wholesome animal spirits."

After two years, the unselfish student could bear no longer the thought that his beloved brother Ezekiel was not to enjoy a college education. When he went home in vacation, he confided to his brother his unhappiness for his sake, and for a whole night they discussed the subject. It was decided that Daniel should consult the father. "This, we knew," said Mr. Webster, "would be a trying thing to my father and mother and two unmarried sisters. My father was growing old, his health not good, and his circumstances far from easy.... The farm was to be carried on, and the family taken care of; and there was nobody to do all this but him, who was regarded as the mainstay—that is to say, Ezekiel. However, I ventured on the negotiation, and it was carried, as other things often are, by the earnest and sanguine manner of youth. I told him that I was unhappy at my brother's prospects. For myself, I saw my way to knowledge, respectability, and self-protection; but, as to him, all looked the other way; that I would keep school, and get along as well as I could, be more than four years in getting through college, if necessary,—provided he also could be sent to study.... He said that to carry us both through college would take all he was worth; that, for himself, he was willing to run the risk; but that this was a serious matter to our mother and two unmarried sisters; that we must settle the matter with them, and, if their consent was obtained, he would trust to Providence, and get along as well as he could."

Captain Webster consulted with his wife; told her that already the farm was mortgaged for Daniel's education, and that if Ezekiel went to college it would take all they possessed. "Well," said she, with her brave mother-heart, "I will trust the boys;" and they lived to make her glad that she had trusted them.

The boy of seventeen went back to Dartmouth to struggle with poverty alone, but he was happy; the boy of nineteen began a new life, studying under Dr. Wood, and, later, entered Dartmouth College.

Daniel, as he had promised, began to earn money to pay his own and his brother's way. By superintending a small weekly paper, called the Dartmouth Gazette, he earned enough to pay his board. In the winter he taught school, and gave the money to Ezekiel. While in college, his wonderful powers in debate began to manifest themselves. He wrote his own declamations. Said one of his classmates: "In his movements he was rather slow and deliberate, except when his feelings were aroused; then his whole soul would kindle into a flame. We used to listen to him with the deepest respect and interest, and no one ever thought of equalling the vigor and flow of his eloquence."

Beside his regular studies, he devoted himself to history and politics. From the old world he learned lessons in finance, in commerce, in the stability of governments, that he was able to use in after life. He remembered what he read. He says, "So much as I read I made my own. When a half-hour or an hour, at most, had elapsed, I closed my book, and thought over what I had read. If there was anything peculiarly interesting or striking in the passage, I endeavored to recall it, and lay it up in my memory, and commonly I could recall it. Then, if, in debate or conversation afterward, any subject came up on which I had read something, I could talk very easily so far as I had read, and then I was very careful to stop." In this manner Mr. Webster became skilled in the art of conversation, and could be the life of any social gathering.

On July 4, 1800, he delivered his first public speech, at the request of the people of Hanover, tracing the history of our country to the grand success of the Revolution.

On leaving college he entered the law office of Mr. T. W. Thompson, of Salisbury. He seems not to have inclined strongly to the law, his tastes leading him toward general literature, but he was guided by the wishes of his father and other friends. His first reading was in the Law of Nations—Vattel, Burlamaqui, and Montesquieu, followed by Blackstone's Commentaries. After four months, he was obliged to quit his studies and earn money for Ezekiel.

He obtained a school at Fryeburg, Maine, promising to teach

for six months for one hundred and seventy-five dollars. Four nights each week he copied deeds, and made in this way two dollars a week. Thirty years afterward he said, "The ache is not yet out of my fingers; for nothing has ever been so laborious to me as writing, when under the necessity of writing a good hand."

When May came with its week of vacation, he says, "I took my quarter's salary, mounted a horse, went straight over all the hills to Hanover, and had the pleasure of putting these, the first earnings of my life, into my brother's hands for his college expenses. Having enjoyed this sincere and high pleasure, I hied me back again to my school and my copying of deeds." Thus at twenty was the great American living out Emerson's sublime motto, "Help somebody," founded on that broadest and sweetest of all commands, "Love one another."

"In these days," says George Ticknor Curtis' delightful life of Webster, "he was always dignified in his deportment. He was usually serious, but often facetious and pleasant. He was an agreeable companion, and eminently social with all who shared his friendship. He was greatly beloved by all who knew him. His habits were strictly abstemious, and he neither took wine nor strong drink. He was punctual in his attendance upon public worship, and ever opened his school with prayer. I never heard him use a profane word, and never saw him lose his temper."

While teaching and copying deeds, he read Adam's "Defence of the American Constitutions," Williams' "Vermont," Mosheim's "Ecclesiastical History," and continued his Blackstone. He walked much in the fields, alone, and thus learned to know himself; gaining that power of thought and mastery of self which are essential to those who would have mastery over others. He said, "I loved this occasional solitude then, and have loved it ever since, and love it still. I like to contemplate nature, and to hold communion, unbroken by the presence of human beings, with 'this universal frame—this wondrous fair.' I like solitude also, as favorable to thoughts less lofty. I like to let the thoughts go free, and indulge excursions. And when thinking is to be done one must, of course, be alone. No man knows himself who does not thus sometimes keep his own company. At a subsequent period of life, I have found that my lonely journeys, when following the court on its circuits, have afforded many an edifying day."

And yet in this busy life he called himself "naturally indolent," which was true, probably. Seeing that most of us do not love work, it is wise that in early life, if we would accomplish anything, we are drilled into habits of industry.

When he went back to the study of law, he says, "I really often despaired. I thought I never could make myself a lawyer, and was almost going back to the business of school-keeping. There are propositions in Coke so abstract, and distinctions so nice, and doctrines embracing so many conditions and qualifications, that it requires an effort not only of a mature mind, but of a mind both strong and mature, to understand him." And yet he adds, "If one can keep up an acquaintance with general literature in the meantime, the law may help to invigorate and unfold the powers of the mind."

He longed, as every ambitious young man longs, for a wider sphere. If he could only go to Boston, and mingle with the cultivated society there!—but this seemed an impossibility. At this time Ezekiel, through a college friend, was offered a private school in Boston. He accepted the position, and wrote to Daniel urging him to come and teach Latin and Greek for an hour and a half each day, thus earning enough to pay his board.

Daniel went to Boston, poor and unknown. His first efforts in finding an office in which to study were unsuccessful, for who cares about a young stranger in a great city? If we looked upon a human being as his Maker looks, doubtless we should be interested in him. He desired to study with some one already prominent. He found his way to the office of Christopher Gore, who was the first district attorney of the United States for Massachusetts, a commissioner to England under Jay's treaty for eight years, Ex-Governor of the State, and ex-senator. Mr. Webster thus narrates his early experience: "A young man, as little known to Mr. Gore as myself, undertook to introduce me to him. We ventured into Mr. Gore's rooms, and my name was pronounced. I was shockingly embarrassed, but Mr. Gore's habitual courtesy of manner gave me courage to speak. I had the grace to begin with an unaffected apology, told him my position was very awkward, my appearance there very like an intrusion; and that if I expected anything but a civil dismission, it was only founded in his known kindness and generosity of character. I was from the country, I said; had studied law for two years; had come to Boston to study a year more; had some respectable acquaintances in New Hampshire, not unknown to him, but had no introduction; that I had heard he had no clerk; thought it possible he would receive one; that I came to Boston to work, not to play; was most desirous, on all accounts, to be his pupil; and all I ventured to ask at present was that he would keep a place for me in his office till I could write to New Hampshire for proper letters, showing me worthy of it. I delivered this speech trippingly on the tongue, though I suspect it was better composed than spoken. Mr. Gore heard me with much encouraging good-nature. He evidently saw my embarrassment;

spoke kind words, and asked me to sit down. My friend had already disappeared. Mr. Gore said what I had suggested was very reasonable, and required little apology.... He inquired, and I told him, what gentlemen of his acquaintance knew me and my father in New Hampshire. Among others, I remember I mentioned Mr. Peabody, who was Mr. Gore's classmate. He talked to me pleasantly for a quarter of an hour; and, when I rose to depart, he said: 'My young friend, you look as though you might be trusted. You say you come to study, and not to waste time. I will take you at your word. You may as well hang up your hat at once; go into the other room; take your book, and sit down to reading it, and write at your convenience to New Hampshire for your letters.'"

The young man must have had the same earnest, frank look as the father when Washington said to him, "Captain Webster, I believe I can trust you," else he would not have won his way so quickly to the lawyer's confidence. Mr. Gore was a man of indefatigable research and great amenity of manners. The younger man probably unconsciously took on the habits of the older, for, says Emerson, "With the great we easily become great."

Webster now read, in addition to books on the common and municipal law, Ward's "Law of Nations," Lord Bacon's "Elements," Puffendorff's "Latin History of England," Gifford's "Juvenal," Boswell's "Tour to the Hebrides," Moore's "Travels," and other works. When we know what books a man or woman reads, we generally know the person. The life in Mr. Gore's office was one long step on the road to fame, and it did not come by chance; it came because, even in timidity, Webster had the courage to ask for a high place.

When about ready for admission to the bar, the position of Clerk of the Court of Common Pleas of Hillsborough County was offered to him, an appointment which had been the desire of the family for him for years. The salary was fifteen hundred dollars. This seemed a fortune indeed. "I could pay all the debts of the family," he says, "could help on Ezekiel—in short, I was independent. I had no sleep that night, and the next morning when I went to the office I stepped up the stairs with a lighter heart than I ever had before." He conveyed the good news to Mr. Gore.

"Well, my young friend," said he, "the gentlemen have been very kind to you; I am glad of it. You must thank them for it. You will write immediately, of course."

"I told him that I felt their kindness and liberality very deeply; that I should certainly thank them in the best manner I was able; but that, I should go up to Salisbury so soon, I hardly thought it was necessary to write. He looked at me as if he was greatly surprised.

105

'Why,' said he, 'you don't mean to accept it, surely!' The bare idea of not accepting it so astounded me that I should have been glad to have found any hole to have hid myself in.... 'Well,' said he, 'you must decide for yourself; but come, sit down, and let us talk it over. The office is worth fifteen hundred a year, you say. Well, it never will be any more. Ten to one, if they find out it is so much, the fees will be reduced. You are appointed now by friends; others may fill their places who are of different opinions, and who have friends of their own to provide for. You will lose your place; or, supposing you to retain it, what are you but a clerk for life? And your prospects as a lawyer are good enough to encourage you to go on. Go on, and finish your studies; you are poor enough, but there are greater evils than poverty: live on no man's favor; what bread you do eat, let it be the bread of independence; pursue your profession, make yourself useful to your friends and a little formidable to your enemies, and you have nothing to fear.'"

Young Webster went home and passed another sleepless night. Then he borrowed some money, hired a sleigh, and started for Salisbury. When he reached his father's house, the pale old man said to him, "Well, Daniel, we have got that office for you."

"Yes, father," was the reply, "the gentlemen were very kind; I must go and thank them."

"They gave it to you without my saying a word about it."

"I must go and see Judge Farrar, and tell him I am much obliged to him."

"Daniel, Daniel," said he, at last, with a searching look, "don't you mean to take that office?"

"No, indeed, father," was the response, "I hope I can do much better than that. I mean to use my tongue in the courts, not my pen; to be an actor, not a register of other men's acts. I hope yet, sir, to astonish your honor in your own court by my professional attainments."

He looked half proud, half sorrowful, and said slowly, "Well, my son, your mother has always said you would come to something or nothing. She was not sure which; I think you are now about settling that doubt for her." He never spoke a word more upon the subject. The fifteen-hundred-dollar clerkship was gone forever, but Daniel had chosen the right road to fame and prosperity.

He returned finally to the quiet town of Boscawen, and, not willing to be separated from his father, began the life of a country lawyer. His practice brought not more than five or six hundred dollars a year, but it gave self-support. He had also time for study. "Study," he said, "is the grand requisite for a lawyer. Men may be born poets, and leap from their cradle painters. Nature may have made them musicians, and called on them only to exercise, and not to acquire, ability; but law is artificial. It is a human science, to be learned, not inspired. Let there be a genius for whom nature has done so much as apparently to have left nothing for application, yet, to make a lawyer, application must do as much as if nature had done nothing. The evil is that an accursed thirst for money violates everything.... The love of fame is extinguished, every ardent wish for knowledge repressed; conscience put in jeopardy, and the best feelings of the heart indurated by the mean, money-catching, abominable practices which cover with disgrace a part of the modern practitioners of the law."

Webster's first speech at the bar was listened to by his proud and devoted father, who did not live to hear him a second time. He died in 1806, at sixty-seven, and was buried beneath a tall pine-tree on his own field. Daniel assumed his debts, and for ten years bore the burden, if that may be called a burden which we do willingly for love's sake.

The next year he removed to Portsmouth. He was now twenty-five, pale, slender, and of refined and apparently delicate organization. He had written considerable for the press, made several Fourth of July orations, and published a little pamphlet, "Considerations on the Embargo Laws."

In June, 1808, when he was twenty-six, he made the wisest choice of his life in his marriage to Grace Fletcher, daughter of Rev. Elijah Fletcher of Hopkinton. She was twenty-seven, a rare combination of intellect and sweetness, just the woman to inspire an educated man by her cultivated and sympathetic mind, and to rest him with her gentle and genial presence. She had a quiet dignity which won respect, and her manners were unaffected, frank, and winning. From the first time he saw her she looked "like an angel" to him, and such she ever remained to his vision.

And now began the happiest years of his life. The small, wooden house in which they lived grew into a palace, because love was there. His first child, little Grace, named for her mother, became the idol of his heart. Business increased and friends multiplied during the nine years he lived at Portsmouth. He was fortunate in having for an almost constant opponent in the law the renowned Jeremiah Mason, fourteen years his senior, and the acknowledged head of the legal profession in New Hampshire. Mr. Webster studied him closely. "He had a habit," said Webster, "of standing quite near to the jury, so near that he might have laid his finger on the foreman's nose; and then he talked to them in a plain conversational way, in short sentences, and using no word that was not level to the comprehension of the least educated man on the panel. This led me to examine my own style, and I set about reforming it altogether." Before this his style had been somewhat florid; afterward it was terse, simple, and graphic.

On July 4, 1812, Webster delivered an oration before the "Washington Benevolent Society," in which he stoutly opposed the war then being carried on with England. The address immediately passed through two editions, and led to his appointment as delegate to an assembly of the people of Rockingham County, to express disapproval of the war. The "Rockingham Memorial," which was presented to the President, was written by Mr. Webster, and showed a thorough knowledge of the condition of affairs, and an ardent devotion to the Union, even though the various sections of the country might differ in opinion. The result of this meeting was the sending of Mr. Webster to Congress, where he took his seat May 24, 1813. He was thirty-one; the poverty, the poor clothes in Dartmouth College, the burden of the father's debts had not kept him from success.

Once in Congress, it was but natural that his influence should be felt. He did not speak often, but when he did speak the House listened. He was placed on the committee on Foreign Relations, with Mr. Calhoun as chairman. He helped to repeal the Embargo Laws, spoke on the Tariff, showing that he was a Free Trader in principle, but favored Protection as far as expediency demanded it, and took strong grounds against the war of 1812. He urged the right and necessity of free speech on all questions. He said, "It is the ancient and undoubted prerogative of this people to canvas public measures and the merits of public men. It is a 'home-bred right,' a fireside privilege. It has ever been enjoyed in every house, cottage, and cabin in the nation.... It is as undoubted as the right of breathing the air, or walking on the earth. Belonging to private life as a right, it belongs to public life as a duty; and it is the last duty which those whose representative I am shall find me to abandon."

He was active in that almost interminable discussion concerning a United States Bank. The first bank, chartered in 1791, had Hamilton for its defender, and Jefferson for its opponent. In 1811, the bank failed to obtain a renewal of its charter. During the war of 1812, the subject was again urged. The Jeffersonians were opposed to any bank; another party favored a bank which should help the government by heavy loans, and be relieved from paying its notes in specie; still another party, to which Webster belonged, favored a bank with reasonable capital, compelled to redeem its notes in specie, and at liberty to make loans or not to the government. On the subject of the currency he made some

108

remarkable speeches, showing a knowledge of the subject perhaps unequalled since Hamilton.

The bank bill passed in 1816, shorn of some of its objectionable features. On April 26, Mr. Webster presented his resolutions requiring all dues to the government to be paid in coin, or in Treasury notes, or in notes of the Bank of the United States, and by a convincing speech aided in its adoption, thus rendering his country a signal service.

During this session of Congress, Webster received a challenge to a duel from John Randolph of Roanoke, and was brave enough to refuse, saying, "It is enough that I do not feel myself bound, at all times and under any circumstances, to accept from any man, who shall choose to risk his own life, an invitation of this sort."

The time had come now in Mr. Webster's life for a broader sphere; he decided to move to Boston. His law practice had never brought more than two thousand dollars a year, and he needed more than this for his growing family. Besides, his house at Portsmouth, costing him six thousand dollars, had been burned, his library and furniture destroyed, and he must begin the world anew.

The loss of property was small compared with another loss close at hand. Grace, the beautiful, precocious first-born, the sunshine of the home, died in her father's arms, smiling full in his face as she died. He wept like a child, and could never forget that parting look.

After settling in Boston, business flowed in upon him, until he earned twenty thousand dollars a year. He would work hard in the early morning hours, coming home tired from the courts in the afternoon. Says a friend, "After dinner, Mr. Webster would throw himself upon the sofa, and then was seen the truly electrical attraction of his character. Every person in the room was drawn immediately into his sphere. The children squeezing themselves into all possible places and postures upon the sofa, in order to be close to him; Mrs. Webster sitting by his side, and the friend or social visitor only too happy to join in the circle. All this was not from invitation to the children; he did nothing to amuse them, he told them no stories; it was the irresistible attraction of his character, the charm of his illumined countenance, from which beamed indulgence and kindness to every one of his family."

Among the celebrated cases which helped Mr. Webster's renown was the Dartmouth College case in 1817. The college was originally a charity school for the instruction of the Indians in the Christian religion, founded by Rev. Eleazer Wheelock. He solicited and obtained subscriptions in England, the Earl of Dartmouth being a generous giver. A charter was obtained from the Crown in 1769, appointing Dr. Wheelock president, and empowering him to name his successor, subject to the approval of the trustees. In 1815 a quarrel began between two opposite political and religious factions. The Legislature was applied to, which changed the name from college to university, enlarged the number of trustees, and otherwise modified the rights of the corporation under the charter from England. The new trustees took possession of the property. The old board brought action against the new, but the courts of New Hampshire decided that the acts of the Legislature were constitutional. The case was appealed to Washington, and on March 10, 1818, Mr. Webster made his famous speech of over four hours, proving that by the Constitution of the United States the charter of an institution is a contract which a State Legislature cannot annul.

In closing he said to the Chief Justice, "This, sir, is my case. It is the case, not merely of that humble institution, it is the case of every college in our land. It is more. It is the case of every eleemosynary institution throughout our country—of all those great charities founded by the piety of our ancestors, to alleviate human misery and scatter blessings along the pathway of life. It is more! It is, in some sense, the case of every man among us who has property of which he may be stripped, for the question is simply this: Shall our State Legislatures be allowed to take that which is not their own, to turn it from its original use, and apply it to such ends or purposes as they in their discretion shall see fit? Sir, you may destroy this little institution; it is weak; it is in your hands! I know it is one of the lesser lights in the literary horizon of our country. You may put it out. But, if you do so, you must carry through your work! You must extinguish, one after another, all those greater lights of science which, for more than a century, have thrown their radiance over our land!

"It is, sir, as I have said, a small college. And yet there are those who love it—"

Here Mr. Webster broke down, overcome by the recollections of those early days of poverty, and the self-sacrifice of the dead father. The eyes of Chief Justice Marshall were suffused with tears, as were those of nearly all present. When Mr. Webster sat down, for some moments the silence was death-like, and then the people roused themselves as though awaking from a dream. Nearly seventy years after this, when the Hon. Mellen Chamberlain, Librarian of the Boston Public Library, gave his eloquent address at the dedication of Wilson Hall, the library building of Dartmouth College, he held in his hand the very copy of Blackstone from which Webster quoted in his great argument, with his autograph on the fly-leaf. Of Webster he said, "His imagination transformed the soulless body corporate—the fiction of the king's prerogative—into a living personality, the object of his filial devotion, the beloved mother whose protection called forth all his powers, and enkindled in his bosom a quenchless love."

Several years later, Webster won the great case of Gibbons vs. Ogden, which settled that the State of New York had no right, under the Constitution, to grant a monopoly of steam navigation, on its waters, to Fulton and Livingston.

He now took an active part in the revision of the Constitution of Massachusetts, helping to do away with the religious test, that a person holding office must declare his belief in the Christian religion. A believer himself, he was unwilling to force his views upon others. December 22, 1820, he delivered an oration at Plymouth, commemorating the two-hundredth anniversary of the landing of the Pilgrims. It was a grand theme, and the theme had a master to handle it. He began simply, "Let us rejoice that we behold this day. Let us be thankful that we have lived to see the bright and happy breaking of the auspicious morn which commences the third century of the history of New England.... Forever honored be this, the place of our fathers' refuge! Forever remembered the day which saw them, weary and distressed, broken in everything but spirit, poor in all but faith and courage, at last secure from the danger of wintry seas, and impressing this shore with the first footsteps of civilized man!"

Then the picture was sketched on a glowing canvas;—the noble Pilgrims; the progress of New England during the century; the grand government under which we live and develop, with the Christian religion for our comfort and our hope. In closing he said, "The hours of this day are rapidly flying, and this occasion will soon be passed. Neither we nor our children can expect to behold its return. They are in the distant regions of futurity, they exist only in the all-creating power of God, who shall stand here, a hundred years hence, to trace through us their descent from the Pilgrims, and to survey, as we have now surveyed, the progress of their country during the lapse of a century. We would anticipate their concurrence with us in our sentiments of deep regard for our common ancestors. We would anticipate and partake the pleasure with which they will then recount the steps of New England's advancement. On the morning of that day, although it will not disturb us in our repose, the voice of acclamation and gratitude, commencing on the Rock of Plymouth, shall be transmitted through millions of the sons of the Pilgrims, till it lose itself in the murmurs of the Pacific seas."

The people heard the oration as though entranced. Said Mr.

111

Ticknor, a man of remarkable culture, "I was never so excited by public speaking before in my life. Three or four times I thought my temples would burst with the gush of blood; for, after all, you must know that I am aware it is no connected and compacted whole, but a collection of wonderful fragments of burning eloquence, to which his whole manner gave tenfold force. When I came out I was almost afraid to come near to him. It seemed to me as if he was like the mount that might not be touched, and that burned with fire."

John Adams wrote him, "If there be an American who can read it without tears, I am not that American.... Mr. Burke is no longer entitled to the praise—the most consummate orator of modern times.... This oration will be read five hundred years hence with as much rapture as it was heard. It ought to be read at the end of every century, and indeed at the end of every year, forever and ever."

From the day he delivered that oration, Mr. Webster was the leading orator of America. From that day he belonged not to Grace Webster alone, not to Massachusetts, not to one political party, but to the people of the United States. Five years after that, he delivered the address at the laying of the corner-stone of Bunker Hill monument. Who does not remember the impassioned words to the survivors of the Revolution, "Venerable men! you have come down to us from a former generation. Heaven has bounteously lengthened out your lives that you might behold this joyous day. You are now where you stood fifty years ago, this very hour, with your brothers and your neighbors, shoulder to shoulder, in the strife for your country. Behold, how altered! The same heavens are indeed over your heads; the same ocean rolls at your feet; but all else, how changed! You hear now no roar of hostile cannon, you see no mixed volumes of smoke and flame rising from burning Charlestown. The ground strewed with the dead and the dying; the impetuous charge; the steady and successful repulse; the loud call to repeated assault, the summoning of all that is manly to repeated resistance; a thousand bosoms freely and fearlessly bared in an instant to whatever of terror there may be in war and death,—all these you have witnessed, but you witness them no more.... All is peace; and God has granted you this sight of your country's happiness, ere you slumber in the grave forever. He has allowed you to behold and to partake the reward of your patriotic toils, and he has allowed us, your sons and countrymen, to meet you here, and in the name of the present generation, in the name of your country, in the name of liberty, to thank you!

"But, alas! you are not all here! Time and the sword have thinned your ranks. Prescott, Putnam, Stark, Brooks, Read,

Pomeroy, Bridge! our eyes seek for you in vain amidst this broken band. You are gathered to your fathers, and live only to your country in her grateful remembrance and your own bright example."

Who has not read that address delivered at Faneuil Hall, Boston, in commemoration of the lives and services of John Adams and Thomas Jefferson, who died July 4, 1826. Who does not remember that imaginary speech of John Adams, "Sink or swim, live or die, survive or perish, I give my hand and my heart to this vote. It is true, indeed, that in the beginning we aimed not at independence. But there's a Divinity which shapes our ends.... Sir, I know the uncertainty of human affairs, but I see, I see clearly through this day's business. You and I, indeed, may rue it. We may not live to see the time when this declaration shall be made good. We may die,—die colonists,—die slaves;—die, it may be, ignominiously and on the scaffold. Be it so. Be it so. If it be the pleasure of Heaven that my country shall require the poor offering of my life, the victim shall be ready at the appointed hour of sacrifice, come when that hour may. But, while I do live, let me have a country, or at least the hope of a country, and that a free country."

Concerning this speech of John Adams, beginning, "Sink or swim, live or die," Mr. Webster said, "I wrote that speech one morning before breakfast, in my library, and when it was finished my paper was wet with my tears." In delivering this oration, his manuscript lay near him on a small table, but he did not once refer to it. As far as possible in his addresses, he preferred Anglo-Saxon words to those with Latin origin; therefore, this great speech is so simple that school-boys the country over can declaim it and understand it.

In 1823, when Webster was forty-one, Boston elected him to Congress. He was, of course, widely known and observed; courtly in physique, impassioned yet calm, easy yet dignified, comprehensive in thought, a lover of and expounder of the Constitution.

The following year he visited Marshfield, on the south-east shore of Massachusetts, and saw the home which he afterward purchased, and which, with its eighteen hundred acres, became the joy of his later years. Here he planted flowers and trees. He would often say to others, "Plant trees, adorn your grounds, live for the benefit of those who shall come after you." Here he watched every sunrise and sunset, every moonrise from new to full, and grew rested and refreshed by these ever recurring glimpses of divine power. He said, "I know the morning; I am acquainted with it, and I love it, fresh and sweet as it is, a daily creation, breaking forth and calling all that have life, and breath, and being, to new adoration, new enjoyments, and new gratitude."

Here he enjoyed the ocean as he had enjoyed it in his boyhood, and years later, when his brain was tired from overwork, he would exclaim, plaintively, "Oh, Marshfield! the Sea! the Sea!"

This year also Webster paid a visit to Thomas Jefferson at Monticello. In his conversation with the ex-President, he told this story of himself, which well illustrates the fact that all the knowledge which we can acquire becomes of use to us at one time or another in life. When a young lawyer in Portsmouth, a blacksmith brought him a case under a will. As the case was a difficult one, he spent one month in the study of it, buying fifty dollars' worth of books to help him in the matter. He argued the case, won it, and received a fee of fifteen dollars. Years after, Aaron Burr sent for him to consult with him on a legal question of consequence. The case was so similar to that of the blacksmith that Webster could cite all the points bearing upon it from the time of Charles II. Mr. Burr was astonished, and suspected he was the counsel for the opposite side. Webster received enough compensation from Burr to cover the loss of time and money in the former case, and gained, besides, Burr's admiration and respect.

In the winter of 1824, Webster's youngest child, Charles, died, at the age of two years. Mrs. Webster wrote her absent husband, "I have dreaded the hour which should destroy your hopes, but trust you will not let this event afflict you too much, and that we both shall be able to resign him without a murmur, happy in the reflection that he has returned to his Heavenly Father pure as I received him.... Do not, my dear husband, talk of your own 'final abode;' that is a subject I never can dwell on for a moment. With you here, my dear, I can never be desolate. Oh, may Heaven, in its mercy, long preserve you!"

Four years later, "the blessed wife," as he called her, went to her "final abode." Mr. Webster watched by her side till death took her. Then at the funeral, in the wet and cold of that January day, he walked close behind the hearse, holding Julia and Fletcher, his two children, by the hand. Her body was placed beneath St. Paul's Church, Boston, beside her children. All were removed afterward to Marshfield.

Webster went back to Washington, having been made United States senator, but he seemed broken-hearted, and unable to perform his duties. He wrote to a friend, "Like an angel of God, indeed. I hope she is in purity, in happiness, and in immortality; but I would fain hope that, in kind remembrance of those she has left, in a lingering human sympathy and human love, she may yet be, as God originally created her, a 'little lower than the angels.' I cannot pursue these thoughts, nor turn back to see what I have written."

Again he wrote, "I feel a vacuum, an indifference, a want of motive, which I cannot describe. I hope my children, and the society of my best friends, may rouse me; but I can never see such days as I have seen. Yet I should not repine; I have enjoyed much, very much; and, if I were to die to-night, I should bless God most fervently that I have lived."

Judge Story spoke of Mrs. Webster as a sister with "her kindness of heart, her generous feelings, her mild and conciliatory temper, her warm and elevated affections, her constancy, purity, and piety, her noble disinterestedness, and her excellent sense."

Later, Mr. Webster married Caroline Le Roy, the daughter of a New York merchant, but no affection ever effaced from his heart the memory of Grace Webster, whom he always spoke of as "the mother of his children."

The next year, 1829, his idolized brother Ezekiel died suddenly at forty-nine, while he was addressing a jury in the court-house at Concord, New Hampshire.

Daniel Webster said of this shock, "I have felt but one such in life; and this follows so soon that it requires more fortitude than I possess to bear it with firmness, and, perhaps, as I ought. I am aware that the case admits no remedy, nor any present relief; and endeavor to console myself with reflecting that I have had much happiness with lost connections, and that they must expect to lose beloved objects in this world who have beloved objects to lose."

Recently, at the home of Kate Sanborn in New York, the grand-niece of Daniel Webster, I met the sweet-faced wife of Ezekiel, young in her feelings and young in face despite her four-score years. Here I saw a picture of the great orator in his youth, the desk on which he wrote, and scores of mementos of Marshfield and "Elms Farms," treasured by the cultivated woman who bears token of her renowned kinship.

With all these sorrows crowded into Mr. Webster's life, he could not cease his pressing work in Congress. Andrew Jackson had become President, and John C. Calhoun had preached his Nullification doctrines till South Carolina was ready to separate herself from the Union, because of her dissatisfaction with the tariff laws. Webster had somewhat changed his views, and had become a supporter of the "American System" of Henry Clay, the system of "protection," because he thought the interests of his constituents demanded it. For himself, he loved agriculture, but he saw the need of fostering manufactures if we would have a great and prosperous country.

On December 29, 1829, Mr. Foote, a senator from Connecticut, introduced a resolution to inquire respecting the sales and surveys of western lands. In a long debate which followed, General Hayne of South Carolina took occasion to chastise New England, in no tender words, for her desire to build up herself in wealth at the expense of the West and South. On January 20, Webster made his first reply to the General, having only a night in which to prepare his speech. The notes filled three pages of ordinary letter paper, while the speech, as reported, filled twenty pages.

Again General Hayne spoke in an able yet personal manner, asserting the doctrines of nullification, and attempting to justify the position of his State in seceding. Mr. Webster took notes while he was speaking, but, as the Senate adjourned, his speech did not come till the following day. Again he had but a night in which to prepare.

When the morning of January 26 came, the galleries, floor, and staircase were crowded with eager men and women. "It is a critical moment," said Mr. Bell, of New Hampshire, to Mr. Webster, "and it is time, it is high time, that the people of this country should know what this Constitution is." "Then," answered Webster, "by the blessing of Heaven they shall learn, this day, before the sun goes down, what I understand it to be."

When Webster began speaking his words were slowly uttered. "Mr. President,—When the mariner has been tossed, for many days, in thick weather, and on an unknown sea, he naturally avails himself of the first pause in the storm, the earliest glance of the sun, to take his latitude, and ascertain how far the elements have driven him from his true course. Let us imitate this prudence, and before we float farther on the waves of this debate, refer to the point from which we departed, that we may at least be able to conjecture where we now are. I ask for the reading of the resolution."

And then with trenchant sarcasm, unanswerable logic, and the intense feeling which belongs to true oratory, Mr. Webster taught the American people the strength and holding power of the Constitution, which a civil war, thirty years later, was to prove unalterably. The speech, which filled seventy printed pages, came from only five pages of notes. When asked how long he was in preparation for the reply to Hayne, he answered, his "whole life."

How often his loving defence of Massachusetts has been quoted! "Mr. President, I shall enter on no encomiums upon Massachusetts. She needs none. There she is—behold her, and judge for yourselves. There is her history: the world knows it by heart. The past, at least, is secure. There is Boston, and Concord, and Lexington, and Bunker Hill,—and there they will remain forever. The bones of her sons, falling in the great struggle for Independence, now lie mingled with the soil of every State, from New England to Georgia; and there they will lie forever. And, sir, where American liberty raised its first voice, and where its youth was nurtured and sustained, there it still lives, in the strength of its manhood and full of its original spirit. If discord and disunion shall wound it—if party strife and blind ambition shall hawk at and tear it—if folly and madness, if uneasiness under salutary and necessary restraint, shall succeed to separate it from that union, by which alone its existence is made sure, it will stand, in the end, by the side of that cradle in which its infancy was rocked: it will stretch forth its arm, with whatever of vigor it may still retain, over the friends who gather round it; and it will fall at last, if fall it must, amidst the proudest monuments of its own glory, and on the very spot of its origin.

"When my eyes shall be turned to behold for the last time the sun in heaven, may I not see him shining on the broken and dishonored fragments of a once glorious Union; on States dissevered, discordant, belligerent; on a land rent with civil feuds, or drenched, it may be, in fraternal blood!—Let their last feeble and lingering glance rather behold the gorgeous ensign of the republic, now known and honored throughout the earth, still full high advanced, its arms and trophies streaming in their original lustre, not a stripe erased or polluted, nor a single star obscured—bearing for its motto no such miserable interrogatory as What is all this worth? Nor those other words of delusion and folly, Liberty first, and Union afterwards—but everywhere, spread all over in characters of living light, blazing on all its ample folds, as they float over the sea and over the land, and in every wind under the whole heavens, that other sentiment, dear to every true American heart— Liberty and Union, now and forever, one and inseparable!"

Of course, this reply to Hayne electrified the country, and Webster began to be mentioned for the presidential chair. No one who ever heard him speak, with his wonderful magnetism, his majestic enthusiasm, his rich, full voice, and his unsurpassed physique, could ever forget the man, his words, or his presence. When he visited Europe, some said, "There goes a king." When Sydney Smith saw him, he exclaimed, "Good Heavens! he is a small cathedral by himself."

Through Jackson's administration Webster was his courteous opponent in most measures, but in the nullification scheme he was heart and hand with the fearless, self-willed general. When Henry Clay brought forward his compromise tariff bill, which pacified the nullifiers, Webster opposed it, believing that, in the face of this opposition to the Constitution, concession was unwise.

In 1833, the famous statesman made an extended journey through the West, and was everywhere honored and fêted. Church-bells were rung, cannon fired, and houses decorated at his coming. Great crowds gathered everywhere to hear him speak.

By this time a party was developing in opposition to the unusual powers exercised by General Jackson, whose great victory at New Orleans had made him the idol of the people. The party was the more easily formed from the financial troubles under Van Buren, he having reaped the harvest of which Jackson had sown the seed. Naturally, Mr. Webster became the leader of this Whig party, so called from the Whig party in England, formed to resist the ultra demands of the king. Massachusetts favored him for the presidency. Boston presented him with a massive silver vase, before an audience of four thousand persons. Philadelphia and Baltimore gave him public dinners. Letters came from various States urging his name upon the National Convention, which met at Harrisburg, Pennsylvania, December 4, 1839. But Mr. Webster had been so prominent that his views upon all public questions were too well known, therefore General William Henry Harrison, of Ohio, an honored soldier of the War of 1812, was chosen, as being a more "available" candidate.

Webster must have been sorely disappointed, as were his friends, but he at once began to work earnestly for his party, spoke constantly at meetings, and helped to elect Harrison, who died one month after the exciting election, at the age of sixty-eight. John Tyler, of Virginia, the Vice-President, succeeded him, and Mr. Webster remained Secretary of State under him, as he had been under Harrison. Here the duties were arduous and complicated.

For many years the north-eastern boundary had been a matter of dispute between England and the United States. Bitter feeling had been engendered also by trouble in Canada in 1837. Several of those in rebellion had fled from Canada to the States, had fitted out an American steamboat, the Carolina, to make incursions into that country. She was burned by a party of Canadians, and an American was killed. McLeod, from Canada, acknowledged himself the slayer, was arrested, and committed for murder. The British were angered by this, as were the Americans by the search of their vessels by British cruisers. Lord Ashburton was finally sent as a special envoy to the United States, and largely through the statesmanship of Mr. Webster the Ashburton treaty was concluded, and war between the nations avoided.

Meantime, President Tyler had vetoed the bill for establishing another United States Bank, and thereby set his own party against him. Most of the cabinet resigned, and although much pressure was brought by the Whig party upon Mr. Webster, that he resign also, he

118

remained till the treaty matter was settled. Then he returned to Marshfield, and devoted himself once more to the law.

He had spent lavishly upon his farm; he had also bought western land, and lost money by his investments. He felt obliged to entertain friends, and this was expensive. Besides, he never kept regular accounts, often in his generosity gave five hundred dollars when he should have given but five, and now found himself embarrassed by debts which were a source of sorrow to his friends as well as to himself, and a source of advantage to his enemies. Thirty-five thousand dollars were now given him by his admirers, from which he received a yearly income.

In 1844, the annexation of Texas was a leading presidential question. Until 1836 she was a province of Mexico, but in 1835 she resorted to arms to free herself. On March 6, 1836, a Texan fort, called the Alamo, was surrounded by eight thousand Mexicans, led by Santa Anna. The garrison was massacred. The next month the battle of San Jacinto was fought, and Texas became independent. When she asked admission to the Union, the Democrats favored and the Whigs opposed, because she would naturally become slave territory. Already, August 30, 1843, the "Liberty Party" had assembled at Baltimore and nominated a candidate for the presidency. The North was becoming agitated on the subject of slavery, but the Whigs avoided both the subjects of slavery and Texas in their platform, and nominated as their presidential candidate not Daniel Webster but Henry Clay.

Again Webster worked earnestly for his party and its nominee, but the Whigs were defeated, as is usually the case when a party fears to touch the great questions which public opinion demands. They learned a lesson when it was too late, and other political parties should profit by their example.

James K. Polk of Tennessee was elected, Texas was admitted to the Union, and the Mexican War resulted. War was declared by Congress May 11, 1846, vigorously prosecuted, and Mexico was defeated. By the terms of the treaty, concluded February 2, 1848, New Mexico and Upper California were given to the United States.

Webster, who had been returned to the Senate by Massachusetts, opposed the war as he had the annexation of Texas. At this time a double sorrow came to him. His second son, Major Edward Webster, a young man of fine abilities, courage, and high sense of honor, died near the city of Mexico, from disease induced by exposure. His body arrived in Boston May 4, and, only three days before, Webster's lovely daughter, Julia, who had married Samuel Appleton of Boston, was carried to her grave by consumption. Her death, at thirty, was beautiful in its resignation and faith, even though she left five little children to the care of others. Her last words were, "Let me go, for the day breaketh," which words were placed upon her tombstone.

Mr. Webster was indeed crushed by this new sorrow. He wrote to his friend Mrs. Ticknor, "I cannot speak of the lost ones; but I submit to the will of God. I feel that I am nothing, less even than the merest dust of the balance; and that the Creator of a million worlds, and the judge of all flesh, must be allowed to dispose of me and mine as to his infinite wisdom shall seem best."

In 1848, when Mr. Webster was sixty-six, the presidency once more eluded his grasp by the nomination of another "available" man, General Zachary Taylor, one of the heroes of the Mexican War. Webster had spoken earnestly for Harrison and Clay; now he was unwilling longer to work for the party which had ignored him and nominated a man whom, though an able soldier, he thought unfitted for the place as a statesman. If it was a mistake to show that he was wounded in spirit, as it undoubtedly was for so great a man, it was nevertheless human.

The thing which Mr. Webster had feared these many years was now coming to pass. A violent agitation of the slavery question in the Territories was upon the nation. For thirty years slavery had been odious to the North, and carefully nurtured by the South. In 1820, when Missouri was admitted as a State, the North insisted that a clause prohibiting slavery should be inserted as a condition of her admission to the Union. Henry Clay devised the compromise by which slavery was prohibited in all the new territory lying north of latitude 36° 30', which was the southern boundary of Missouri. This line was called Mason and Dixon's line, from the names of the two surveyors who ran the boundary line between Maryland and Pennsylvania.

Year by year the hatred of slavery had intensified at the North. February 1, 1847, David Wilmot of Pennsylvania introduced in Congress his famous proviso, by which slavery was to be excluded from all territory thereafter acquired or annexed by the United States. And now, in 1849, the conflict on the slavery question was more virulent than ever. California, having framed a constitution prohibiting slavery, applied for admission to the Union. New Mexico asked for a territorial government and for the exclusion of slavery.

The South claimed that the Missouri Compromise, extending to the Pacific coast, guaranteed the right to introduce slavery into California and New Mexico, and threatened secession from the Union. Again Henry Clay settled the matter,—for a time only, as it proved,—by his famous Compromise of 1850, by which California was admitted as a free State, the Territories taken from Mexico left to decide the slavery question as they chose, the slave-trade abolished in the District of Columbia, more effectual enforcement of the Fugitive Slave Law demanded, with some other minor provisions.

The Fugitive Slave Law, which provided for the return of the fugitives without trial by jury, and expected Christian people to aid the slave-dealers in capturing their slaves, was especially obnoxious to the North. Some of the States had passed "Personal Liberty Bills," punishing as kidnappers persons who sought to take away alleged slaves.

Mr. Webster saw with dismay all this bitterness, and knew that the Union which he loved was in danger. He hoped to avert civil war, perhaps to still the tumult forever, and so gave his great heart and brain to the Clay compromise. On March 7, 1850, he delivered in Congress his famous speech on the Compromise bill. The Senate chamber was crowded with an intensely excited audience. Mr. Webster discussed the whole history of slavery, opposed the Wilmot Proviso, because he thought every part of the country settled as to slavery, either by law or nature,—he could not look into the future and see Kansas,—and then condemned the course of the North in its resistance to the Fugitive Slave Law, which he held to be constitutional. The words in reference to restoring fugitive slaves created a storm of indignation at the North, which had looked upon Webster as a great anti-slavery leader, and who had said in the oration at Plymouth, "I hear the sound of the hammer, I see the smoke of the furnaces where manacles and fetters are still forged for human limbs. I see the visages of those who, by stealth and at midnight, labor in this work of hell, foul and dark, as may become the artificers of such instruments of misery and torture. Let that spot be purified, or let it cease to be of New England. Let it be purified, or let it be set aside from the Christian world; let it be put out of the circle of human sympathies and human regards, and let civilized man henceforth have no communion with it." In his speech to Hayne he had said, "I regard domestic slavery as one of the greatest evils, both moral and political."

Probably Mr. Webster had not changed his mind at all in regard to the enormity of slavery, but he hoped to save the Union from war. He indeed helped to postpone the conflict, but if the presidency had before this been a possibility to him, it became now an impossibility forever, and his own words had done it.

President Taylor died July 9, 1850, when the discussion of the Compromise matter was at its height, and Millard Fillmore became President. He at once made Webster Secretary of State. Mr. Webster bore bravely the reproaches of the North. He said, "I cared for nothing, I was afraid of nothing, but I meant to do my duty. Duty performed makes a man happy; duty neglected makes a man unhappy.... If the fate of John Rogers had stared me in the face, if I had seen the stake, if I had heard the fagots already crackling, by the blessing of Almighty God I would have gone on and discharged the duty which I thought my country called upon me to perform."

At the next national Whig convention, General Winfield Scott was nominated to the presidency. Multitudes throughout the country were disappointed that Webster was not chosen. Boston gave him a magnificent reception. Marshfield welcomed him with a gathering of thousands of people nine miles from his home, who escorted him thither, scattering garlands along the way. "I remember how," says Charles Lanman, "after the crowd had disappeared, he entered his house fatigued beyond measure, and covered with dust, and threw himself into a chair. For a moment his head fell upon his breast, as if completely overcome, and he then looked up like one seeking something he could not find. It was the portrait of his darling but departed daughter, Julia, and it happened to be in full view. He gazed upon it for some time in a kind of trance, and then wept like one whose heart was broken, and these words escaped his lips, 'Oh, I am so thankful to be here. If I could only have my will, never, never would I again leave this home!'"

Here he was happy. Here he had gathered a large library, many of his books being on science, of which he was very fond. Of geology and physical geography he had made a careful study. Humboldt's "Cosmos" was an especial favorite.

In the spring of 1852, Mr. Webster fell from his carriage, and from this fall he never entirely recovered. In the fall he made his will, and wrote these words for his monument, "Lord, I believe; help thou mine unbelief. Philosophical argument, especially that drawn from the vastness of the universe in comparison with the apparent insignificance of this globe, has sometimes shaken my reason for the faith that is in me; but my heart has assured and reassured me that the Gospel of Jesus Christ must be a Divine Reality.

"The Sermon on the Mount cannot be a merely human production. This belief enters into the very depth of my conscience. The whole history of man proves it."

Mr. Webster had repeatedly given his testimony in favor of the Christian religion. "Religion," he said, "is a necessary and indispensable element in any great human character. There is no living without it. Religion is the tie that connects man with his Creator, and holds him to his throne. If that tie be all sundered, all broken, he floats away, a worthless atom in the universe; its proper attractions all gone, its destiny thwarted, and its whole future nothing but darkness, desolation, and death."

Once, at a dinner party of gentlemen, he was asked by one present, "What is the most important thought that ever occupied your mind?"

The reply came slowly and solemnly, "My individual responsibility to God!"

When the last of October came, Mr. Webster was nearing the end of life. About a week before he died he asked that a herd of his best oxen might be driven in front of his windows, that he might see their honest faces and gentle eyes. A man who thus loves animals must have a tender heart.

A few hours before Mr. Webster died, he said slowly, "My general wish on earth has been to do my Maker's will. I thank him now for all the mercies that surround me.... No man, who is not a brute, can say that he is not afraid of death. No man can come back from that bourne; no man can comprehend the will or the works of God. That there is a God all must acknowledge. I see him in all these wondrous works—himself how wondrous!

"The great mystery is Jesus Christ—the Gospel. What would the condition of any of us be if we had not the hope of immortality?... Thank God, the Gospel of Jesus Christ brought life and immortality to light, rescued it—brought it to light." He then began to repeat the Lord's prayer, saying earnestly, "Hold me up, I do not wish to pray with a fainting voice."

He longed to be conscious when death came. At midnight he said, "I still live," his last coherent words. A little after three he ceased to breathe.

He was buried as he had requested to be, "without the least show or ostentation," on October 29, 1852. The coffin was placed upon the lawn, and more than ten thousand persons gazed upon the face of the great statesman. One unknown man, in plain attire, said as he looked upon him, all unconscious that anybody might hear his words, "Daniel Webster, the world without you will seem lonesome." Six of his neighbors bore him to his grave and laid him beside Grace and his children.

When the Civil War came, which Mr. Webster had done all in his power to avert, it took the last child out of his family: Fletcher, a colonel of the Twelfth Massachusetts volunteers, fell in the battle of August 29, 1862, near Bull Run.

HENRY CLAY

Henry Clay, the "mill-boy of the Slashes," was born April 12, 1777, in Hanover County, Virginia, in a neighborhood called the "Slashes," from its low, marshy ground. The seventh in a family of eight children, says Dr. Calvin Colton, in his "Life and Times of Henry Clay," he came into the home of Rev. John Clay, a true-hearted Baptist minister, poor, but greatly esteemed by all who knew him. Mr. Clay used often to preach out-of-doors to his impecunious flock, who, beside loving him for his spiritual nature, admired his fine voice and manly presence.

When Henry was four years old the father died, leaving the wife to struggle for her daily bread, rich only in the affection which poverty so often intensifies and makes heroic. She was a devoted mother, a person of more than ordinary mind, and extremely patriotic, a quality transmitted to her illustrious son.

Says Hon. Carl Schurz, in his valuable Life of Clay, "There is a tradition in the family that, when the dead body of the father was still lying in the house, Colonel Tarleton, commanding a cavalry force under Lord Cornwallis, passed through Hanover County on a raid, and left a handful of gold and silver on Mrs. Clay's table as a compensation for some property taken or destroyed by his soldiers; but that the spirited woman, as soon as Tarleton was gone, swept the money into her apron and threw it into the fireplace. It would have been in no sense improper, and more prudent, had she kept it, notwithstanding her patriotic indignation."

Anxious that her children be educated, Mrs. Clay sent them to the log school-house in the neighborhood, to learn reading, writing, and arithmetic from Peter Deacon, an Englishman, who seems to have succeeded well in teaching, when sober. The log house was a small structure, with earth floor, no windows, and an entrance which served for continuous ventilation, as there was no door to keep out cold or heat. Henry had nothing of consequence to remember of this school save the marks of a whipping received from Peter Deacon when he was angry.

As soon as school hours were over each day, he had to work to help support the family. Now the bare-footed boy might be seen ploughing; now, mounted on a pony guided by a rope bridle, with a bag of meal thrown across the horse's back, he might be seen going from his home to Mrs. Darricott's mill, on the Pamunky River. The people nicknamed him "The mill-boy of the Slashes," and, years later, when the same bare-footed, mother-loving boy was nominated for the presidency, the term became one of endearment and pride to hundreds of thousands, who knew by experience what a childhood of toil and hardship meant. He became the idol of the poor not less than of the rich, because he could sympathize in their privations, and sympathy is usually born of suffering. Perchance we ought to welcome bitter experiences, for he alone has power who has great sympathy.

After some years of widowhood, Mrs. Clay married Captain Henry Watkins of Richmond, Virginia, and, though she bore him seven children, he did not forget to be a father to the children of her former marriage. When Henry was fourteen, Captain Watkins placed him in Richard Denny's store in Richmond. For a year the boy sold groceries and dry-goods in the retail store, reading in every moment of leisure. His step-father thought rightly that a boy who was so eager to read should have better advantages, and therefore applied to his friend, Colonel Tinsley, for a position in the office of the Clerk of the High Court of Chancery, the clerk being the brother of the colonel.

"There is no vacancy," said the clerk.

"Never mind," said the colonel, "you must take him;" and so he did.

The glad mother cut and made for Henry an ill-fitting suit of gray "figinny" (Virginia) cloth, cotton and silk mixed, and starched his linen to a painful stiffness. When he appeared in the clerk's office he was tall and awkward, and the occupants at the desks could scarcely restrain their mirth at the appearance of the new-comer. Henry was put to the task of copying. The clerks wisely remained quiet, and soon found that the boy was proud, ambitious, quick, willing to work, and superior to themselves in common-sense and the use of language.

Every night when they went in quest of amusement young Clay went home to read. It could not have been mere chance which attracted to the studious, bright boy the attention of George Wythe, the Chancellor of the High Court of Chancery. He was a noted and noble man, one of the signers of the Declaration of Independence, for ten years teacher of jurisprudence at William and Mary's College, a man so liberal in his views in the days of slavery that he emancipated all his slaves and made provision for their maintenance; the same great man in whose office Thomas Jefferson gained inspiration in his youth.

George Wythe selected Clay for his amanuensis in writing out

125

the decisions of the courts. He soon became greatly attached to the boy of fifteen, directed his reading, first in grammatical studies, and then in legal and historical lines. He read Homer, Plutarch's Lives, and similar great works. The conversation of such a man as Mr. Wythe was to Clay what that of Christopher Gore was to Daniel Webster, or that of Judge Story to Charles Sumner. Generally men who have become great have allied themselves to great men or great principles early in life. When Clay had been four years with the chancellor he naturally decided to become a lawyer. Poverty did not deter him; hard work did not deter him. Those who fear to labor must not take a step on the road to fame.

Clay entered the office of Attorney-General Robert Brooke, a man prominent and able. Here he studied hard for a year, and was admitted to the bar, having gained much legal knowledge in the previous four years. During this year he mingled with the best society of Richmond, his own intellectual ability, courteous manners, and good cheer making him welcome, not less than the well known friendship of Chancellor Wythe for him. Clay organized a debating society, and the "mill-boy of the Slashes" quite astonished, not only the members but the public as well, by his unusual powers of oratory.

The esteem of Richmond society did not bring money quickly enough to the enterprising young man. His parents had removed to Kentucky, and he decided to go there also, "and grow up with the country." He was now twenty-one, poor, not as thoroughly educated as he could have wished, but determined to succeed, and when one has this determination the battle is half won. That he regretted his lack of early opportunities, a speech made on the floor of Congress years afterward plainly showed. In reply to Hon. John Randolph he said, "The gentleman from Virginia was pleased to say that in one point, at least, he coincided with me in an humble estimate of my grammatical and philological acquisitions. I know my deficiencies. I was born to no proud patrimonial estate. I inherited only infancy, ignorance, and indigence. I feel my defects. But, so far as my situation in early life is concerned, I may, without presumption, say it was more my misfortune than my fault. But, however I regret my want of ability to furnish the gentleman with a better specimen of powers of verbal criticism, I will venture to say it is not greater than the disappointment of this committee as to the strength of his argument."

When Clay arrived in Lexington, Kentucky, he found not the polished society of Richmond, but a genial, warm-hearted, high-spirited race of men and women, who cordially welcomed the young lawyer with his sympathetic manner and distinguished air, the result of an inborn sense of leadership. Soon after he began to practise law, he joined a debating society, and, with his usual good-sense, did not take an active part until he became acquainted with the members.

One evening, after a subject had been long debated, and the vote was to be taken, Clay, feeling that the matter was not exhausted, rose to speak. At first he was embarrassed, and began, "Gentlemen of the jury!" The audience laughed. Roused to self-control by this mistake, his words came fast and eloquent, till the people held their breath in amazement. From that day, Lexington knew that a young man of brilliancy and power had come within her borders.

Nearly fifty years later, he said in the same city, when he retired from public life, "In looking back upon my origin and progress through life, I have great reason to be thankful. My father died in 1781, leaving me an infant of too tender years to retain any recollection of his smiles or endearments. My surviving parent removed to this State in 1792, leaving me, a boy fifteen years of age, in the office of the High Court of Chancery, in the city of Richmond, without guardian, without pecuniary means of support, to steer my course as I might or could. A neglected education was improved by my own irregular exertions, without the benefit of systematic instruction. I studied law principally in the office of a lamented friend, the late Governor Brooke, then attorney-general of Virginia, and also under the auspices of the venerable and lamented Chancellor Wythe, for whom I had acted as amanuensis. I obtained a license to practise the profession from the judges of the court of appeals of Virginia, and established myself in Lexington in 1797, without patrons, without the favor or countenance of the great or opulent, without the means of paying my weekly board, and in the midst of a bar uncommonly distinguished by eminent members. I remember how comfortable I thought I should be if I could make one hundred pounds, Virginia money, per year, and with what delight I received the first fifteen-shilling fee. My hopes were more than realized. I immediately rushed into a successful and lucrative practice."

His cases at first were largely criminal. His first marked case was that of a woman who, in a moment of passion, shot her sister-in-law. Clay could not bear to see a woman hanged, and she heretofore the respected wife of a respected man. He pleaded "temporary delirium," and saved her life.

It is said that no murderer ever suffered the extreme penalty of the law who was defended by Henry Clay. He saved the life of one Willis, accused of an atrocious murder. Meeting the man later, he said, "Ah! Willis, poor fellow, I fear I have saved too many like you who ought to be hanged." When Clay was public prosecutor, he took up the case of a slave, much valued for his intelligence and honor, who, in the absence of his owner, had been unmercifully treated by an overseer. In self-defence the slave killed the overseer with an axe. Clay argued that had the deed been done by a free man it would have been man-slaughter, but by a slave, who should have submitted, it was murder. The colored man was hanged, meeting death heroically. Clay was so overcome by the painful result of his own unfortunate reasoning that he at once resigned his position, and never ceased to be sorry for his connection with the affair.

Sometimes the ending of a case was ludicrous as well as pathetic. Two Germans, father and son, were indicted for murder in the first degree. The mother and wife were present, and, of course, intensely interested. When Clay obtained the acquittal of the accused, the old lady rushed through the crowd, flung her arms around the neck of the stylish young attorney, and clung to him so persistently that it was difficult for him to free himself!

He soon began to engage more exclusively in civil suits, especially those growing out of the land laws of Virginia and Kentucky, and quickly acquired a leading position at the bar. He had already married, at twenty-two, Lucretia Hart, eighteen years old, the daughter of Colonel Thomas Hart, a well known and respected citizen of Lexington. She was a woman of practical common-sense, devoted to him, and a tender mother to their eleven children, six daughters and five sons.

As soon as Mr. Clay had earned sufficient money he bought Ashland, an estate of six hundred acres, a mile and a half south-east from Lexington court-house. A spacious brick mansion, with flower gardens and groves, made it in time one of the most attractive places in the South. Here, later, Clay entertained Lafayette, Webster, Monroe, and other famous men from Europe and America.

Mr. Clay began his political life when but twenty-two. Kentucky, in 1799, in revising her constitution, considered a project for the gradual abolition of slavery in the State. Clay was an ardent advocate of the measure. He wrote in favor of it in the press, and spoke earnestly in its behalf in public. He, however, received more censure than praise for the position he took, but his conduct was in keeping with his declaration years later: "I had rather be right than be President."

All his life he rejoiced that he had thus early favored the abolition of slavery. He said, thirty years later, "Among the acts of my life which I look back to with most satisfaction is that of my having coöperated with other zealous and intelligent friends to procure the establishment of that system in this State. We were overpowered by numbers, but submitted to the decision of the majority with that grace which the minority in a republic should ever yield to that decision. I have, nevertheless, never ceased, and shall never cease, to regret a decision the effects of which have been to place us in the rear of our neighbors, who are exempt from slavery, in the state of agriculture, the progress of manufactures, the advance of improvements, and the general progress of society."

From this time Clay spoke on all important political questions. Once, when he and George Nicholas had spoken against the alien and sedition laws of the Federalists, so pleased were the Kentuckians that both speakers were placed in a carriage and drawn through the streets, the people shouting applause. Thus foolishly are persons—usually young men—willing to be considered horses through their excitement!

When Clay was twenty-six, so effective had been his eloquence that he was elected to the State Legislature. Who would have prophesied this when he carried meal to Mrs. Darricott's mill! Reading evenings, when other boys roamed the streets, had been an important element in this success; friendship with those older and stronger than himself had given maturity of thought and plan.

When he was thirty he was chosen to the United States Senate, to fill the unexpired term of another. At once, despite his youth, he took an active part in debate, was placed on important committees, and advocated "internal improvements," as he did all the rest of his life, desiring always that America become great and powerful. He was happy in this first experience at the national capital. He wrote home to his wife's father: "My reception in this place has been equal, nay, superior to my expectations. I have experienced the civility and attention of all I was desirous of obtaining. Those who are disposed to flatter me say that I have acquitted myself with great credit in several debates in the Senate. But, after all I have seen, Kentucky is still my favorite country. There amidst my dear family I shall find happiness in a degree to be met with nowhere else."

As soon as Clay was home again, Kentucky sent him to her State Legislature, where he was elected speaker. Already the conflicts between England and France under Napoleon had seriously affected our commerce by the unjust decrees of both nations. Mr. Clay strongly denounced the Orders in Council of the British, and praised Jefferson for the embargo. He urged, also, partly as a retaliatory measure, and partly as a measure of self-protection, that the members of the Legislature wear only such clothes as were made by our own manufacturers. Humphrey Marshall, a strong Federalist, and a man of great ability, denounced this resolution as the work of a demagogue. The result was a duel, in which, after Clay and Marshall were both slightly wounded, the seconds prevented further bloodshed. Once before this Clay had accepted a challenge, and the duel was prevented only by the interference of friends. Had death resulted at either time, America would have missed from her record one of the brightest and fairest names in her history.

When Clay was thirty-three he was again sent to the Senate of the United States, to fill an unexpired term of two years. At the end of that time Kentucky was too proud of him to allow his returning to private life. He was therefore elected to the House of Representatives, and took his seat November 4, 1811. He was at once chosen speaker, an honor conferred for seven terms, fourteen years.

"Henry Clay stands," says Carl Schurz, "in the traditions of the House of Representatives as the greatest of its speakers. His perfect mastery of parliamentary law, his quickness of decision in applying it, his unfailing presence of mind and power of command in moments of excitement and confusion, the courteous dignity of his bearing, are remembered as unequalled by any one of those who had preceded or who have followed him."

Here in the excitement of debate he was happy. He could speak at will against the British, who had seized more than nine hundred American ships, and the French more than five hundred and fifty. When several thousand Americans had been impressed as British seamen, the hot blood of the Kentuckian demanded war. He said in Congress, "We are called upon to submit to debasement, dishonor, and disgrace; to bow the neck to royal insolence, as a course of preparation for manly resistance to Gallic invasion! What nation, what individual was ever taught in the schools of ignominious submission these patriotic lessons of freedom and independence?... An honorable peace is attainable only by an efficient war. My plan would be to call out the ample resources of the country, give them a judicious direction, prosecute the war with the utmost vigor, strike wherever we can reach the enemy, at sea or on land, and negotiate the terms of a peace at Quebec or at Halifax. We are told that England is a proud and lofty nation, which, disdaining to wait for danger, meets it half way. Haughty as she is, we once triumphed over her, and, if we do not listen to the counsels of timidity and despair, we shall again prevail. In such a cause, with the aid of Providence, we must come out crowned with success; but if we fail, let us fail like men, lash ourselves to our gallant tars, and expire together in one common struggle, fighting for FREE TRADE AND SEAMEN'S RIGHTS."

The War of 1812 came, even though New England strongly opposed it. The country was poorly prepared for a great contest by land or by sea, but Clay's enthusiasm seemed equal to a dozen armies. He cheered every regiment by his hope and his patriotism. When defeats came at Detroit and in Canada, Josiah Quincy of Massachusetts, leader of the Federalists, said, "Those must be very young politicians, their pin-feathers not yet grown, and, however they may flutter on this floor, they are not fledged for any high or distant flight, who think that threats and appealing to fear are the ways of producing any disposition to negotiate in Great Britain, or in any other nation which understands what it owes to its own safety and honor."

Clay answered in a two-days speech that was never forgotten. He scourged the Federalists with stinging words: "Sir, gentlemen appear to me to forget that they stand on American soil; that they are not in the British House of Commons, but in the chamber of the House of Representatives of the United States; that we have nothing to do with the affairs of Europe, the partition of territory and sovereignty there, except so far as these things affect the interests of our own country. Gentlemen transform themselves into the Burkes, Chathams, and Pitts of another country, and forgetting, from honest zeal, the interests of America, engage with European sensibility in the discussion of European interests.... I have no fears of French or English subjugation. If we are united we are too powerful for the mightiest nation in Europe, or all Europe combined. If we are separated and torn asunder, we shall become an easy prey to the weakest of them. In the latter dreadful contingency, our country will not be worth preserving.

"The war was declared because Great Britain arrogated to herself the pretension of regulating our foreign trade, under the delusive name of retaliatory orders in council—a pretension by which she undertook to proclaim to American enterprise, 'Thus far shalt thou go, and no further'—orders which she refused to revoke, after the alleged cause of their enactment had ceased; because she persisted in the practice of impressing American seamen; because she had instigated the Indians to commit hostilities against us; and because she refused indemnity for her past injuries upon our commerce. I throw out of the question other wrongs. The war in fact was announced on our part to meet the war which she was waging on her part."

The speech electrified the country. The army was increased, the nation encouraged, and the war carried to a successful issue. Such a power had Clay become that Madison talked of making him commander-in-chief of the army, but Gallatin dissuaded him, saying, "What shall we do without Clay in Congress?"

When the war was nearing its end—before Jackson had fought his famous battle at New Orleans—and a treaty of peace was to be effected, the President appointed five commissioners to confer with the British government: John Quincy Adams, Clay, Bayard, Jonathan Russell, Minister to Sweden, and Albert Gallatin.

They reached Ghent, in the Netherlands, July 6, 1814, a company of earnest men, not always in accord, but desirous of accomplishing the most possible for America. Adams was able, courageous, irritable, and sometimes domineering; Clay, impetuous, spirited, genial, making friends of the British commissioners as they played at whist—he never allowed cards to come into his home at Ashland; Gallatin, discreet, a peace-maker, and dignified counsellor.

For five months the commissioners argued, waited to see if their respective countries would accede to the terms proposed, and finally settled an honorable peace. Then Clay, Adams, and Gallatin spent three months in London negotiating a treaty of commerce. Clay had meantime heard of the battle of New Orleans, and said, "Now I can go to England without mortification." In Paris he met Madame de Staël. "I have been in England," said she, "and have been battling for your cause there. They were so much enraged against you that at one time they thought seriously of sending the Duke of Wellington to lead their armies against you."

"I am very sorry," replied Clay, "that they did not send the duke."

"And why?" she asked.

"Because if he had beaten us, we should have been in the condition of Europe, without disgrace. But if we had been so fortunate as to defeat him, we should have greatly added to the renown of our arms."

When Clay returned to America, he was welcomed in New York and Lexington with public dinners. That the war had produced good results was well stated in his Lexington address. "Abroad, our character, which, at the time of its declaration, was in the lowest state of degradation, is raised to the highest point of elevation. It is impossible for any American to visit Europe without being sensible of this agreeable change in the personal attentions which he receives, in the praises which are bestowed on our past exertions, and the predictions which are made as to our future prospects. At home, a government, which, at its formation, was apprehended by its best friends, and pronounced by its enemies to be incapable of standing the shock, is found to answer all the purposes of its institution."

Clay was now famous; commanding in presence, with a winsome rather than handsome face, exuberant in spirits, generous by nature, polite to the poorest, self-possessed, with a voice unsurpassed, if ever equalled, for its musical tone; a man who made friends everywhere and among all classes, and never lost them; who was always a gentleman, because always kind at heart. Manner, which Emerson calls the "finest of the fine arts," gave Clay the "mastery of palace and fortune" wherever he went. That voice and hand-grasp, that remembrance of a face and a name, won him countless admirers.

President Madison offered him the mission to Russia, which he declined, as also a place in the Cabinet, as Secretary of War, preferring to speak on all those matters which helped to build up America. On the question of the United States Bank he made a strong speech against its constitutionality, which Andrew Jackson said later was his most convincing authority when he destroyed the bank. Clay's views changed in after years, and made him at bitter enmity with Andrew Jackson and John Tyler, both of whom vigorously opposed a bank, with its vast capital and consequent power in politics.

Clay's desire for the rapid development of America led him to become a "protectionist," and the leader of the so-called "American system," as opposed to Free Trade or the Foreign System. He believed that only as we encourage our own manufactures can we become a powerful nation, paying high wages, shutting out the products of the cheap labor of Europe, increasing our home market, and becoming independent of the foreign market. Clay's speeches were read the country over, and won him thousands of followers.

Like others in public life, he now and then gave offence to his constituents. He had voted for a bill to increase the pay of members

133

of Congress from six dollars a day to a salary of fifteen hundred dollars a year. To the farmers of Kentucky this amount seemed far too great. He one day met an old hunter who had always voted for him, but was now determined to vote against a man so extravagant in his ideas!

"My friend," said Clay, "have you a good rifle?"

"Yes."

"Did it ever flash?"

"Yes; but only once."

"What did you do with the rifle when it flashed?—throw it away?"

"No; I picked the flint, tried again, and brought down the game."

"Have I ever flashed, except upon the compensation bill?"

"No."

"Well, will you throw me away?"

"No, Mr. Clay; I will pick the flint and try you again."

Mr. Clay was returned to Congress, and voted for the repeal of the fifteen hundred dollar salary.

The subject which was to surpass all other subjects in interest, and well-nigh destroy the Union, was coming into prominence—slavery. Henry Clay, from a boy, when George Wythe, the Virginia chancellor, freed his slaves, had looked upon human bondage as a curse. He used to say, "If I could be instrumental in eradicating this deepest stain from the character of our country, and removing all cause of reproach on account of it, by foreign nations; if I could only be instrumental in ridding of this foul blot that revered State that gave me birth, or that not less beloved State which kindly adopted me as her son, I would not exchange the proud satisfaction which I should enjoy for the honor of all the triumphs ever decreed to the most successful conqueror.

"When we consider the cruelty of the origin of negro slavery, its nature, the character of the free institutions of the whites, and the irresistible progress of public opinion throughout America, as well as in Europe, it is impossible not to anticipate frequent insurrections among the blacks in the United States; they are rational beings like ourselves, capable of feeling, of reflection, and of judging of what naturally belongs to them as a portion of the human race. By the very condition of the relation which subsists between us, we are enemies of each other. They know well the wrongs which their ancestors suffered at the hands of our ancestors, and the wrongs which they believe they continue to endure, although they

134

may be unable to avenge them. They are kept in subjection only by the superior intelligence and superior power of the predominant race."

At the North, anti-slavery sentiments had intensified; at the South, where slavery was at first regarded as an evil, the consequent ease and wealth from slave labor had changed public opinion, and had made the people jealous of northern discussion. Through the invention of the cotton-gin, by Eli Whitney, the value of cotton exports had quadrupled in twenty years, and the value of slaves had trebled. Comparatively good feeling was maintained by the two sections of the country as long as for every slave State admitted to the Union a free State was also admitted.

In 1818, the people of Missouri desired to be admitted to the Union. Mr. Tallmadge of New York proposed that the further introduction of slavery should be prohibited, and that all children born within the said State should be free at the age of twenty-five years. The discussion grew strong and bitter. Two years later the inhabitants of the State proceeded to adopt a constitution which forbade free negroes from coming into the territory or settling in it. The discussion grew more bitter still. Threats of disunion and civil war were heard. Jefferson wrote from his Monticello home, "The Missouri question is the most portentous one that ever threatened the Union. In the gloomiest moments of the Revolutionary War I never had any apprehension equal to that I feel from this source."

A senator from Illinois, Mr. Thomas, proposed that no restriction as to slavery be imposed upon Missouri, but that in all the rest of the territory ceded by France to the United States, north of 36° 30', this being the southern boundary of Missouri, there should be no slavery. Then Mr. Clay, with his intense love for the Union, bent all his energies to effect this compromise suggested by Thomas. He spoke earnestly in its behalf, and went from member to member, persuading and beseeching with all his genius and winsomeness. When Clay had effected the passage of the bill, the "great pacificator" became more beloved than ever. He had saved the Union, and now was talked of as the successor to President Monroe.

Clay was now forty-seven, the polished orator, the consummate leader, one of the great trio whom all visitors to Washington wished to look upon: Clay, Webster, and Calhoun. Kentucky was earnest in her support of Clay as President.

When the time came for voting, six candidates were before the people: John Quincy Adams, Jackson, Clay, Calhoun, Clinton of

New York, and Crawford of Georgia. Hon. Thomas H. Benton of Missouri was an ardent supporter of Clay, and travelled over several States speaking in his behalf.

Clay was anxious for the position, but would do nothing unworthy to obtain it. He wrote to a friend, "On one resolution, my friends may rest assured, I will firmly rely, and that is, to participate in no intrigue, to enter into no arrangements, to make no promises or pledges; but that, whether I am elected or not, I will have nothing to reproach myself with. If elected, I will go into the office with a pure conscience, to promote with my utmost exertions the common good of our country, and free to select the most able and faithful public servants. If not elected, acquiescing most cheerfully in the better selection which will thus have been made, I will at least have the satisfaction of preserving my honor unsullied and my heart uncorrupted."

After the vote had been taken, as no candidate received a clear majority, the election necessarily went to the House of Representatives. Though Jackson received the most electoral votes, Clay, not friendly to him, used his influence for Adams and helped obtain his election. Clay was, of course, bitterly censured by the followers of Jackson, and when Adams made him Secretary of State the cry of "bargain and sale" was heard throughout the country. Though both Adams and Clay denied any promise between them, the Jackson men believed, or professed to believe it, and helped in later years to spoil his presidential success. Adams said, "As to my motives for tendering him the Department of State when I did, let the man who questions them come forward. Let him look around among the statesmen and legislators of the nation and of that day. Let him then select and name the man whom, by his preëminent talents, by his splendid services, by his ardent patriotism, by his all-embracing public spirit, by his fervid eloquence in behalf of the rights and liberties of mankind, by his long experience in the affairs of the Union, foreign and domestic, a President of the United States, intent only upon the honor and welfare of his country, ought to have preferred to Henry Clay."

Returning to Kentucky before taking the position of Secretary of State, his journey thither was one constant ovation. Public dinners were given him in Virginia, Pennsylvania, and Ohio. In the midst of this prosperity, sorrow laid her hand heavily upon the great man's heart. His children were his idols. They obeyed him because they loved him and were proud of him. Lucretia, named for her mother, a delicate and much beloved daughter, died at fourteen.

136

Eliza, a most attractive girl, with her father's magnetic manners, died on their journey to Washington. A few days after her death, another daughter, Susan Hart, then Mrs. Durolde of New Orleans, died, at the age of twenty.

There was work to be done for the country, and Mr. Clay tried to put away his sorrow that he might do his duty. As Secretary of State he helped to negotiate treaties with Prussia, Denmark, Austria, Russia, and other nations. The opposition to Adams and Clay became intense. The Jackson party felt itself defrauded. John Randolph of Virginia was an outspoken enemy, closing a scathing speech with the words, "by the coalition of Blifil and Black George— by the combination, unheard of till then, of the Puritan with the blackleg."

Clay was indignant, and sent Randolph a challenge, which he accepted. On the night before the duel, Randolph told a friend that he had determined not to return Clay's fire. "Nothing," he said, "shall induce me to harm a hair of his head. I will not make his wife a widow and his children orphans. Their tears would be shed over his grave; but when the sod of Virginia rests on my bosom, there is not in this wide world one individual to pay this tribute upon mine."

The two men met on the banks of the Potomac, near sunset. Clay fired and missed his adversary, while Randolph discharged his pistol in the air. As soon as Clay perceived this he came forward and exclaimed, "I trust in God, my dear sir, that you are unhurt; after what has occurred, I would not have harmed you for a thousand worlds." Years afterward, a short time before Randolph's death, as he was on his way to Philadelphia, he stopped in Washington, and was carried into the Senate chamber during its all-night session. Clay was speaking. "Hold me up," he said to his attendants; "I have come to hear that voice."

At the presidential election of 1828 Andrew Jackson was the successful candidate, and Clay retired to his Ashland farm, where he took especial delight in his fine horses, cattle, and sheep. But he was soon returned to the Senate by his devoted State.

The tariff question was now absorbing the public mind. The South, under Calhoun's leadership, had been opposed to protection, which they believed aided northern manufacturers at the expense of southern agriculturists. When the tariff bill of 1832 was passed, and South Carolina talked of nullification and secession, Clay said: "The great principle which lies at the foundation of all free government is that the majority must govern, from which there can be no appeal but the sword. That majority ought to govern wisely, equitably, moderately, and constitutionally; but govern it must, subject only to that terrible appeal. If ever one or several States, being a minority, can, by menacing a dissolution of the Union, succeed in forcing an abandonment of great measures deemed essential to the interests and prosperity of the whole, the Union from that moment is practically gone. It may linger on in form and name, but its vital spirit has fled forever."

South Carolina passed her nullification ordinance, and prepared to resist the collection of revenues at Charleston. Then Jackson, with his undaunted courage and indomitable will, ordered a body of troops to South Carolina, and threatened to hang Calhoun and his nullifiers as "high as Haman."

Then the "great pacificator" came forward to heal the wounds between North and South, and preserve the Union. He prepared his "Compromise Bill," which provided for a gradual reduction of duties till the year 1842, when twenty per cent. at a home valuation should become the rate on dutiable goods. He spent much time and thought on this bill, visiting the great manufacturers of the country, and urging them to accede for the sake of peace.

After this bill passed he was more esteemed than ever. He visited by request the Northern and Eastern States, and spoke to great gatherings of people in nearly all the large cities. A platform having been erected on the heights of Bunker Hill, Edward Everett addressed him in the presence of an immense audience, and Clay responded with his usual eloquence. The young men of Boston presented him a pair of silver pitchers, weighing one hundred and fifty ounces. The young men of Troy, New York, gave him a superbly mounted rifle. Other cities made him expensive presents.

After the first four years of Jackson's "reign," as it was called by those who deprecated the unusual power held by the executive, Clay was again nominated for the presidency by the Whigs, and again defeated, Jackson receiving two hundred and nineteen electoral votes and Clay only forty-nine.

Again in 1840, after the four years' term of Van Buren, the protégé of Jackson, all eyes turned toward Clay as the coming President. But already he had been twice the nominee and been twice defeated. The anti-slavery element had become a serious factor in party plans. The secretary of the American Anti-Slavery Society in New York wrote Clay: "I should consider the election of a slave-holder to the presidency a great calamity to the country." The slave-holders meantime denounced Clay as an abolitionist.

When the Whig national convention met, December 4, 1839, they chose, not Clay, but General William Henry Harrison, a good man and a successful soldier, but a very different man from the popular Clay. The statesman was sorely disappointed. "I am," he said, "the most unfortunate man in the history of parties: always run by my friends when sure to be defeated, and now betrayed for a nomination when I or any one would be sure of an election."

His friends throughout the country were grieved and indignant. But Clay supported with all his power the true-hearted old soldier, who, when elected, offered him the first place in the Cabinet, which was declined. Harrison died a month after his inauguration, and John Tyler became President. Clay and Tyler differed constantly, till Clay determined to retire from the Senate. He said: "I want rest, and my private affairs want attention. Nevertheless, I would make any personal sacrifice if, by remaining here, I could do any good; but my belief is I can effect nothing, and perhaps my absence may remove an obstacle to something being done by others." When it became known that Clay would make a farewell address, the Senate chamber was crowded.

He spoke of his long career of public service, and the memorable scenes they had witnessed together. His feelings nearly overcame him as he said: "I emigrated from Virginia to the State of Kentucky now nearly forty-five years ago; I went as an orphan boy who had not yet attained the age of majority, who had never recognized a father's smile nor felt his warm caresses, poor, penniless, without the favor of the great, with an imperfect and neglected education, hardly sufficient for the ordinary business and common pursuits of life; but scarce had I set foot upon her generous soil when I was embraced with parental fondness, caressed as though I had been a favorite child, and patronized with liberal and unbounded munificence. From that period the highest honors of the State have been freely bestowed upon me; and when, in the darkest hour of calumny and detraction, I seemed to be assailed by all the rest of the world, she interposed her broad and impenetrable shield, repelled the poisoned shafts that were aimed for my destruction, and vindicated my good name from every malignant and unfounded aspersion. I return with indescribable pleasure to linger a while longer, and mingle with the warm-hearted and whole-souled people of that State; and, when the last scene shall forever close upon me, I hope that my earthly remains will be laid under her green sod with those of her gallant and patriotic sons."

When Clay reached Lexington he was welcomed like a prince. A great public feast was given in his honor. In his speech to the people he said: "I have been accused of ambition, often accused of ambition. If to have served my country during a long series of years with fervent zeal and unshaken fidelity, in seasons of peace and war, at home and abroad, in the legislative halls and in an executive department; if to have labored most sedulously to avert the embarrassment and distress which now overspread this Union, and, when they came, to have exerted myself anxiously, at the extra session and at this, to devise healing remedies; if to have desired to introduce economy and reform in the general administration, curtail enormous executive power, and amply provide, at the same time, for the wants of the government and the wants of the people, by a tariff which would give it revenue and then protection; if to have earnestly sought to establish the bright but too rare example of a party in power faithful to its promises and pledges made when out of power,—if these services, exertions, and endeavors justify the accusation of ambition, I must plead guilty to the charge.

"I have wished the good opinion of the world; but I defy the most malignant of my enemies to show that I have attempted to gain it by any low or grovelling acts, by any mean or unworthy sacrifices, by the violation of any of the obligations of honor, or by a breach of any of the duties which I owed to my country."

In 1844, at the Whig convention at Baltimore, May 1, Clay was unanimously nominated for the presidency, with a great shout that shook the building. It seemed as though his hour of triumph had come at last. James K. Polk was the Democratic nominee. Another party now appeared, the "Liberty Party," with James G. Birney of Kentucky as its candidate. He was an able lawyer, and a man who had liberated his slaves through principle. The contest was one of the most acrimonious in our national history. Texas was clamoring for admission to the Union, with the Mexican War sure to result. The Whigs feared to commit themselves on the slavery question. When the votes were counted Birney had received over sixty-two thousand, enough to throw the election into the hands of the Democrats. The abolitionists had done what they were willing to do,—bury the Whig party, that from its grave might arise another party, which should fearlessly grapple with slavery, and they accomplished their desire, when, in 1860, the Republican party made Abraham Lincoln President.

The disappointment to Mr. Clay was extreme, but he bore it bravely. His friends all over the country seemed broken-hearted. Letters of sorrow poured into Ashland. "I write," said one, "with an aching heart, and ache it must. God Almighty save us! Although our hearts are broken and bleeding, and our bright hopes are crushed, we feel proud of our candidate. God bless you! Your countrymen do bless you. All know how to appreciate the man who has stood in the first rank of American patriots. Though unknown to you, you are by no means a stranger to me." Another wrote: "I have buried a revolutionary father, who poured out his blood for his country; I have followed a mother, brothers, sisters, and children to the grave; and, although I hope I have felt, under all these afflictions, as a son, a brother, and a father should feel, yet nothing has so crushed me to the earth, and depressed my spirits, as the result of our late political contest."

"Permit me, a stranger, to address you. From my boyhood I have loved no other American statesman so much except Washington. I write from the overflowing of my heart. I admire and love you more than ever. If I may never have the happiness of seeing you on earth, may I meet you in heaven."

A lady wrote, "I had indulged the most joyous anticipations in view of that political campaign which has now been so ingloriously ended. I considered that the nation could never feel satisfied until it had cancelled, in some degree, the onerous obligations so long due to its faithful and distinguished son."

Another lady wrote, "My mind is a perfect chaos when I dwell upon the events which have occurred within the last few weeks. My heart refused to credit the sad reality. Had I the eloquence of all living tongues, I could not shadow forth the deep, deep sorrow that has thrilled my inmost soul. The bitterest tears have flowed like rain-drops from my eyes. Never, till now, could I believe that truth and justice would not prevail."

A lady in Maryland, ninety-three years old, wrought for Clay a counterpane of almost numberless pieces. New York friends sent a silver vase three feet high. The ladies of Tennessee sent a costly vase. Tokens of affection came from all directions. But the grief was so great that in some towns business was almost suspended, while the people talked "of the late blow that has fallen upon our country."

Other troubles were pressing upon Mr. Clay's heart. By heavy expenditures and losses through his sons, his home had become involved to the extent of fifty thousand dollars. The mortgage was to be foreclosed, and Henry Clay would be penniless. A number of friends had learned these facts, and sent him the cancelled obligation. He was overcome by this proof of affection, and exclaimed, "Had ever any man such friends or enemies as Henry Clay!"

Two years later, his favorite son, Colonel Henry Clay, was killed under General Taylor, in the battle of Buena Vista. "My life has been full of domestic affliction," said the father, "but this last is the severest among them." A few years before, while in Washington, a brilliant and lovely married daughter had died. When Mr. Clay opened the letter and read the sad news, he fainted, and remained in his room for days.

Mr. Clay was now seventy years old. Chastened by sorrow, he determined to unite with the Episcopal Church. Says one who was present in the little parlor at Ashland, "When the minister entered the room on this deeply solemn and interesting occasion, the small assembly, consisting of the immediate family, a few family connections, and the clergyman's wife, rose up. In the middle of the room stood a large centre-table, on which was placed, filled with water, the magnificent cut-glass vase presented to Mr. Clay by some gentlemen of Pittsburg. On one side of the room hung the large picture of the family of Washington, himself an Episcopalian by birth, by education, and a devout communicant of the church; and immediately opposite, on a side-table, stood the bust of the lamented Harrison, with a chaplet of withered flowers hung upon his head, who was to have been confirmed in the church the Sabbath after he died,—fit witnesses of such a scene. Around the room were suspended a number of family pictures, and among them the portrait of a beloved daughter, who died some years ago, in the triumphs of that faith which her noble father was now about to embrace; and the picture of the late lost son, who fell at the battle of Buena Vista. Could these silent lookers-on at the scene about transpiring have spoken from the marble and the canvas, they would heartily have approved the act which dedicated the great man to God."

In 1848, Clay was again talked of for the presidency, but the party managers considered General Taylor, of the Mexican War, a more available candidate, and he was nominated and elected. Clay was again unanimously chosen to the Senate for six years from March 4, 1849. Seven years before, he had said farewell. Now, at seventy-two, he was again to debate great questions, and once more save the nation from disruption and civil war,—for a time; he hoped, for all time.

The territory obtained from Mexico became a matter of contention as to whether it should be slave territory or not. California asked to be admitted to the Union without slavery. The North favored this, while the South insisted that the Missouri Compromise of 1820, which forbade slavery north of 36° 30', if continued to the Pacific Ocean, would entitle them to California. Already the Wilmot Proviso, which sought to exclude slavery from all territory hereafter acquired by the United States, had aroused bitter feeling at the South. Clay, loving the Union beyond all things

142

else, thought out his compromise of 1850. As he walked up to the Capitol to make his last great speech upon the measure, he said to a friend accompanying him, "Will you lend me your arm? I feel myself quite weak and exhausted this morning." The friend suggested that he postpone his speech.

"I consider our country in danger," replied Clay; "and if I can be the means in any measure of averting that danger, my health and life are of little consequence."

Great crowds had come from Philadelphia, New York, Boston, and elsewhere to hear the speech, which occupied two days. He said: "War and dissolution of the Union are identical; they are convertible terms; and such a war!... If the two portions of the confederacy should be involved in civil war, in which the effort on the one side would be to restrain the introduction of slavery into the new territories, and, on the other side, to force its introduction there, what a spectacle should we present to the contemplation of astonished mankind! An effort to propagate wrong! It would be a war in which we should have no sympathy, no good wishes, and in which all mankind would be against us, and in which our own history itself would be against us."

For six months the measure was debated. Clay came daily to the Senate chamber, so ill he could scarcely walk, but determined to save the Union. "Sir," said the grand old man, "I have heard something said about allegiance to the South. I know no South, no North, no East, no West, to which I owe any allegiance.... Let us go to the fountain of unadulterated patriotism, and, performing a solemn lustration, return divested of all selfish, sinister, and sordid impurities, and think alone of our God, our country, our conscience, and our glorious Union.... If Kentucky to-morrow unfurls the banner of resistance unjustly, I never will fight under that banner. I owe a paramount allegiance to the whole Union,—a subordinate one to my own State. When my State is right, when it has a cause for resistance, when tyranny and wrong and oppression insufferable arise, I will then share her fortunes; but if she summons me to the battlefield, or to support her in any cause which is unjust against the Union, never, never will I engage with her in such a cause!"

Finally the Compromise Bill of 1850 was substantially adopted. Among its several provisions were the admission of California as a free State, the abolition of the slave-trade in the District of Columbia, the organization of the Territories of New Mexico and Utah without conditions as to slavery, and increased stringency of the Fugitive Slave Laws.

Mr. Clay's hopes as to peace seemed for a few brief months to be realized. Then the North, exasperated by the provisions of the Fugitive Slave Bill, by which all good citizens were required to aid slave-holders in capturing their fugitive slaves, began to resist the bill by force. Clay could do no more. He must have foreseen the bitter end. Worn and tired, he went to Cuba to seek restoration of health.

In 1852 he was urged to allow his name to be used again for the presidency. It was too late now. He returned to Washington at the opening of the thirty-second Congress, but he entered the Senate chamber but once. During the spring, devoted friends and two of his sons watched by his bedside. He said: "As the world recedes from me, I feel my affections more than ever concentrated on my children and theirs."

The end came peacefully, June 29, 1852, when he was seventy-six. On July 1 the body lay in state in the Senate chamber, and was then carried to Lexington. In all the principal cities through which the cortege passed, Baltimore, Philadelphia, New York, Albany, Buffalo, Cleveland, Cincinnati, and others, thousands gathered to pay their homage to the illustrious dead, weeping, and often pressing their lips upon the shroud. On July 10, when the body, having reached Lexington, was ready for burial, nearly a hundred thousand persons were gathered. In front of the Ashland home, on a bier covered with flowers, stood the iron coffin. Senators and scholars, the rich and the poor, the white and the black, mourned together in their common sorrow. The great man had missed the presidency, but he had not missed the love of a whole nation. The "mill-boy of the Slashes," winsome, sincere, had, unaided, become the only and immortal Henry Clay.

CHARLES SUMNER

Henry Ward Beecher said of Charles Sumner: "He was raised up to do the work preceding and following the war. His eulogy will be, a lover of his country, an advocate of universal liberty, and the most eloquent and high-minded of all the statesmen of that period in which America made the transition from slavery to liberty."

"The most eloquent and high-minded." Great praise, but worthily bestowed!

Descended from an honorable English family who came to Massachusetts in 1637, settling in Dorchester, and the son of a well known lawyer, Charles Sumner came into the world January 6, 1811, with all the advantages of birth and social position. That he cared comparatively little for the family coat-of-arms of his ancestors is shown by his words in his address on "The True Grandeur of Nations." "Nothing is more shameful for a man than to found his title to esteem not on his own merits, but on the fame of his ancestors. The glory of the fathers is, doubtless, to their children, a most precious treasure; but to enjoy it without transmitting it to the next generation, and without adding to it yourselves,—this is the height of imbecility."

Sumner added to the "glory of the fathers," not by ease and self-indulgence, not by conforming to the opinions of the society about him, but by a life of labor, and heroic devotion to principle. He had such courage to do the right as is not common to mankind, and such persistency as teaches a lesson to the young men of America.

Charles was the oldest of nine children, the twin brother of Matilda, who grew to a beautiful womanhood, and died of consumption at twenty-one. The family home was at No. 20 Hancock Street, Boston, a four-story brick building.

Charles Pinckney Sumner, the father, a scholarly and well bred man of courtly manners, while he taught his children to love books, had the severity of nature which forbade a tender companionship between him and his oldest son. This was supplied, however, by the mother, a woman of unusual amiability and good-sense, who lived to be his consolation in the struggles of manhood, and to be proud and thankful when the whole land echoed his praises.

The boy was tall, slight, obedient, and devoted to books. He was especially fond of reading and repeating speeches. When sent to dancing-school he showed little enjoyment in it, preferring to go to the court-room with his father, to listen to the arguments of the lawyers. When he visited his mother's early home in Hanover, he had the extreme pleasure of reciting in the country woods the orations which he had read in the city.

In these early days he was an aspiring lad, with a manner which made his companions say he was "to the manor born." The father had decided to educate him in the English branches only, thus fitting him to earn his living earlier, as his income from the law, at this time, was not large. Charles, however, had purchased some Latin books with his pocket money, and surprised his father with the progress he had made by himself when ten years old. He was therefore, at this age, sent to the Boston Latin School. So skilful was he in the classics that at thirteen he received a prize for a translation from Sallust, and at fifteen a prize for English prose and another for a Latin poem. At the latter age he was ready to enter Harvard College. He had desired to go to West Point, but, fortunately, there was no opening. The country needed him for other work than war. To lead a whole nation by voice and pen up to heroic deeds is better than to lead an army.

All this time he read eagerly in his spare moments, especially in history, enjoying Gibbon's "Rome," and making full extracts from it in his notebooks. At fourteen he had written a compendium of English history, from Cæsar's conquest to 1801, which filled a manuscript book of eighty-six pages.

His first college room at Harvard was No. 17 Stoughton Hall. "When he entered," says one of his class-mates, "he was tall, thin, and somewhat awkward. He had but little inclination for engaging in sports or games, such as kicking foot-ball on the Delta, which the other students were in almost the daily habit of enjoying. He rarely went out to take a walk; and almost the only exercise in which he engaged was going on foot to Boston on Saturday afternoon, and then returning in the evening. He had a remarkable fondness for reading the dramas of Shakespeare, the works of Walter Scott, together with reviews and magazines of the higher class. He remembered what he read, and quoted passages afterwards with the greatest fluency.... In declamation he held rank among the best; but in mathematics there were several superior. He was always amiable and gentlemanly in deportment, and avoided saying anything to wound the feelings of his class-mates." One of the chief distinguishing marks of a well bred man is that he speaks ill of no one and harshly to no one.

In Sumner's freshman year his persistency showed itself, as in his childhood, when, in quarrelling with a companion over a stick, he held it till his bleeding hands frightened his antagonist, who ran away. By the laws of the college, students wore a uniform, consisting of an Oxford cap, coat, pantaloons, and vest of the color known as "Oxford mixed." In summer a white vest was allowed. Sumner, having a fancy for a buff vest, purchased one, wore it, and was summoned before the teachers for non-conformity to rules. He insisted, with much eloquence, that his vest was white. Twice he was admonished, and finally, as the easiest way to settle with the good-principled but persistent student, it was voted by the board, "that in future Sumner's vest be regarded as white!"

In scholarship in college he ranked among the first third. He gave much time to general reading, especially the old English authors, Milton, Pope, Dryden, Addison, Goldsmith. Hazlitt's "Select British Poets" and Harvey's "Shakespeare" he kept constantly on his table in later life, ready for use. The latter, which he always called The Book, was found open on the day of his death, with the words marked in Henry VI:—

"Would I were dead! if God's good will were so;
For what is in this world but grief and woe?"

On leaving college, Sumner's mind was not made up as to his future work. He was somewhat inclined to the law, but questioned his probable success in it. He spent a year at home in study, mastering mathematics, which he so disliked, and reading Tacitus, Juvenal, Persius, Hume, Hallam, and the like. In the winter he composed an essay on commerce, and received the prize offered by the "Boston Society for the Diffusion of Useful Knowledge." Daniel Webster, the president of the society, gave the prize, Liebner's "Encyclopædia Americana," to Sumner, taking his hand and calling him his "young friend." He did not know that this youth would succeed him in the Senate, and thrill the nation by his eloquence, as Webster himself had done.

Sumner's class-mates were proud that he had gained this prize, and one wrote to another, "Our friend outstrips all imagination. He will leave us all behind him…. He has been working hard to lay a foundation for the future. I doubt whether one of his class-mates has filled up the time since commencement with more, and more thorough labor; and to keep him constant he has a pervading ambition,—not an intermittent, fitful gust of an affair, blowing a hurricane at one time, then subsiding to a calm, but a strong, steady breeze, which will bear him well on in the track of honor."

In the fall of 1831 Sumner had decided to study law, and began in earnest at the Harvard Law School. Early and late he was among his books, often until two in the morning. He soon knew the place of each volume in the law library, so that he could have found it in the dark. He read carefully in common law, French law, and international law; procured a common-place book, and wrote out tables of English kings and lord-chancellors, sketches of lawyers, and definitions and incidents from Blackstone. He made a catalogue of the law library, and wrote articles for legal magazines. He went little into society, because he preferred his books. Judge Story, a man twice his own age, became his most devoted friend, and to the end of his life Sumner loved him as a brother.

Chief Justice Story, whom Lord Brougham called the "greatest justice in the world," was a man of singularly sweet nature, appreciative of the beautiful and the pure, as well as a man of profound learning. The influence of such a lovable and strong nature over an ambitious youth, who can estimate?

The few friends Sumner made among women were, as a rule, older than himself, a thing not unusual with intellectual men. He chose those whose minds were much like his own, and who were appreciative, refining, and stimulating. Brain and heart seemed to be the only charms which possessed any fascination for him.

The eminent sculptor, W. W. Story of Rome, says, "Of all men I ever knew at his age, he was the least susceptible to the charms of women. Men he liked best, and with them he preferred to talk. It was in vain for the loveliest and liveliest girl to seek to absorb his attention. He would at once desert the most blooming beauty to talk to the plainest of men. This was a constant source of amusement to us, and we used to lay wagers with the pretty girls that with all their art they could not keep him at their side a quarter of an hour. Nor do I think we ever lost one of these bets. I remember particularly one dinner at my father's house, when it fell to his lot to take out a charming woman, so handsome and full of esprit that any one at the table might well have envied him his position. She had determined to hold him captive, and win her bet against us. But her efforts were all in vain. Unfortunately, on his other side was a dry old savant, packed with information; and within five minutes Sumner had completely turned his back on his fair companion and engaged in a discussion with the other, which lasted the whole dinner. We all laughed. She cast up her eyes deprecatingly, acknowledged herself vanquished, and paid her bet. Meantime, Sumner was wholly unconscious of the jest or of the laughter. He had what he wanted—sensible men's talk. He had mined the savant as he mined every one

148

he met, in search of ore, and was thoroughly pleased with what he got."

In manner Sumner was natural and sincere, friendly to all, winning at the first moment by his radiant smile. A sunny face is a constant benediction. How it blesses and lifts burdens from aching hearts! Sumner had heart-aches like all the rest of mankind, but his face beamed with that open, kindly expression which is as sweet to hungering humanity as the sunshine after rain. And this "genial illuminating smile," says Mr. Story, "he never lost."

These days in the law school were happy days for the lover of learning. Forty years afterward, Mr. Sumner said, in an address to the colored law students of Howard University, Washington, "These exercises carry me back to early life.... I cannot think of those days without fondness. They were the happiest of my life.... There is happiness in the acquisition of knowledge, which surpasses all common joys. The student who feels that he is making daily progress, constantly learning something new,—who sees the shadows by which he was originally surrounded gradually exchanged for an atmosphere of light,—cannot fail to be happy. His toil becomes a delight, and all that he learns is a treasure,—with this difference from gold and silver, that it cannot be lost. It is a perpetual capital at compound interest."

While at the law school, Sumner wrote a friend, "A lawyer must know everything. He must know law, history, philosophy, human nature; and, if he covets the fame of an advocate, he must drink of all the springs of literature, giving ease and elegance to the mind, and illustration to whatever subject it touches. So experience declares, and reflection bears experience out.... The lower floor of Divinity Hall, where I reside, is occupied by law students. There are here Browne and Dana of our old class, with others that I know nothing of,—not even my neighbor, parted from me by a partition wall, have I seen yet, and I do not wish to see him. I wish no acquaintances, for they eat up time like locusts. The old class-mates are enough." To another he wrote, "Determine that you will master the whole compass of law; and do not shrink from the crabbed page of black-letter, the multitudinous volumes of reports, or even the gigantic abridgments. Keep the high standard in your mind's eye, and you will certainly reach some desirable point.... You cannot read history too much, particularly that of England and the United States. History is the record of human conduct and experience; and it is to this that jurisprudence is applied.... Above all love and honor your profession. You can make yourself love the law, proverbially dry as it is, or any other study. Here is an opportunity for the

149

exercise of the will. Determine that you will love it, and devote yourself to it as to a bride."

When the study at the law school was over, Sumner returned to Boston, and entered the office of Benjamin Rand, Court Street, a man distinguished for learning rather than for oratory. The young lawyer succeeded fairly well, though he loved study better than general practice. Two years later he gave instruction at the law school when Judge Story was absent, and then reported his opinions in the Circuit Court, in three volumes. He assisted Professor Greenleaf in preparing "Reports of the Decisions of the Supreme Court of Maine," revised, with much labor, Dunlap's "Admiralty Practice," and edited "The American Jurist."

In the midst of this hard work he spent a brief vacation at Washington, writing to his father, "I shall probably hear Calhoun, and he will be the last man I shall ever hear speak in Washington. I probably shall never come here again. I have little or no desire ever to come again in any capacity. Nothing that I have seen of politics has made me look upon them with any feeling other than loathing. The more I see of them the more I love law, which, I feel, will give me an honorable livelihood."

When he visited Niagara, he wrote home, "I have sat for an hour contemplating this delightful object, with the cataract sounding like the voice of God in my ears. But there is something oppressive in hearing and contemplating these things. The mind travails with feelings akin to pain, in the endeavor to embrace them. I do not know that it is so with others; but I cannot disguise from myself the sense of weakness, inferiority, and incompetency which I feel."

When Sumner was twenty-six, he determined to carry out a life-long plan of visiting Europe, to study its writers, jurists, and social customs. He needed five thousand dollars for this purpose. He had earned two thousand, and, borrowing three from three friends, he started December 8, 1837. Emerson gave him a letter of introduction to Carlyle, Story to some leading lawyers, and Washington Allston to Wordsworth. Judge Story said in his letter, "Mr. Sumner is a practising lawyer at the Boston bar, of very high reputation for his years, and already giving the promise of the most eminent distinction in his profession; his literary and judicial attainments are truly extraordinary. He is one of the editors, indeed, the principal editor, of 'The American Jurist,' a quarterly journal of extensive circulation and celebrity among us, and without a rival in America. He is also the reporter of the court in which I preside, and has already published two volumes of reports. His private character, also, is of the best kind for purity and propriety."

His friend Dr. Lieber gave him some good suggestions about travelling. "Plan your journey. Spend money carefully. Keep steadily a journal. Never think that an impression is too vivid to be forgotten. Believe me, time is more powerful than senses or memory. Keep little books for addresses. Write down first impressions of men and countries."

Just before Sumner started from New York, he wrote to his little sister, Julia, then ten years old, "I am very glad, my dear, to remember your cheerful countenance.... Let it be said of you that you are always amiable.... Cultivate an affectionate disposition. If you find that you can do anything which will add to the pleasure of your parents, or anybody else, be sure to do it. Consider every opportunity of adding to the pleasure of others as of the highest importance, and do not be unwilling to sacrifice some enjoyment of your own, even some dear plaything, if by doing so you can promote the happiness of others. If you follow this advice, you will never be selfish or ungenerous, and everybody will love you."

To his brother George, six years younger than himself, he wrote, "Do not waste your time in driblets. Deem every moment precious,—far more so than the costliest stones.... Keep some good book constantly on hand to occupy every stray moment."

As soon as Sumner reached Paris he devoted himself to the study of the language, so as to be able to speak what he could write already. He attended lectures given by the professors of colleges, became acquainted with Victor Cousin, the noted writer on morals and metaphysics, and the friend of authors, lawyers, and journalists. He said, years later, in an eloquent tribute to Judge Story: "It has been my fortune to know the chief jurists of our time in the classical countries of jurisprudence,—France and Germany. I remember well the pointed and effective style of Dupin, in one of his masterly arguments before the highest court of France; I recall the pleasant converse of Pardessus, to whom commercial and maritime law is under a larger debt, perhaps, than to any other mind, while he descanted on his favorite theme; I wander in fancy to the gentle presence of him with flowing silver locks who was so dear to Germany, Thibaut, the expounder of Roman law, and the earnest and successful advocate of a just scheme for the reduction of the unwritten law to the certainty of a written text; from Heidelberg I pass to Berlin, where I listen to the grave lecture and mingle in the social circle of Savigny, so stately in person and peculiar in countenance, whom all the continent of Europe delights to honor; but my heart and my judgment, untravelled, fondly turn with new love and admiration to my Cambridge teacher and friend.

Jurisprudence has many arrows in her quiver, but where is one to compare with that which is now spent in the earth?"

After some months in Paris, Sumner went to England, remaining ten months, and receiving attentions rarely if ever accorded to an American. He used some letters of introduction, but generally he was welcomed to the houses of lords and authors simply because the young man of learning was honored for his refinement and nobility of soul. He was admitted to the clubs, attended debates in Parliament, was present at the coronation of Queen Victoria in Westminster Abbey, sat on the bench at Westminster Hall, dined often with Lord Brougham, Sir William Hamilton, Jeffrey of the Edinburgh Review, Lord Morpeth the Chief Secretary for Ireland, Hallam, Carlyle, Lord Holland, Lord Houghton, Grote, Sydney Smith, Macaulay, Landor, Leigh Hunt, and scores of others, the greatest in the kingdom. An English writer said: "He presents in his own person a decisive proof that an American gentleman, without official rank or widespread reputation, by mere dint of courtesy, candor, an entire absence of pretension, an appreciating spirit, and a cultivated mind, may be received on a perfect footing of equality in the best English circles, social, political, and intellectual."

Sumner wrote back to his friends in America: "I have made myself master of English practice and English circuit life. I cannot sufficiently express my admiration of the heartiness and cordiality which pervade all the English bar. They are truly a band of brothers, and I have been received among them as one of them. I have visited many—perhaps I may say most—of the distinguished men of these glorious countries (England, Scotland, and Ireland), at their seats, and have seen English country life, which is the height of refined luxury, in some of its most splendid phases. For all the opportunities I have had I feel grateful."

Sumner found, what all travellers find, that cultivated, well bred people all speak a common language, that of universal courtesy and kindness. The English did not ask if he had wealth or distinguished parentage; it was enough that he was intelligent on all topics, considerate, gentle in manner, a gentleman in every possible situation.

Every letter home teemed with descriptions of visits to Wordsworth, then sixty-nine years of age; to Macaulay, whom Sydney Smith called "a tremendous machine for colloquial oppression;" to the beautiful Caroline Norton, the poet, "one of the brightest intellects I have ever met," with "the grace and ease of the woman, with a strength and skill of which any man might well be proud;" to Lord Brougham, with "a fulness of information and physical spirits, which make him more commanding than all."

Sumner spent three months in Rome, at first studying the language from six to twelve hours a day. He became the friend of the artist Thomas Crawford, then poor, but with high ambition. He wrote his praises home to his friends, induced them to buy one of his earliest works and exhibit it in Boston; cheered the half-despairing artist by assuring him that he would be "a great and successful sculptor, and be living in a palace," all of which came true. A noble nature, indeed, that could pause in its own aspiring work and lift another to fame and success!

Six months were spent in Germany by Sumner, where he studied language and law as earnestly as he had in France and Italy. The rich, full days of literary intercourse were coming to an end. He wrote to his intimate friend Longfellow: "I shall soon be with you; and I now begin to think of hard work, of long days filled with uninteresting toil and humble gains. I sometimes have a moment of misgiving, when I think of the certainties which I abandoned for travel, and of the uncertainties to which I return. But this is momentary; for I am thoroughly content with what I have done. If clients fail me; if the favorable opinion of those on whom professional reputation depends leaves me; if I find myself poor and solitary,—still I shall be rich in the recollection of what I have seen, and will make companions of the great minds of these countries I have visited."

In the spring of 1840 Sumner was home again, having been abroad for two and one-half years. The father and his sister Jane, a lovely girl of seventeen, had both died during his absence. He went at once to the Hancock Street home, and began his professional labors from nine till five or six in the afternoon. In the evening he read as formerly till midnight or later, going every Saturday evening to spend the night with Longfellow at Craigie House.

This affection for Longfellow never changed. When the poet went abroad in 1842, Sumner wrote him, "We are all sad at your going; but I am more sad than the rest, for I lose more than they do. I am desolate. It was to me a source of pleasure and strength untold to see you; and, when I did not see you, to feel that you were near, with your swift sympathy and kindly words. I must try to go alone,— hard necessity in this rude world of ours, for our souls always in this life need support and gentle beckonings, as the little child when first trying to move away from its mother's knee. God bless you, my dear friend, from my heart of hearts. My eyes overflow as I now trace these lines."

Sumner was full of incident and vivid description of his life abroad, and the most charming homes of Boston were open to him whenever he had the time to visit, which was seldom. The letters from Europe made the long days of law practice less monotonous. He wrote much on legal matters; and now, at thirty-three, undertook to edit the "Equity Reports" of Francis Vesey, Jr., numbering twenty volumes, for two thousand dollars. By the terms agreed upon, a volume was to be ready each fortnight. He worked night and day, took no recreation, and soon broke down in health; and his life was despaired of. He welcomed death, for he had before this time become somewhat despondent. Most of his friends were married, and some, like Prescott and Longfellow, had come to fame already. He felt that his life was not showing the results of which his youth gave promise.

Had he found at this time "the perfect woman" for whom he used to tell his friends he was seeking, and made her his wife, there would doubtless have come into his life satisfaction and rest. That he did not marry was the more strange since women admired him for the qualities which are especially attractive to the sex; a knightly sense of honor, fidelity in friendship, fearlessness, and affectionate confidence.

Sumner recovered his health, while his beloved sister Mary, at the age of twenty-two, faded from his sight by consumption. He wrote his brother George: "She herself wished to die; and I believe that we all became anxious at last that the angel should descend to bear her aloft. From the beautiful flower of her life the leaves had all gently fallen to the earth; and there remained but little for the hand of death to pluck. During the night preceding the morning on which she left us, she slept like a child; and within a short time of her death, when asked if she were in pain, she said, 'No; angels are taking care of me.'"

To Charles Sumner this death was an incomparable loss. She was especially beautiful and lovely, and the idol of his heart. Possibly it helped to make him ready for his great work.

Into most lives, especially those designed for great deeds, there seem to come decisive moments when events open the door from the darkness of obscurity into the noonday glare of fame. Such a time came to Sumner in 1845. He was asked to deliver the usual Fourth of July address at Tremont Temple, Boston, as Charles Francis Adams, Horace Mann, and others had done in previous years. He chose for his subject "The True Grandeur of Nations," showing that the "true grandeur" is peace and not war. He dealt vigorously with the Mexican War, then impending, as a result of the

154

annexation of Texas, with consequent enlargement of slave territory.

Sumner was now thirty-four, well developed physically, his face handsome and radiant as ever, with the smile of his boyhood, his voice clear and resonant, his mind full to overflowing. He spoke for two hours, without notes. He said: "The true greatness of a nation cannot be in triumphs of the intellect alone. Literature and art may widen the sphere of its influence; they may adorn it; but they are in their nature but accessories. The true grandeur of humanity is in moral elevation, sustained, enlightened, and decorated by the intellect of man.... In our age there can be no peace that is not honorable; there can be no war that is not dishonorable. The true honor of a nation is to be found only in deeds of justice and beneficence, securing the happiness of its people,—all of which are inconsistent with war. In the clear eye of Christian judgment, vain are its victories, infamous are its spoils. He is the true benefactor, and alone worthy of honor, who brings comfort where before was wretchedness; who dries the tear of sorrow; who pours oil into the wounds of the unfortunate; who feeds the hungry, and clothes the naked; who unlooses the fetter of the slave; who does justice; who enlightens the ignorant; who, by his virtuous genius in art, in literature, in science, enlivens and exalts the hours of life; who, by words or actions, inspires a love for God and for man. This is the Christian hero; this is the man of honor in a Christian land."

The believers in war felt somewhat hurt by Sumner's plainness of speech, but the city of Boston and the State of Massachusetts awoke to the knowledge of an eloquent man in their midst, who had doubtless a work before him. Mrs. Lydia Maria Child wrote him: "How I did thank you for your noble and eloquent attack upon the absurd barbarism of war! It was worth living for to have done that, if you never do anything more. But the soul that could do that will do more."

Chancellor Kent wrote him, "I am very strongly in favor of the institution of a congress of nations or system of arbitration without going to war. Every effort ought to be made by treaty stipulation, remonstrance, and appeal to put a stop to the resort to brutal force to assert claims of right. The idea of war is horrible. I remember I was very much struck, even in my youth, by the observation (I think it was in Tom Paine's 'Crisis') that 'he who is the author of war lets loose the whole contagion of hell, and opens a vein that bleeds a nation to death.'"

Seven thousand copies of this oration were distributed by the Peace Societies of England, and it had a wide reading in our own country.

Sumner was now called upon to speak with Garrison, Phillips, and others, on the question of the annexation of Texas with her slave territory. He said, "God forbid that the votes and voices of the freemen of the North should help to bind anew the fetters of the slave! God forbid that the lash of the slave-dealer should be nerved by any sanction from New England! God forbid that the blood which spurts from the lacerated quivering flesh of the slave should soil the hem of the white garments of Massachusetts."

The educated Boston lawyer, the friend of hosts of authors and jurists on both sides of the ocean, the accomplished and aristocratic scholar, Sumner had placed himself among the despised Abolitionists! Many of his friends stood aghast, even refusing to recognize him on the street. This act required great moral heroism, but he was equal to the occasion. The door had opened to fame and immortality, even though they came to him through contumely and well-nigh martyrdom.

In 1846, Mr. Sumner spoke before the Phi Beta Kappa Society of Harvard University: "We stand on the threshold of a new age, which is preparing to recognize new influences. The ancient divinities of violence and wrong are retreating to their kindred darkness. The sun of our moral universe is entering a new ecliptic, no longer deformed by those images, Cancer, Taurus, Leo, Sagittarius, but beaming with the mild radiance of those heavenly signs, Faith, Hope, and Charity.

> "'There's a fount about to stream;
> There's a light about to beam;
> There's a warmth about to glow;
> There's a flower about to blow;
> There's a midnight blackness changing
> Into gray:
> Men of thought and men of action,
> Clear the way!'"

Theodore Parker wrote to the orator, "You have planted a seed, 'out of which many and tall branches shall arise,' I hope. The people are always true to a good man who truly trusts them. You have had opportunity to see, hear, and feel the truth of that oftener than once. I think you will have enough more opportunities yet; men will look for deeds noble as the words a man speaks."

And Charles Sumner became as noble as the words he had spoken. It makes us stronger to commit ourselves before the world. We are compelled to live up to the standard of our speech, or be adjudged hypocrites.

Before the Boston Mercantile Library Association, Sumner read a brilliant paper on "White Slavery in the Barbary States," and gave an address before Amherst College on "Fame and Glory." He spoke earnestly in the Whig conventions, asking them to come out against slavery. He urged Daniel Webster, the Defender of the Constitution, to become the "Defender of Humanity," "by the side of which that earlier title shall fade into insignificance, as the Constitution, which is the work of mortal hands, dwindles by the side of man, who is created in the image of God." But the words of entreaty came too late; the Whig party did not dare take up the cause of human freedom.

In 1851, when Sumner was forty, the new era of his life came. The Free-Soil party, organized August 9, 1848, the successor of the "Liberty" party formed eight years earlier, wanted him as their leader. Would he separate from the Whigs? Yes, for he had said, "Loyalty to principle is higher than loyalty to party. The first is a heavenly sentiment from God; the other is a device of this earth.... I wish it to be understood that I belong to the party of freedom,—to that party which plants itself on the Declaration of Independence and the Constitution of the United States.... It is said that we shall throw away our votes, and that our opposition will fail. Fail, sir! No honest, earnest effort in a good cause ever fails. It may not be crowned with the applause of man; it may not seem to touch the goal of immediate worldly success, which is the end and aim of so much of life; but still it is not lost. It helps to strengthen the weak with new virtue, to arm the irresolute with proper energy, to animate all with devotion to duty, which in the end conquers all. Fail! Did the martyrs fail when with their precious blood they sowed the seed of the Church?... Did the three hundred Spartans fail when, in the narrow pass, they did not fear to brave the innumerable Persian hosts, whose very arrows darkened the sun? No! Overborne by numbers, crushed to earth, they have left an example which is greater far than any victory. And this is the least we can do. Our example shall be the source of triumph hereafter."

Millard Fillmore had signed the hated Fugitive Slave Bill, and Webster had made his disastrous speech of March 7, 1850, urging conformity to the demands of the bill. Sumner's hour had come. By a union of the Free-Soil and Democratic parties, he was elected to the Senate of the United States for six years, over the eloquent Robert C. Winthrop, the Whig candidate. The contest was bitter. Sumner would give no pledges, and said he would not walk across the room to secure the election. On Monday, December 1, 1851, he took his seat. Devotion to principle had gained him an exalted position.

Months went by before he could possibly obtain a hearing on the slavery question, on which issue he had been elected. Finally, the long sought opportunity came by introducing an amendment that the Fugitive Slave Bill should be repealed. He spoke for four hours as only Charles Sumner could speak. Despised by the slave-holders, they listened to his burning words. In closing, he said: "Be admonished by those words of oriental piety,—'Beware of the groans of wounded souls. Oppress not to the utmost a single heart; for a solitary sigh has power to overset a whole world.'"

Mr. Polk of Tennessee said to him: "If you should make that speech in Tennessee, you would compel me to emancipate my niggers."

The vote on the repeal stood: Yeas, four; nays, forty-seven. Alas! how many years he wrought before the repeal came.

Sumner had been heard not merely by Congress; he had been heard by two continents. Henceforward, for twenty-three years, he was to be in Congress the great leader in the cause of human freedom.

In 1854 the advocates of slavery brought forward the Kansas-Nebraska Bill, by which a large territory, at the recommendation of Stephen A. Douglas, was to be left open for slavery or no slavery, as the dwellers therein should decide. On the night of the passage of this bill, Sumner made an eloquent protest. "Sir, the bill which you are now about to pass is at once the worst and the best bill on which Congress ever acted. Yes, sir, WORST and BEST at the same time.

"It is the worst bill, inasmuch as it is a present victory of slavery.... It is the best, for it prepares the way for that 'All hail hereafter,' when slavery must disappear.... Thus, sir, now standing at the very grave of freedom in Kansas and Nebraska, I lift myself to the vision of that happy resurrection by which freedom will be secured hereafter, not only in these Territories but everywhere under the national government. More clearly than ever before, I now see 'the beginning of the end' of slavery. Proudly I discern the flag of my country as it ripples in every breeze, at last become in reality, as in name, the flag of freedom,—undoubted, pure, and irresistible. Am I not right, then, in calling this bill the best on which Congress ever acted?

"Sorrowfully I bend before the wrong you are about to enact. Joyfully I welcome all the promises of the future."

After the passage of the bill the excitement at the North was intense. Public meetings were held, denouncing the new scheme of the slave-power to acquire more territory. So bitter grew the feeling that Sumner was urged by his friends to leave Washington, lest harm come to him; but he walked the streets unarmed. "He was assailed," said the noble Joshua R. Giddings of Ohio, "by the whole slave-power in the Senate, and, for a time, he was the constant theme of their vituperation. The maddened waves rolled and dashed against him for two or three days, until eventually he obtained the floor himself; then he arose and threw back the dashing surges with a power of inimitable eloquence utterly indescribable."

The Kansas-Nebraska Bill produced its legitimate result,—civil war in the Territory. Slave-holders rushed in from Missouri, bringing their slaves with them; free men came from the East to build homes, school-houses, and churches on these fertile lands. The struggles at the ballot-box over illegal elections were followed by struggles on the battle-field. At the village of Ossawatomie twenty-eight Free State men led by John Brown defeated on the open prairie fifty-six Slave State men. Houses were burned, and men murdered. Two State constitutions were adopted: one at Lecompton, representing the pro-slavery element; the other at Lawrence, representing the anti-slavery party. Finally, the President, in 1855, appointed a military governor to restore Kansas to order. But, while order might be restored there, the whole country seemed on the verge of civil war.

Meantime the Republican party had been formed in 1854, the outgrowth of the "Liberty" and "Free Soil" parties. A "Bill for the Admission of Kansas into the Union" having been presented, Sumner made his celebrated speech "The Crime against Kansas," on the 19th and 20th of May, 1856. He spoke eloquently and fearlessly, arousing more than ever the hot blood of the South. Two days later, as Mr. Sumner was sitting at his desk in the Senate chamber, his head bent forward in writing, the Senate having adjourned, Preston S. Brooks, a nephew of Mr. Butler, a senator of South Carolina, stood before him. "I have read your speech twice over, carefully," he said. "It is a libel on South Carolina and Mr. Butler, who is a relative of mine." Instantly he struck Mr. Sumner on the back of the head, with his hollow gutta-percha cane, making a long and fearful gash, repeating the blows in rapid succession. Sumner wrenched the desk from the floor, to which it was screwed, but, unable to defend himself, fell forward bleeding and insensible. He was carried by his friends to a sofa in the lobby, and during the night lay pale and bewildered, scarcely speaking to any one about him.

The indignation and horror of the North beggar description. That a man, in this age of free speech, should be publicly beaten, and that by a member of the House of Representatives, was, of course, a disgrace to the nation. Said Joseph Quincy: "Charles

159

Sumner needs not our sympathy. If he dies his name will be immortal—his name will be enrolled with the names of Warren, Sidney, and Russell; if he lives he is destined to be the light of the nation." Wendell Phillips said: "The world will yet cover every one of those scars with laurels. He must not die! We need him yet, as the van-guard leader of the hosts of Liberty. Nay, he shall yet come forth from that sick-chamber, and every gallant heart in the commonwealth be ready to kiss his very footsteps."

Brooks was censured by the House of Representatives, resigned his seat, and died the following year. Sumner returned to Boston as soon as he was able. Houses were decorated for his coming, and banners flung to the breeze with the words, "Welcome, Freedom's Defender," "Massachusetts loves, honors, will sustain and defend her noble Sumner." The home on Hancock Street was surrounded by a dense crowd. He appeared at the window with his widowed mother, and bowed to their cheers. For several months he enjoyed the tender care of this mother, now almost alone. Her son Horace had been lost in the ship Elizabeth, July 16, 1850, when Margaret Fuller, her husband, and child were drowned. Albert, a sea-captain, had been lost with his wife and only daughter on their way to France. And now, perhaps, her distinguished son Charles was to give his life to help bring freedom to four millions in slavery.

In 1857 Sumner was almost unanimously reëlected to the Senate for six years, but Brooks had done his dreadful work too well. Broken in health, he sailed for Europe. Nearly twenty years before he had gone to meet the honored and famous, his future all unknown; now he went as the stricken leader of a great cause, one of the most able and eloquent men of the new world. Twenty years before he was restless and unhappy because he did not see his life-work before him; now he was happy in spite of physical agony, because he knew he was helping humanity.

After travelling in Switzerland, Germany, and Great Britain, he returned and took his seat in Congress, but, finding his health still impaired, he sailed again to Europe. He regretted to leave the country, but was, as he says, "often assured and encouraged to feel that to every sincere lover of civilization my vacant chair was a perpetual speech." On this second visit he came under the treatment of Dr. Brown-Séquard, who, when asked by Mr. Sumner what would cure him, replied, "Fire." At once the dreadful remedy was applied. The physician says, when he first met the senator, "He could not make use of his brain at all. He could not read a newspaper, could not write a letter. He was in a frightful state as regards the activity of the mind, as every effort there was most painful to him.... I told him the truth,—that there would be more effect, as I thought, if he did not take chloroform; and so I had to submit him to the martyrdom of the greatest suffering that can be inflicted on mortal man. I burned him with the first moxa. I had the hope that after the first application he would submit to the use of chloroform; but for five times after that he was burned in the same way, and refused to take chloroform. I have never seen a patient who submitted to such treatment in that way."

Sumner wrote home: "It is with a pang unspeakable that I find myself thus arrested in the labors of life and in the duties of my position. This is harder to bear than the fire."

Four years elapsed before he regained his health; indeed his death finally resulted from the attack of Brooks. No sooner had he returned to the Senate than he made another great speech against slavery. The country was agitated by the coming presidential election. John Brown had captured, with a force of twenty-two men, the United States arsenal at Harper's Ferry, with the fallacious hope of setting the slaves at liberty. He was of course overpowered, his sons killed at his side, as others of his sons had been on the Kansas battlefields, and he led out to execution, December 2, 1859, with a radiant face and an overflowing heart, because he knew that his death would arouse the nation to action.

Mr. Sumner spoke to an immense audience at Cooper Institute, urging the election of Abraham Lincoln. By this election, he said, "we shall save the Territories from the five-headed barbarism of slavery; we shall save the country and the age from that crying infamy, the slave-trade; we shall help save the Declaration of Independence, now dishonored and disowned in its essential, life-giving truth,—the equality of men.... A new order of things will begin; and our history will proceed on a grander scale, in harmony with those sublime principles in which it commenced. Let the knell sound!—

> "'Ring out the old, ring in the new!
> Ring out the false, ring in the true!
> Ring out a slowly dying cause,
> And ancient forms of party strife!
> Ring in the nobler modes of life,
> With sweeter manners, purer laws.'"

A "new order of things" was indeed begun. South Carolina very soon seceded from the Union, and other southern States followed her example. Sumner now spoke and wrote constantly. He

161

urged Massachusetts to be "firm, FIRM, FIRM! against every word or step of concession.... More than the loss of forts, arsenals, or the national capital, I fear the loss of our principles."

In 1861, Mr. Sumner was made chairman of the Committee on Foreign Relations. How different his position from that day, ten years before, when he stood almost alone in the Senate, a hated abolitionist!

When the war began, he saw with prophetic eye the necessity of emancipating the slaves. He urged it in his public speeches. When Lincoln hesitated and the country feared the result, he said to a vast assembly at Cooper Institute, "There has been the cry, 'On to Richmond!' and still another worse cry, 'On to England!' Better than either is the cry, 'On to freedom!'"

As the war went forward he was ever at his post, working for Henry Wilson's bill for the abolishing of slavery in the District of Columbia, for the recognition of the independence of Hayti and Liberia, for the final suppression of the coastwise trade in slaves, for the employment of colored troops in the army, and for a law that "no person shall be excluded from the cars on account of color," on various specified lines of railroad. He spoke words of encouragement constantly to the North, "This is no time to stop. Forward! Forward! Thus do I, who formerly pleaded so often for peace, now sound to arms; but it is because, in this terrible moment, there is no other way to that sincere and solid peace without which there will be endless war.... Now, at last, by the death of slavery, will the republic begin to live; for what is life without liberty?

"Stretching from ocean to ocean, teeming with population, bountiful in resources of all kinds, and thrice happy in universal enfranchisement, it will be more than conqueror, nothing too vast for its power, nothing too minute for its care."

He wrote for the magazines on the one great subject. He helped organize the Freedman's Bureau, which he called the "Bridge from Slavery to Freedom." He urged equal pay to colored soldiers. He was invaluable to President Lincoln. Though they did not always think alike, Lincoln said to Sumner, "There is no person with whom I have more advised throughout my administration than with yourself."

When Lincoln was assassinated, Sumner wept by his bedside. "The only time," said an intimate friend, "I ever saw him weep." When he delivered his eloquent eulogy on Lincoln in Boston, he said, "That speech, uttered on the field of Gettysburg, and now sanctified by the martyrdom of its author, is a monumental act. In the modesty of his nature, he said, 'The world will little note, nor long remember, what we say here; but it can never forget what they did here.'

"He was mistaken. The world noted at once what he said, and will never cease to remember it. The battle itself was less important than the speech. Ideas are more than battles."

And so the great slavery pioneer and the great emancipator will go down in history together. How the world worships heroic manhood! Those who, with sweet and unselfish natures, seek not their own happiness, but are ready to die if need be for the right and the truth!

Sumner aided in those three grand amendments to the Constitution, the thirteenth, fourteenth, and fifteenth. "Neither slavery nor involuntary servitude, except as a punishment for crime, whereof the party shall have been duly convicted, shall exist within the United States, or any place subject to their jurisdiction.... All persons born or naturalized in the United States, and subject to the jurisdiction thereof, are citizens of the United States and of the State wherein they reside. No State shall make or enforce any law which shall abridge the privileges or immunities of citizens of the United States; nor shall any State deprive any person of life, liberty, or property, without due process of law, nor deny to any person within its jurisdiction the equal protection of the laws.... The right of citizens of the United States to vote shall not be denied or abridged by the United States, or by any State, on account of race, color, or previous condition of servitude."

In June, 1866, Mr. Sumner came home to say good-bye to his dying mother. True to her noble womanhood, she urged that he should not be sent for, lest the country could not spare him from his work. Beautiful self-sacrifice of woman! Heaven can possess nothing more angelic. O mother, wife, and loved one, know thine unlimited powers, and hold them forever for the ennobling of men!

When Mrs. Sumner was buried, her son turned away sorrowfully, and exclaimed, "I have now no home." He had a house in Washington, where he had lived for many years, but it was only home to him where a sweet-faced and sweet-voiced woman loved him.

In 1869, Mr. Sumner made his remarkable speech on the "Alabama" claims, which for a time caused some bitter feeling in England. This vessel, built at Liverpool, and manned by a British crew, was sent out by the Confederate government, and destroyed sixty-six of our vessels, with a loss of ten million dollars. In 1864, she was overtaken in the harbor of Cherbourg, France, by Captain Winslow, commander of the steamer Kearsarge, and sunk, after an hour's desperate fighting. Her commander, Captain Raphael Semmes, was picked up by the English Deerhound, and taken to Southampton. In the summer of 1872, a board of arbitration met at Geneva, Switzerland, and awarded the United States over fifteen million dollars as damages, which Great Britain paid.

On May 12, 1870, Mr. Sumner introduced his supplementary Civil-Rights Bill, declaring that all persons, without regard to race or color, are entitled to equal privileges afforded by railroads, steamboats, hotels, places of amusement, institutions of learning, religion, and courts of law. His maxim was, "Equality of rights is the first of rights."

He supported Horace Greeley for President, thus separating himself from the Republican party, and carrying out his life-long opinion that principle is above party. After another visit to Europe, in 1872, when he was sixty-one years old, feeling that, the war being over and slavery abolished, the two portions of the country should forget all animosity and live together in harmony, he introduced a resolution in the Senate, "That the names of battles with fellow-citizens shall not be continued in the army register or placed on the regimental colors of the United States."

Massachusetts hastily passed a vote of censure upon her idolized statesman, which she was wise enough to rescind soon after. This latter action gave Mr. Sumner great comfort. He said, "The dear old commonwealth has spoken for me, and that is enough."

In his freestone house, full of pictures and books, overlooking Lafayette Square in Washington, on March 11, 1874, Charles Sumner lay dying. The day previous, in the Senate, he had complained to a friend of pain in the left side. On the morning of the eleventh he was cold and well nigh insensible. At ten o'clock he said to Judge Hoar, "Don't forget my Civil-Rights Bill." Later, he said, "My book! my book is not finished.... I am so tired! I am so tired!"

He had worked long and hard. He passed into the rest of the hereafter at three o'clock in the afternoon. Grand, heroic soul! whose life will be an inspiration for all coming time.

The body, enclosed in a massive casket, upon which rested a wreath of white azaleas and lilies, was borne to the Capitol, followed by a company of three hundred colored men and a long line of carriages. The most noticeable among the floral gifts, says Elias Nason, in his Life of Sumner, "was a broken column of violets and white azaleas, placed there by the hands of a colored girl. She had been rendered lame by being thrust from the cars of a railroad, whose charter Mr. Sumner, after hearing the girl's story, by a resolution, caused to be revoked." From there it was carried to the State House in Boston, and visited by at least fifty thousand people. In the midst of the beautiful floral decorations was a large heart of flowers, from the colored citizens of Boston, with the words, "Charles Sumner, you gave us your life; we give you our hearts."

Through a dense crowd the coffin was borne to Mount Auburn cemetery, and placed in the open grave just as the sun was setting, Longfellow, Holmes, Emerson, and other dear friends standing by. The grand old song of Luther was sung, "Ein feste Burg ist unser Gott." Strange contrast! the quiet, unknown Harvard law student;— the great senator, doctor of laws, author, and orator. Sumner had his share of sorrow. He lived to see seven of his eight brothers and sisters taken away by death. He who had longed for domestic bliss did not find it. He married, when he was fifty-five, Mrs. Alice Mason Hooper, but the companionship did not prove congenial, and a divorce resulted, by mutual consent.

He forgot the heart-hunger of his early years in living for the slaves and the down-trodden, whether white or black. Through all his struggles he kept a sublime hope. He used to say, "All defeats in a good cause are but resting-places on the road to victory at last." He had defeats, as do all, but he won the victory.

Well says Hon. James G. Blaine, in his "Twenty Years of Congress," "Mr. Sumner must ever be regarded as a scholar, an orator, a philanthropist, a philosopher, a statesman, whose splendid and unsullied fame will always form part of the true glory of the nation."

"He belongs to all of us, in the North and in the South," said Hon. Carl Schurz, in his eulogy delivered in Music Hall, Boston, "to the blacks he helped to make free, and to the whites he strove to make brothers again. On the grave of him whom so many thought to be their enemy, and found to be their friend, let the hands be clasped which so bitterly warred against each other. Upon that grave let the youth of America be taught, by the story of his life, that not only genius, power, and success, but, more than these, patriotic devotion and virtue, make the greatness of the citizen."

U. S. GRANT

What Longfellow wrote of Charles Sumner may well be applied to Grant:—

> "Were a star quenched on high,
> For ages would its light,
> Still travelling downward from the sky,
> Shine on our mortal sight.
>
> "So when a great man dies,
> For years beyond our ken
> The light he leaves behind him lies
> Upon the paths of men."

The light left by General Grant will not fade out from American history. To be a great soldier is of course to be immortal; but to be magnanimous to enemies, heroic in affections, a master of self, without vanity, honest, courageous, true, invincible,—such greatness is far above the glory of battlefields. Such greatness he possessed, who, born in comparative obscurity, came to be numbered in that famous trio, dear to every American heart: Washington, Lincoln, Grant.

Ulysses Simpson Grant was born April 27, 1822, in a log house at Mount Pleasant, Ohio. The boy seems to have had the blood of soldiers in his veins, for his great-grandfather and great-uncle held commissions in the English army in 1756, in the war against the French and Indians, and both were killed. His grandfather served through the entire war of the Revolution.

His father, Jesse R. Grant, left dependent upon himself, learned the trade of a tanner, and by his industry made a home for himself and family. Unable to attend school more than six months in his life, he was a constant reader, and through his own privations became the more anxious that his children should be educated.

Ulysses was the first-born child of Jesse Grant and Hannah Simpson, who were married in June, 1821. When their son was about a year old, they moved to Georgetown, Ohio, and here the boy passed a happy childhood, learning the very little which the schools of the time were able to impart.

He was not fond of study, and enjoyed the more active life of the farm. He says in his personal memoirs: "While my father carried

166

on the manufacture of leather and worked at the trade himself, he owned and tilled considerable land. I detested the trade, preferring almost any other labor; but I was fond of agriculture, and of all employment in which horses were used. We had, among other lands, fifty acres of forest within a mile of the village. In the fall of the year, choppers were employed to cut enough wood to last a twelve-month. When I was seven or eight years of age, I began hauling all the wood used in the house and shops. I could not load it on the wagons, of course, at that time, but I could drive, and the choppers would load, and some one at the house unload. When about eleven years old, I was strong enough to hold a plough. From that age until seventeen I did all the work done with horses, such as breaking up the land, furrowing, ploughing corn and potatoes, bringing in the crops when harvested, hauling all the wood, besides tending two or three horses, a cow or two, and sawing wood for stoves, etc., while still attending school. For this I was compensated by the fact that there never was any scolding or punishing by my parents; no objection to rational enjoyments, such as fishing, going to the creek a mile away to swim in summer, taking a horse and visiting my grandparents in the adjoining county, fifteen miles off, skating on the ice in winter, or taking a horse and sleigh when there was snow on the ground."

The indulgent father allowed his son some unique experiences. Ulysses, at fifteen, having made a journey to Flat Rock, Kentucky, seventy miles away, with a carriage and two horses, took a fancy to a saddle-horse and offered to trade one which he was driving, for this animal. The owner hesitated about trading with a lad, but finally consented, and the untried colt was hitched to the carriage with his new mate. After proceeding a short distance, the animal became frightened by a dog, kicked, and started to run over an embankment. Ulysses, nothing daunted, took from his pocket a large handkerchief, tied it over the horse's eyes, and sure that the terrified creature would see no more dogs, though he trembled like an aspen leaf, drove peacefully homeward.

Young Grant was as truthful as he was calm and courageous. He tells this story of himself. "There was a Mr. Ralston living within a few miles of the village, who owned a colt which I very much wanted. My father had offered twenty dollars for it, but Ralston wanted twenty-five. I was so anxious to have the colt that after the owner left I begged to be allowed to take him at the price demanded. My father yielded, but said twenty dollars was all the horse was worth, and told me to offer that price; if it was not accepted, I was to offer twenty-two and a half, and if that would not get him, to give

167

the twenty-five. I at once mounted a horse and went for the colt. When I got to Mr. Ralston's house, I said to him: 'Papa says I may offer you twenty dollars for the colt; but if you won't take that, I am to offer twenty-two and a half; and if you won't take that, to give you twenty-five.' It would not require a Connecticut man to guess the price finally agreed upon....

"I could not have been over eight years at the time. This transaction caused me great heart-burning. The story got out among the boys of the village, and it was a long time before I heard the last of it. Boys enjoy the misery of their companions, at least village boys in that day did, and in later life I have found that all adults are not free from the peculiarity. I kept the horse until he was four years old, when he went blind, and I sold him for twenty dollars. When I went to Maysville to school, in 1836, at the age of fourteen, I recognized my colt as one of the blind horses working on the tread-wheel of the ferry-boat."

All this time the father was desirous of an education for his child. The son of a neighbor had been appointed to West Point, and had failed in his examinations. Mr. Grant applied for his son. "Ulysses," he said one day, "I believe you are going to receive the appointment." "What appointment!" was the response. "To West Point. I have applied for it." "But I won't go," said the impetuous boy. But the father's will was law, and the son began to prepare himself. He bought an algebra, but, having no teacher, he says, it was Greek to him. He had no love for a military life, and looked forward to the West Point experience only as a new opportunity to travel East and see the country.

At seventeen he took passage on a steamer for Pittsburg, in the middle of May, 1839. Fortunately the accommodating boat remained for several days at every port, for passengers or freight, and meantime the curious boy used his eyes to learn all that was possible. When he reached Harrisburg, he rode to Philadelphia on the first railroad which he had ever seen except the one on which he had just crossed the summit of the Alleghany Mountains. "In travelling by the road from Harrisburg," he says, "I thought the perfection of rapid transit had been reached. We travelled at least eighteen miles an hour, when at full speed, and made the whole distance averaging probably as much as twelve miles an hour. This seemed like annihilating space. I stopped five days in Philadelphia; saw about every street in the city, attended the theatre, visited Girard College (which was then in course of construction), and got reprimanded from home afterwards, for dallying by the way so long....

"I reported at West Point on the 30th or 31st of May, and about two weeks later passed my examinations for admission, without difficulty, very much to my surprise. A military life had no charms for me, and I had not the faintest idea of staying in the army even if I should be graduated, which I did not expect. The encampment which preceded the commencement of academic studies was very wearisome and uninteresting. When the 28th of August came—the date for breaking up camp and going into barracks—I felt as though I had been at West Point always, and that if I stayed to graduation I would have to remain always. I did not take hold of my studies with avidity, in fact I rarely ever read over a lesson the second time during my entire cadetship. I could not sit in my room doing nothing. There is a fine library connected with the academy, from which cadets can get books to read in their quarters. I devoted more time to these than to books relating to the course of studies. Much of the time, I am sorry to say, was devoted to novels, but not those of a trashy sort. I read all of Bulwer's then published, Cooper's, Marryat's, Scott's, Washington Irving's works, Lever's, and many others that I do not now remember. Mathematics was very easy to me, so that when January came I passed the examination, taking a good standing in that branch. In French, the only other study at that time in the first year's course, my standing was very low. In fact, if the class had been turned the other end foremost, I should have been near the head."

The years at West Point did not go by quickly; only the ten weeks of vacation which seemed shorter than one week in school. Sometimes at the academy a great general, like Winfield Scott, came to review the cadets. "With his commanding figure," says young Grant, "his quite colossal size, and showy uniform, I thought him the finest specimen of manhood my eyes had ever beheld, and the most to be envied. I could never resemble him in appearance, but I believe I did have a presentiment, for a moment, that some day I should occupy his place on review—although I had no intention then of remaining in the army. My experience in a horse trade ten years before, and the ridicule it caused me, were too fresh in my mind for me to communicate this presentiment to even my most intimate chum." How often into lives there comes a feeling that there is a specified work to be done by us that no other person can or will ever do!

When the years were over at West Point, each "four times as long as Ohio years," young Grant was anxious to enter the cavalry, especially as he had suffered from a cough for six months, and his family feared consumption. Having gone home, he waited anxiously for his new uniform. "I was impatient," he says, "to get on my uniform and see how it looked, and probably wanted my old schoolmates, particularly the girls, to see me in it. The conceit was knocked out of me by two little circumstances that happened soon after the arrival of the clothes, which gave me a distaste for military uniform that I never recovered from. Soon after the arrival of the suit I donned it, and put off for Cincinnati on horseback. While I was riding along a street of that city, imagining that every one was looking at me with a feeling akin to mine when I first saw General Scott, a little urchin, bareheaded, barefooted, with dirty and ragged pants held up by a single gallows—that's what suspenders were called then—and a shirt that had not seen a washtub for weeks, turned to me and cried: 'Soldier, will you work? No sir-ee; I'll sell my shirt first!' The horse trade and its dire consequences were recalled to mind.

"The other circumstance occurred at home. Opposite our house in Bethel stood the old stage tavern where 'man and beast' found accommodation. The stable-man was rather dissipated, but possessed of some humor. On my return, I found him parading the streets, and attending in the stable, barefooted, but in a pair of sky-blue nankeen pantaloons—just the color of my uniform trousers—with a strip of white cotton sheeting sewed down the outside seams in imitation of mine. The joke was a huge one in the minds of many of the people, and was much enjoyed by them; but I did not appreciate it so highly."

In September, 1843, Grant reported for duty at Jefferson Barracks, St. Louis, the largest military post in the United States at that time. His hope was to become assistant professor of mathematics at West Point, and he would have been appointed had not the Mexican War begun soon after.

A new page was now to be turned in the eventful life of the young officer; when he was to have, as Emerson beautifully says of love, "the visitation of that power to his heart and brain which created all things anew; which was the dawn in him of music, poetry, and art; which made the face of nature radiant with purple light; the morning and the night varied enchantments; when a single tone of one voice could make the heart bound, and the most trivial circumstance associated with one form is put in the amber of memory; when he became all eye when one was present, and all memory when one was gone; ... when the moonlight was a pleasing fever, and the stars were letters, and the flowers ciphers, and the air was coined into song; when all business seemed an impertinence, and all the men and women running to and fro in the streets were pictures."

At West Point, Grant's class-mate was F. T. Dent, whose family resided five miles west of Jefferson Barracks. "Two of his unmarried brothers," says Grant, "were living at home at that time, and, as I had taken with me from Ohio my horse, saddle, and bridle, I soon found my way out to White Haven, the name of the Dent estate. As I found the family congenial, my visits became frequent. There were at home, besides the young men, two daughters, one a school miss of fifteen, the other a girl of eight or nine. There was still an older daughter, of seventeen, who had been spending several years at boarding-school in St. Louis, but who, though through school, had not yet returned home.... In February she returned to her country home. After that I do not know but my visits became more frequent; they certainly did become more enjoyable. We would often take walks, or go on horseback together to visit the neighbors, until I became quite well acquainted in that vicinity.... If the fourth infantry had remained at Jefferson Barracks it is possible, even probable, that this life might have continued for some years without my finding out that there was anything serious the matter with me; but in the following May a circumstance occurred which developed my sentiment so palpably that there was no mistaking it."

This "circumstance" was the annexation of Texas, the probability of a war with Mexico, and the necessity of leaving Jefferson Barracks for the Texan frontier. Alas! now that days full of hope, and the sweet realization of a divine companionship had come, they must have sudden ending. Grant took a brief furlough, went to say good-bye to his father and mother, and then to White Haven to see Julia Dent. In crossing a swollen stream, his uniform was wet through, but he donned the suit of a future brother-in-law, and appeared before his beloved to ask her hand in marriage, to receive her acceptance, and then to hasten to the scene of action. He saw her but once in the next four years and three months; four anxious years to her, when death often stared her lover in the face.

As soon as Texas was admitted to the Union, in 1845, the "army of occupation," as the three thousand men under General Zachary Taylor were called, advanced to the Rio Grande and built a fort. When the first hostile gun was fired, Grant says, "I felt sorry that I had enlisted. A great many men, when they smell battle afar off, chafe to get into the fray. When they say so themselves, they generally fail to convince their hearers that they are as anxious as they would like to make believe, and as they approach danger they become more subdued. This rule is not universal, for I have known a few men who were always aching for a fight when there was no

171

enemy near, who were as good as their word when the battle did come on. But the number of such men is small."

The first battle was at Palo Alto, meaning "tall trees or woods," six miles from the Rio Grande. Early in the forenoon of May 8, Taylor's three thousand men were drawn up in line of battle, opposed by superior numbers. The infantry was armed with flintlock muskets and paper cartridges charged with powder, buckshot, and ball. "At the distance of a few hundred yards," says Grant, "a man might fire at you all day without your finding it out." The artillery consisted of two batteries and two eighteen-pounder iron guns, with three or four twelve-pounder howitzers throwing shell. The firing was brisk on both sides. One cannon-ball passed near Grant, killing several of his companions. After a hard day's fight, the enemy retreated in the night. The war had now begun in earnest, and the man who at the first hostile gun "felt sorry that he had enlisted" was ready to brave danger on any field.

In the hard-fought battle of Monterey, between sixty-five hundred men under Taylor and ten thousand Mexicans, Grant's curiosity got the better of his judgment, and, leaving the camp, where he had been ordered to remain, he mounted a horse and rode to the front. He made the charge with the men, when about a third of their number were killed. He loaned his horse to the adjutant of the regiment, Lieutenant Hoskins, who was soon killed, and Grant was designated to act in his place.

The ammunition became low, and to return for it was so dangerous that the general commanding did not like to order any one to fetch it, so called for a volunteer. Grant modestly says, "I volunteered to go back to the point we had started from.... My ride back was an exposed one. Before starting, I adjusted myself on the side of my horse furthest from the enemy, and with only one foot holding to the cantle of the saddle, and an arm over the neck of the horse exposed, I started at full run. It was only at street-crossings that my horse was under fire, but these I crossed at such a flying rate that generally I was past and under cover of the next block of houses before the enemy fired. I got out safely, without a scratch."

When Monterey was conquered, and the garrison marched out as prisoners, young Grant was moved to pity, as he says in his Memoirs, thus showing a gentle nature, which he bore years later when thousands were falling around him, and he was still obliged to say, "Forward."

After the capture of Vera Cruz and the surprise at Cerro Gordo, where three thousand Mexicans were made prisoners, the army advanced toward the City of Mexico. Between three and four miles from the city stood Molino del Rey, the "mill of the King," an old stone structure, one story high, flat-roofed, and several hundred feet long. Sandbags were laid along the roof, and good marksmen fought behind them. Near by was Chepultepec, three hundred feet high, fortified on the top and on its rocky sides. From the front, guns swept the approach to Molino. Yet, on the morning of September 8, the assault upon Molino was made, young Grant being among the foremost. The loss was severe, especially among commissioned officers.

Grant says, "I was with the earliest of the troops to enter the mills. In passing through to the north side, looking toward Chepultepec, I happened to notice that there were armed Mexicans still on top of the building, only a few feet from many of our men. Not seeing any stairway or ladder reaching to the top of the building, I took a few soldiers, and had a cart that happened to be standing near brought up, and, placing the shafts against the wall, and chocking the wheels so that the cart could not back, used the shafts as a sort of ladder, extending to within three or four feet of the top. By this I climbed to the roof of the building, followed by a few men, but found a private soldier had preceded me by some other way. There were still quite a number of Mexicans on the roof, among them a major and five or six officers of lower grades, who had not succeeded in getting away before our troops occupied the building. They still had their arms, while the soldier before mentioned was walking as sentry, guarding the prisoners he had surrounded, all by himself. I halted the sentinel, received the swords from the commissioned officers, and proceeded, with the assistance of the soldiers now with me, to disable the muskets by striking them against the edge of the wall, and throwing them to the ground below."

Five days after the fall of Molino, Chepultepec was taken, with severe loss. Grant was mentioned in the official report as having "behaved with distinguished gallantry." Just before the City of Mexico fell into our hands, Grant was made first lieutenant. Promotion had not come rapidly. It is sometimes better if success does not come to us early in life. To learn how to work steadily, day after day, with an unalterable purpose; to learn how to concentrate thought and will-power, how to conquer self through failure and hope deferred, is often essential for him who is to govern either by physical or moral power.

After Mexico fell, and General Scott lived in the halls of the Montezumas, he controlled the city as a Havelock or a Gordon might have done; and Grant learned by observation the best of all lessons for a soldier, to be magnanimous to a fallen foe. He learned other valuable lessons in this war; made the acquaintance of the officers with whom he was to measure his strength, in the most stupendous war of modern times, twenty years later.

When the treaty of peace was signed between our country and Mexico, February 2, 1848, whereby we paid fifteen million dollars for the territory ceded to us, Grant obtained leave of absence for four months. One person must have been inexpressibly thankful that his life had been spared. Four years, and she had seen him but once! How noble we often become by the mellowing power of circumstances which prevent our having our own way! Discipline may be only another word for achievement.

U. S. Grant and Julia Dent were married August 22, 1848, when he was twenty-six, and began a life of affection and helpfulness, which grew brighter till the end came on Mt. McGregor. There was reason why the affection lasted through all the years; in the best sense they lived for each other. Those who find their happiness outside the home are apt to find little inside the home. Devotion begets devotion, and men and women must expect to receive only what they give. Affection scattered produces a scanty harvest.

The winter of 1848 was spent at the post at Sackett's Harbor, New York; the next two years at Detroit, Michigan. In 1852, Grant was ordered to the Pacific coast. And now the young husband and wife must be separated; she to go to her home in St. Louis, and he to the then unsettled West. When Aspinwall was reached the streets of the town were a foot under water, in a blazing, tropical sun. Cholera broke out among the troops, as it had among the inhabitants, and a third of the people died. The crossing of the Isthmus of Panama, on the backs of mules, was tedious and trying. San Francisco was reached early in September. The gold-mining fever was at its height. Soon the troops passed up to Fort Vancouver, on the Columbia River, and a quiet and dull life began. Measles and small-pox were killing the Indians so rapidly that the gun of the white man was superfluous as an agent of destruction.

In 1854, six years after Grant's marriage, despairing of supporting his wife and two children on the Pacific coast with his pay as an army officer, he resigned. His prospects now were not bright. Without a profession, save that of arms, he was to begin, at thirty-two, a struggle for support, which must have tested the affection of the woman who married the young officer in her hopeful girlhood. She owned a farm in St. Louis, and thither they moved as their home. He says of the farm: "I had no means to stock it. A house had to be built also. I worked very hard, never losing a day because of bad weather, and accomplished the object in a moderate way. If nothing else could be done, I would load a cord of wood on a wagon and take it to the city for sale. I managed to keep along very well until 1858, when I was attacked by fever and ague. I had suffered very severely and for a long time from this disease while a boy in Ohio. It lasted now over a year, and, while it did not keep me in the house, it did interfere greatly with the amount of work I was able to perform. In the fall of 1858 I sold out my stock, crops, and farming utensils at auction, and gave up farming."

Four years of struggling had not paid pecuniarily. Poverty is not a pleasant school in which to be nurtured. Blessings upon those who do not grow harsh or discontented with its bitter lessons. To keep sunshine in the face when want knocks at the heart is to win the victory in a dreadful battle. And yet many are able to accomplish this, and brighten with their happy faces lives more prosperous than their own.

In the winter of 1858 Captain Grant established a partnership with a cousin of his wife in the real estate business. Again separation came. The little family were left on the farm while the father tried another method of earning a living for them. "Our business," he says, "might have become prosperous if I had been able to wait for it to grow. As it was, there was no more than one person could attend to, and not enough to support two families. While a citizen of St. Louis, and engaged in the real estate agency business, I was a candidate for the office of county engineer, an office of respectability and emolument which would have been very acceptable to me at that time. The incumbent was appointed by the county court, which consisted of five members. My opponent had the advantage of birth over me (he was a citizen by adoption), and carried off the prize. I now withdrew from the co-partnership with Boggs, and, in May, 1860, removed to Galena, Illinois, and took a clerkship in my father's store."

He was once more in the tannery business, which he had so hated when a boy. It is well that men and women are spurred to duty because somebody depends upon them for daily food, otherwise this life of often uncongenial labor would be unbearable. We rarely do what we like to do in this world;—we do what the merciless goad of circumstance forces us to do. He is wise who goes to his work with a smile.

The year 1860 opened upon a new era in this country. Slavery and anti-slavery had struggled together till the election of Abraham Lincoln to the presidency told that the decisive hour had come. The nation could no longer exist "half slave and half free."

When Mr. Lincoln was inaugurated, March 4, 1861, the Southern States seceded, one after another, until eleven had separated from the Union. Most of the Southern forts were already in the hands of the Confederates. Fort Sumter, in the harbor of Charleston, still remained under the control of the Union. While besieged by the South, an effort was made to send supplies to our starving garrison. The fort was fired upon April 11, 1861, and that shot, like the one at Concord, was "heard round the world."

From that hour slavery was doomed. The President issued his first call for seventy-five thousand volunteers for ninety days. The North and West seemed to respond as one man. The intense excitement reached the little town of Galena. The citizens were at once called together. Business was suspended. In the evening the court-house was packed. Captain Grant was asked to conduct the meeting. The people naturally turned to one who understood battles, when they saw war close at hand. With much embarrassment Grant presided. The leather business was finished for him from that eventful night. The women of Galena were as deeply interested as the men. They came to Grant to obtain a description of the United States uniform for infantry, subscribed and bought the material, procured tailors to cut the garments, and made them with their own willing hands. More and more, with their superior education, women are to play an important part in this country, both in peace and war.

Captain Grant was now asked by Governor Yates, of Illinois, to go into the adjutant-general's office, and render such assistance as he could, which position he accepted, but he modestly says, "I was no clerk, nor had I any capacity to become one. The only place I ever found in my life to put a paper so as to find it again was either a side coat-pocket or the hands of a clerk or secretary more careful than myself. But I had been quartermaster, commissary, and adjutant in the field. The army forms were familiar to me, and I could direct how they should be made out."

Though a man of few words, those few could be effective if Grant chose to use them. Meeting in St. Louis, in a street-car, a young braggart, who said to him, "Where I came from, if a man dares to say a word in favor of the Union we hang him to a limb of the first tree we come to," Grant replied, "We are not so intolerant in St. Louis as we might be. I have not seen a single rebel hung yet, nor heard of one. There are plenty of them who ought to be, however." The young man did not continue the conversation. In May, 1861, Grant wrote a letter to the adjutant-general of the army at Washington, saying that, as he had been in the regular army for fifteen years, and educated at government expense, he tendered his services for the war. No notice was ever taken of the letter, and, of course, no answer was returned. Soon after he spent a week with his parents, in Covington, Kentucky. Twice he called upon Major-General McClellan, at Cincinnati, just across the river, whom he had known slightly in the Mexican War, with the hope that he would be offered a position on his staff. But he failed to see the general, and returned to Illinois. He was not to serve under McClellan. A different destiny awaited him.

President Lincoln now called for three hundred thousand men to enlist for three years or the war. Governor Yates appointed Grant colonel of the Twenty-First Illinois regiment. Another separation from wife and children had come; the beginning of a great career had come also. The regiment repaired to Springfield, Illinois, and, after some time spent in drill, was ordered to move against Colonel Thomas Harris, encamped at the little town of Florida. There was no bravado in the man who had fought so bravely in all the battles of the Mexican War. He says: "As we approached the brow of the hill from which it was expected we could see Harris' camp, and possibly find his men ready formed to meet us, my heart kept getting higher and higher until it felt to me as though it was in my throat. I would have given anything then to have been back in Illinois, but I had not the moral courage to halt and consider what to do; I kept right on. When we reached a point from which the valley below was in full view, I halted. The place where Harris had been encamped a few days before was still there, and the marks of a recent encampment were plainly visible, but the troops were gone. My heart resumed its place. It occurred to me at once that Harris had been as much afraid of me as I had been of him. This was a view of the question I had never taken before, but it was one I never forgot afterwards. From that event to the close of the war, I never experienced trepidation upon confronting an enemy, though I always felt more or less anxiety. I never forgot that he had as much reason to fear my forces as I had his. The lesson was valuable."

Soon after this Lincoln asked the Illinois delegation in Congress to recommend some citizens of the State for the position of brigadier-general, and Grant, to his great surprise, was recommended first on a list of seven. After his appointment he spent several weeks in Missouri, whither he had been ordered. His first battle was at Belmont, where, in a severe engagement of four hours, the loss on our side was 485, and the Confederate loss 642. Grant's horse was shot under him. After the battle the Confederates received reënforcements, and there was danger that our men could not return to the transports on which they had come to Belmont. "We are surrounded," they cried.

"Well," said their cool leader, "if that be so, we must cut our way out as we cut our way in;" and so they did.

Grant, meantime, rode out into a cornfield alone to observe the enemy. While there, as he afterwards learned, the Southern General Polk and one of his staff saw the Union soldier, and said to their men, "There is a Yankee; you may try your marksmanship on him if you wish;" but, strangely enough, nobody fired, and Grant's valuable life was spared.

He soon perceived that he was the only man between the Confederates and the boats. His horse seemed to realize the situation. Grant says: "There was no path down the bank, and every one acquainted with the Mississippi River knows that its banks, in a natural state, do not vary at any great angle from the perpendicular. My horse put his fore feet over the bank without hesitation or urging, and, with his hind feet well under him, slid down the bank and trotted aboard the boat, twelve or fifteen feet away, over a single gangplank. I dismounted and went at once to the upper deck.... When I first went on deck I entered the captain's room, adjoining the pilot-house, and threw myself on a sofa. I did not keep that position a moment, but rose to go out on the deck to observe what was going on. I had scarcely left when a musket-ball entered the room, struck the head of the sofa, passed through it, and lodged in the boat." Thus again was his life saved.

Until February of the following year, 1862, little was done by the troops, except to become ready for the great work before them. The enemy occupied strong points on the Tennessee and Cumberland rivers, at Forts Henry and Donelson, points as essential to us as to them. These Grant determined to take, if possible. Truly said President Lincoln, "Wherever Grant is things move. I have noticed that from the beginning."

On February 2 the expedition started against Fort Henry, with about seventeen thousand men. Several gun-boats, under Commodore Foote, accompanied the army. At a given hour the troops and gun-boats moved together, the one to invest the garrison, the other to attack the fort. After a severe fight of an hour and a half every gun was silenced. General Lloyd Tilghman surrendered, with his seventeen heavy guns, ammunition, and stores.

Fort Donelson must now be taken, strongly fortified as it was. It stood on high ground, with rifle-pits running back two miles from the river, and was defended by fifteen heavy guns, two carronades,

178

and sixty-five pieces of artillery. Outside the rifle-pits, trees had been felled, so that the tops lay toward the attacking army. Our men had no shelter from the snow and rain in this midwinter siege. No campfires could be allowed where the enemy could see them. In the march from Fort Henry to Fort Donelson numbers of the tired troops had thrown away their blankets and overcoats, and there was much real suffering. But war means discomfort and woe as well as death itself.

At three o'clock, February 14, Commodore Foote's gun-boats attacked the water batteries, and after a severe encounter several of them were disabled. The one upon which the commodore stood was hit about sixty times, one shot killing the pilot, carrying away the wheel, and wounding the commander. The night came on intensely cold. The next morning, the enemy, taking heart, came against the national forces to cut their way out. Then Grant rode among his men, saying, "Whichever party first attacks now will whip, and the rebels will have to be very quick if they beat me.... Fill your cartridge-boxes quick, and get into line; the enemy is trying to escape, and he must not be permitted to do so."

Our men worked their way through the abatis of trees, took the outer line of rifle-pits, and bivouacked within the enemy's lines. A driving storm of snow and hail set in, and many soldiers were frozen on that dismal night. There must have been little sleep amid the firing of the Confederate pickets and the groans of the wounded on that frozen ground.

During the night the Confederate Generals Floyd and Pillow left the fort with three thousand men and Forrest with another thousand. On the morning of February 16, Brigadier-General S. B. Buckner sent a note to General Grant, suggesting an armistice. The following reply was returned at once:—

> "Sir,—Yours of this date, proposing armistice and appointment of commissioners to settle terms of capitulation, is just received. No terms except an unconditional and immediate surrender can be accepted. I propose to move immediately upon your works."

From that day U. S. Grant became to the people of the North "Unconditional Surrender" Grant; precious words, indeed, to the army as well as the people, to whom decisive action meant peace at last.

General Buckner considered the terms "ungenerous and unchivalrous," but he surrendered his sixty-five guns, seventeen thousand six hundred small arms, and nearly fifteen thousand troops. Our loss in killed, wounded, and missing was about two thousand; the Confederate loss was believed to be about twenty-five hundred.

This victory, the first great victory of the war, caused much rejoicing at the North, and Grant was at once made major-general of volunteers. Two weeks from this time he was virtually under arrest for not conforming to orders which he never received, but he was soon restored to his position. The country was to learn later, what Lincoln learned early in the war, that one head for an army is better than several heads.

The next great battle under Grant was at Shiloh, near Pittsburg Landing. On the morning of April 6, 1862, the Confederates, under General Albert Sidney Johnston and Beauregard, rushed upon the national lines. All day Sunday the battle raged, and at night the Union forces had fallen back a mile in the rear of their position in the morning. Sherman, who commanded the ridge on which stood the log meeting-house of Shiloh, was twice shot, once in the hand and once in the shoulder, a third ball passing through his hat. Grant could well say of this brave officer, "I never deemed it important to stay long with Sherman."

During the night after the desperate battle the rain fell in torrents upon the two armies, who slept upon their arms. General Grant's headquarters were under a tree, a few hundred yards back from the river. "Some time after midnight," he says, "growing restive under the storm and the continuous rain, I moved back to the log house under the bank. This had been taken as a hospital, and all night wounded men were brought in, their wounds dressed, a leg or an arm amputated, as the case might require, and everything being done to save life or alleviate suffering. The sight was more unendurable than encountering the enemy's fire, and I returned to my tree in the rain."

In battle, the great general could look on men falling about him apparently unmoved; when the battle was over, he could not bear the sight of pain. The men revered him, because, while he led them into death, he almost surely led them into victory.

On April 7 the battle raged all along the line, and the enemy were everywhere driven back. At three o'clock Grant gathered up a couple of regiments, formed them into line of battle, and marched them forward, going in front himself to prevent long-range firing. The command "Charge" was given, and it was executed with loud cheers and a run, and the enemy broke. Grant came near losing his life. A ball struck the metal scabbard of his sword, just below the hilt, and broke it nearly off. Night closed upon a victorious Union army, but the victory had been gained at a fearful cost.

"Shiloh," says General Grant, "was the severest battle fought at the West during the war, and but few in the East equalled it for hard, determined fighting. I saw an open field, in our possession on the second day, over which the Confederates had made repeated charges the day before, so covered with dead that it would have been possible to walk across the clearing, in any direction, stepping on dead bodies, without a foot touching the ground. On our side national and Confederate troops were mingled together in about equal proportions; but on the remainder of the field nearly all were Confederates. On one part, which had evidently not been ploughed for several years, probably because the land was poor, bushes had grown up, some to the height of eight or ten feet. There was not one of these left standing unpierced by bullets. The smaller ones were all cut down."

During the first day the brave Albert Sidney Johnston was wounded. He would not leave the battle-field, but continued in the saddle, giving commands, till, exhausted by loss of blood, he was taken from his horse, and died soon after. The Union loss was reported to be over thirteen thousand. Some estimate the losses as not less than fifteen thousand on each side. Up to this time, Grant had hoped that a few such victories as Fort Donelson would dishearten the South; now he saw that conquest alone could compel peace, with a brave and heroic people, of our own blood and race. From this time the work of laying waste the enemy's country began, with the hope that the sooner supplies were exhausted the sooner peace would be possible.

On October 25, the battle of Corinth having been fought October 3, General Grant was placed in command of the Department of the Tennessee, and began the Vicksburg campaign. The capture of this place would afford free navigation of the Mississippi. For three months plan after plan was tried for the reduction of this almost impregnable position. Sherman made a direct attack at the only point where a landing was practicable, and failed. Grant's army was stationed on the west bank of the river, on marshy ground, full of malaria, from recent rains. The troops were ill of fever, measles, and small-pox, and many died. There could be found scarcely enough dry land on which to pitch their tents.

It was finally decided to cut a canal across the peninsula in front of Vicksburg, that the gun-boats might safely pass through to a point below the city. Four thousand men began work on the canal, but a sudden rise in the river broke the dam and stopped the work. A second method was tried, by breaking levees and widening and connecting streams between Lake Providence, seventy miles above

Vicksburg, through the Red River, into the Mississippi again four hundred miles below, but this project was soon abandoned. Meantime, the North had become restless, and many clamored for Grant's removal, declaring him incompetent, but, amid all the reproaches, he kept silent. When Lincoln was urged to make a change, he said simply, "I rather like the man; I think we'll try him a little longer!"

At length it was decided to attempt to run the gun-boats past the batteries, march the troops down the west bank of the river, cross over to the east side, and attack the rear of Vicksburg. The steamers were protected as far as possible with bales of hay, cotton, and grain, for the boilers could not bear the enemy's fire. On the 16th of April, 1863, on a dark night, the fleet was ready for the dangerous passage. As soon as the boats were discovered, the batteries opened fire, piles of combustibles being lighted along the shore that proper aim might be taken against the fleet. Every transport was struck. As fast as the shots made holes, the men put cotton bags in the openings. For nearly three hours the eight gun-boats and three steamers were under a merciless fire. The Henry Clay was disabled, and soon set on fire by the bursting of a shell in the cotton packed about her boilers. Grant watched the passage of the fleet from a steamer in the river, and felt relieved as though the victory were close at hand.

Soon after, the whole force of thirty-three thousand men were crossed below Vicksburg. Fifty miles to the east, the Confederate General Joseph E. Johnston had a large army, which must be crippled before Vicksburg could be besieged. Port Gibson, near the river, was first taken by our troops; then Raymond, May 12; Jackson, May 18; Champion Hill, May 16; and then Black River Bridge. Grant had beaten Johnston in the rear; now he must beat Pemberton with his nearly fifty thousand men shut up in Vicksburg.

On May 19, the city of Vicksburg was completely invested by our troops. Says General Grant, "Five distinct battles had been fought and won by the Union forces; the capital of the State had fallen, and its arsenals, military manufactories, and everything useful for military purposes had been destroyed; an average of about one hundred and eighty miles had been marched by the troops engaged; but five days' rations had been issued, and no forage; over six thousand prisoners had been captured, and as many more of the enemy had been killed or wounded; twenty-seven heavy cannon, and sixty-one field-pieces had fallen into our hands; and four hundred miles of the river, from Vicksburg to Port Hudson, had become ours."

And now the siege began. By June 30, there were two hundred and twenty guns in position, besides a battery of heavy guns, manned and commanded by the navy. The besiegers had no mortars, save those of the navy in front of the city, but they took tough logs, bored them out for six or twelve-pound shells, bound them with strong iron bands, and used them effectively in the trenches of the enemy.

The eyes of the whole country were centred on Vicksburg. Mines were dug by both armies, and exploded. Among the few men who reached the ground alive after having been thrown up by the explosions was a colored man, badly frightened. Some one asked how high he had gone up. "Dunno, massa; but tink 'bout t'ree mile," was the reply.

Meantime, the people in Vicksburg were living in caves and cellars to escape the shot and shell. Starvation began to stare them in the face. Flour was sold at five dollars a pound; molasses at ten and twelve dollars a gallon. Yet the brave people held out against surrender. A Confederate woman, says General Badeau, in his graphic "Military History of U. S. Grant," asked Grant, tauntingly, as he stopped at her house for water, if he ever expected to get into Vicksburg.

"Certainly," he replied.

"But when?"

"I cannot tell exactly when I shall take the town; but I mean to stay here till I do, if it takes me thirty years."

All through the siege, the men of both armies talked to each other; the Confederates and Unionists calling each other respectively "Yanks" and "Johnnies." "Well, Yank, when are you coming into town?"

"We propose to celebrate the Fourth of July there, Johnnie."

The Vicksburg paper said, prior to the Fourth, in speaking of the Yankee boast that they would take dinner in Vicksburg that day, "The best receipt for cooking a rabbit is, 'First ketch your rabbit!'" The last number of the paper was issued on July 4, and said, "The Yankees have caught the rabbit."

On July 3, at ten o'clock, white flags began to appear on the enemy's works, and two men were seen coming towards the Union lines, bearing a white flag. They bore a message from General Pemberton, asking that an armistice be granted, and three commissioners appointed to confer with a like number named by Grant. "I make this proposition to save the further effusion of blood," said General Pemberton, "which must otherwise be shed to a frightful extent, feeling myself fully able to maintain my position for a yet indefinite period."

To this Grant replied: "The useless effusion of blood you propose stopping by this course can be ended at any time you choose, by the unconditional surrender of the city and garrison. Men who have shown so much endurance and courage as those now in Vicksburg will always challenge the respect of an adversary, and, I can assure you, will be treated with all the respect due to prisoners of war."

In the afternoon of July 3, Grant and Pemberton met under a stunted oak-tree, a few hundred yards from the Confederate lines. They had known each other in the Mexican War. A kindly conference was held, and honorable terms of surrender agreed upon, the officers taking their side-arms and clothing, and staff and cavalry officers one horse each. When the men passed out of the works they had so gallantly defended, not a cheer went up from our men nor was a remark made that could cause pain. The garrison surrendered at Vicksburg numbered over thirty-one thousand men, with sixty thousand muskets, and over one hundred and seventy cannon. Five days later, Port Hudson, lower on the river, surrendered, with six thousand prisoners and fifty-one guns.

There was great rejoicing at the North. Lincoln wrote to Grant: "My dear general, I do not remember that you and I have ever met personally. I write this now as a grateful acknowledgment for the almost inestimable service you have done the country. I write to say a word further. When you first reached the vicinity of Vicksburg, I thought you should do what you finally did, march the troops across the neck, run the batteries with the transports, and then go below; and I never had any faith, except a general hope that you knew better than I, that the Yazoo Pass expedition and the like could succeed. When you got below and took Port Gibson, Grand Gulf, and vicinity, I thought you should go down the river and join General Banks, and when you turned northward, east of the Big Black, I feared it was a mistake. I wish now to make the personal acknowledgment that you were right and I was wrong."

Rare is that soul which is able to see itself in the wrong, and rarer still one which has the generosity to acknowledge it.

In October, Grant, who had now been made a major-general in the regular army, as he had before been appointed to the same rank in the volunteers, was placed in command of the military division of the Mississippi. Later he defeated Bragg at Chattanooga, November 24 and 25, 1863, in the memorable battles of Missionary Ridge and Lookout Mountain. General Halleck said in his annual report, "Considering the strength of the rebel position and the difficulty of storming his intrenchments, the battle of Chattanooga must be considered the most remarkable in history. Not only did the officers and men exhibit great skill and daring in their operations on the field, but the highest praise is due to the commanding general for his admirable dispositions for dislodging the enemy from a position apparently impregnable."

How our brave men fought at Missionary Ridge and Lookout Mountain has never been more graphically and touchingly told than by the late lamented Benjamin F. Taylor: "They dash out a little way and then slacken; they creep up hand over hand, loading and firing, and wavering and halting, from the first line of works to the second; they burst into a charge, with a cheer, and go over it. Sheets of flame baptize them; plunging shots tear away comrades on left and right; it is no longer shoulder to shoulder; it is God for us all! Under tree-trunks, among rocks, stumbling over the dead, struggling with the living, facing the steady fire of eight thousand infantry poured down upon their heads as if it were the old historic curse from heaven, they wrestle with the Ridge. Ten, fifteen, twenty minutes go by, like a reluctant century. The batteries roll like a drum. Between the second and last lines of rebel works is the torrid zone of the battle. The hill sways up like a wall before them at an angle of forty-five degrees, but our brave mountaineers are clambering steadily on—up—upward still!... They seem to be spurning the dull earth under their feet, and going up to do Homeric battle with the greater gods."

When this costly victory had been gained, President Lincoln appointed a day of national thanksgiving. Congress passed a unanimous vote of thanks to Grant and his officers and men, and ordered a medal to be struck in his honor: his face on one side, surrounded by a laurel wreath; on the other side, Fame seated on the American eagle, holding in her right hand a scroll with the words, Corinth, Vicksburg, Mississippi River, and Chattanooga.

Early in 1864, a distinguished honor was paid him. Since the death of Washington, only one man had been appointed a lieutenant-general in the army of the United States,—Winfield Scott. Congress now revived this grade, and on March 1, 1864, Lincoln appointed Grant to this position. On March 9, before the President and his cabinet, his commission was formally presented to him, Lincoln saying, "As the country herein trusts you, so, under God, it will sustain you." Grant now had all the Union armies under his control—over seven hundred thousand men. When he was in the Galena leather store, men said his life was a failure! Was it a failure now? And yet he was the same modest, unostentatious man as when he tried farming to support his beloved family.

Immediately Grant planned two great campaigns: one against Richmond, which was defended by Lee; the other against Atlanta, under Sherman, defended by Joseph E. Johnston. Sherman's march

185

to the sea immortalized him; Grant's march to Richmond was the crowning success in the greatest of modern wars. President Lincoln reposed the utmost confidence in Grant. He wrote him: "The particulars of your plans I neither know nor seek to know. You are vigilant and self-reliant, and, pleased with this, I wish not to obtrude any constraints or restraints upon you. While I am very anxious that any great disaster or the capture of our men in great numbers shall be avoided, I know these points are less likely to escape your attention than they would be mine. If there is anything wanting which is within my power to give, do not fail to let me know it. And now, with a brave army and a just cause, may God sustain you."

The end was coming. On May 4, 1864, Grant crossed the Rapidan with the Army of the Potomac, about one hundred and twenty thousand men, intending to put his forces between Lee and Richmond. Lee, perceiving this design, met the army at the Wilderness, a portion of country covered by a dense forest. The undergrowth was so heavy that it was scarcely possible to see more than one hundred paces in any direction. All day long, May 5, a bloody battle was waged in the woods.

Says Private Frank Wilkeson, "I heard the hum of bullets as they passed over the low trees. Then I noticed that small limbs of trees were falling in a feeble shower in advance of me. It was as though an army of squirrels were at work cutting off nut and pine-cone laden branches preparatory to laying in their winter's store of food. Then, partially obscured by a cloud of powder smoke, I saw a straggling line of men clad in blue. They were not standing as if on parade, but they were taking advantage of the cover afforded by trees, and they were firing rapidly. Their line officers were standing behind them or in line with them. The smoke drifted to and fro, and there were many rifts in it.... We had charged, and charged, and charged again, and had gone wild with battle fever. We had gained about two miles of ground. We were doing splendidly. I cast my eyes upward to see the sun, so as to judge of the time, as I was hungry, and wanted to eat, and I saw that it was still low above the trees. The Confederates seemed to be fighting more stubbornly, fighting as though their battle-line was being fed with more troops. They hung on to the ground they occupied tenaciously, and resolutely refused to fall back further. Then came a swish of bullets and a fierce exultant yell, as of thousands of infuriated tigers. Our men fell by scores. Great gaps were struck in our lines. There was a lull for an instant, and then Longstreet's men sprang to the charge. It was swiftly and bravely made, and was within an ace of being successful. There was great confusion in our line. The men wavered badly. They

186

fired wildly. They hesitated.... The regimental officers held their men as well as they could. We could hear them close behind us, or in line with us, saying, 'Steady, men, steady, steady, steady!' as one speaks to frightened and excited horses."

Grant says, "More desperate fighting has not been witnessed on this continent than that of May 5 and 6.... The ground fought over had varied in width, but averaged three-quarters of a mile. The killed and many of the severely wounded of both armies lay within this belt where it was impossible to reach them. The woods were set on fire by the bursting shells, and the conflagration raged. The wounded who had not strength to move themselves were either suffocated or burned to death. Finally the fire communicated with our breastworks in places. Being constructed of wood, they burned with great fury. But the battle still raged, our men firing through the flames until it became too hot to remain longer."

After a loss of from fourteen to fifteen thousand men on each side, Lee remained in his intrenchments and Grant still moved on toward Richmond. The armies met at Spottsylvania Court-House, and here was fought one of the bloodiest battles of the war, with about the same loss as in the Wilderness. Sometimes the conflict was hand to hand, men using their guns as clubs, being too close to fire. In one place a tree, eighteen inches in diameter, was cut entirely down by musket balls. Grant wrote to Washington, May 11: "We have now ended the sixth day of very hard fighting. The result up to this time is much in our favor. But our losses have been heavy, as well as those of the enemy. We have lost to this time eleven general officers killed, wounded, and missing, and probably twenty thousand men. I think the loss of the enemy must be greater. We have taken over four thousand prisoners in battle, whilst he has taken from us but few except a few stragglers. I am now sending back to Belle Plain all my wagons for a fresh supply of provisions and ammunition, and purpose to fight it out on this line if it takes all summer."

After this came the battles of Drury's Bluff, North Anna, Totopotomoy, and Cold Harbor, with its brilliant assault and deadly repulse, with a loss of from ten to fourteen thousand men on the latter field.

Lee had now been driven so near to Richmond, and the swamps of the Chickahominy were so impassable, that Grant determined to move his army, one hundred and fifteen thousand men, south of the James River and attack Richmond in the rear. The move was hazardous, but he reached City Point safely. General Butler here joined him, and the siege of Petersburg, twenty miles below Richmond, began, and was continued through the winter and spring.

On July 30, 1864, a mine was exploded under one of the enemy's forts. The gallery to the mine was over five hundred feet long from where it entered the ground to the point where it was under the enemy's works. Eight chambers had been left, requiring a ton of powder each to charge them. It exploded at five o'clock in the morning, making a crater twenty feet deep and about one hundred feet in length. Instantly one hundred and ten cannon and fifty mortars commenced work to cover our troops as they entered the enemy's lines. "The effort," says Grant, "was a stupendous failure. It cost us about four thousand men, mostly, however, captured, and all due to inefficiency on the part of the corps commander and the incompetency of the division commander who was sent to lead the assault."

Meanwhile Sheridan had destroyed the power of the South in the Shenandoah valley. Again the army began its march toward Richmond. On April 1, 1865, the battle of Five Forks was fought, nearly six thousand Confederates being taken prisoners; then Petersburg was captured, and on April 3 General Weitzel took possession of Richmond, the enemy having evacuated it, the city having been set on fire before their departure.

For five days Lee's army was pursued with more or less fighting. On April 7, Grant wrote a letter to Lee, saying: "The results of the last week must convince you of the hopelessness of further resistance on the part of the Army of Northern Virginia in this struggle. I feel that it is so, and regard it as my duty to shift from myself the responsibility of any further effusion of blood, by asking of you the surrender of that portion of the Confederate States Army known as the Army of Northern Virginia."

Lee replied, "I reciprocate your desire to avoid useless effusion of blood, and therefore, before considering your proposition, ask the terms you will offer on condition of its surrender."

The answer came: "Peace being my great desire, there is but one condition I would insist upon, namely: that the men and officers surrendered shall be disqualified for taking up arms again against the government of the United States, until properly exchanged."

A place of meeting was designated, and on April 9 Grant and Lee met at the house of a Mr. McLean, at Appomattox Court-House. Grant says, "When I had left camp that morning, I had not expected so soon the result that was then taking place, and consequently was

188

in rough garb, and I was without a sword, as I usually was when on horseback on the field, and wore a soldier's blouse for a coat, with the shoulder-straps of my rank to indicate to the army who I was. When I went into the house I found General Lee. We greeted each other, and, after shaking hands, took our seats. I had my staff with me, a good portion of whom were in the room during the whole of the interview.

"What General Lee's feelings were I do not know. As he was a man of much dignity, with an impassible face, it was impossible to say whether he felt inwardly glad that the end had finally come, or felt sad over the result, and was too manly to show it. Whatever his feelings, they were entirely concealed from my observation; but my own feelings, which had been quite jubilant on the receipt of his letter, were sad and depressed. I felt like anything rather than rejoicing at the downfall of a foe who had fought so long and valiantly, and had suffered so much for a cause, though that cause was, I believe, one of the worst for which a people ever fought, and one for which there was the least excuse. I do not question, however, the sincerity of the great mass of those who were opposed to us.

"General Lee was dressed in a full uniform which was entirely new, and was wearing a sword of considerable value, very likely the sword which had been presented by the State of Virginia; at all events, it was an entirely different sword from the one that would ordinarily be worn in the field. In my rough travelling suit, the uniform of a private, with the straps of a lieutenant-general, I must have contrasted very strangely with a man so handsomely dressed, six feet high, and of faultless form. But this was not a matter that I thought of until afterwards."

When the terms of surrender were completed, Lee remarked that his men had been living for some days on parched corn exclusively, and asked for rations and forage, which were cordially granted. "When news of the surrender first reached our lines," says Grant, "our men commenced firing a salute of a hundred guns in honor of the victory. I at once sent word, however, to have it stopped. The Confederates were now our prisoners, and we did not want to exult over their downfall." True and noble spirit! Twenty-seven thousand five hundred and sixteen officers and men were paroled at Appomattox. At the North, crowds came together to pray and give thanks, in the churches, that the war was over. Mourning garb seemed to be in every house, and the joy was sanctified by tears. The Army of the Potomac marched to Washington, and was disbanded June 30.

The great war was ended. In July, 1866, Congress created the rank of general for the heroic, true-hearted, grand man, of quiet manner but indomitable will, who had saved the Union. He was now but forty-four years of age, and what a record!

Two years later, in 1868, at the Chicago Republican national convention. Grant was unanimously nominated to the presidency. After the assassination of Lincoln, and the disagreement between Congress and Andrew Johnson in the matter of reconstruction, it was believed that Grant would "settle things." To the committee from the convention who announced his nomination to him, he said, "I shall have no policy of my own to enforce against the will of the people."

During the eight years of Grant's presidency, from 1869 to 1877, the country was prosperous, save the financial depression of 1873. The Alabama claims were settled, whereby our country received from Great Britain fifteen million five hundred thousand dollars damages. Grant favored the annexation of the island of Santo Domingo, but the measure was defeated by Congress. The International Exposition was held in Philadelphia in 1876, with an average daily attendance, for five months, of over sixty-one thousand persons. While a large number of the people advocated a third term for General Grant, a nation loving freedom hesitated to establish such a precedent, and Rutherford B. Hayes was chosen President. It was well, in the exciting times preceding this election, when the number of votes for Hayes and Tilden was decided by an electoral commission, that a strong hand was on the helm of State, to keep the peace.

After all these years of labor, General Grant determined to make the tour of the world, and, with his family and a few others, sailed for Europe, May 17, 1877. From the moment they arrived on the other side of the ocean to their return, no American ever received such an ovation as Grant. Thousands crowded the docks at Liverpool, and the mayor gave an address of welcome. At Manchester, ten thousand people listened to his brief address. "As I have been aware," he said, "for years of the great amount of your manufactures, many of which find their ultimate destination in my own country, so I am aware that the sentiments of the great mass of the people of Manchester went out in sympathy to that country during the mighty struggle in which it fell to my lot to take some humble part."

In London, the present Duke of Wellington gave him a grand banquet at Apsley House. At Marlborough House, the Prince of Wales gave him private audience. The freedom of the city of London was presented to him in a gold casket, supported by golden American eagles, standing on a velvet plinth decorated with stars and stripes. He and his family dined with the Queen, at Windsor Castle.

In Scotland, the freedom of the city of Edinburgh was conferred upon him. At a grand ovation at Newcastle, between forty and fifty thousand people were gathered on the moor to see the illustrious general. To the International Arbitration Union in Birmingham he said, "Nothing would afford me greater happiness than to know, as I believe will be the case, that at some future day the nations of the earth will agree upon some sort of congress which shall take cognizance of international questions of difficulty, and whose decisions will be as binding as the decision of our Supreme Court is binding upon us." In Belgium, the king called upon him, and gave a royal banquet in his honor. In Berlin, Bismarck called twice to see him, shaking hands cordially, and saying, "Glad to welcome General Grant to Germany." In Turkey, he was presented with some beautiful Arabian horses by the Sultan. King Humbert of Italy and the Czar of Russia showed him marked attentions. In Norway and Sweden, Spain, China, Egypt, and India, he was everywhere received as the most distinguished general of the age.

On his return to America, at San Francisco and Sacramento, thousands gathered to see him. At Chicago, he said, in addressing the Army of the Tennessee, "Let us be true to ourselves, avoid all bitterness and ill-feeling, either on the part of sections or parties toward each other, and we need have no fear in future of maintaining the stand we have taken among nations, so far as opposition from foreign nations goes." In Philadelphia, where he was royally entertained by his friend Mr. George W. Childs, he said to the Grand Army of the Republic, "What I want to impress upon you is that you have a country to be proud of, and a country to fight for, and a country to die for if need be.... In no other country is the young and energetic man given such a chance by industry and frugality to acquire a competence for himself and family as in America. Abroad it is difficult for the poor man to make his way at all. All that is necessary is to know this in order that we may become better citizens." On his return to New York, he was presented by his friends with a home in that city, and also with the gift of two hundred and fifty thousand dollars.

He was soon prevailed upon to enter a banking firm with Ferdinand Ward and James D. Fish. The bank failed, Grant found himself financially ruined, and the two partners were sent to prison. He was now to struggle again for a living, as in the early days in the Galena leather store. A timely offer came from the Century magazine, to write his experiences in the Civil War. Very simply, so that an uneducated person could understand, Grant modestly and fairly described the great battles in which he was of necessity the central figure. Unused to literary labor, he bent himself to the task, working seven and eight hours a day.

On October 22, 1884, cancer developed in the throat, and for nine months Grant fought with death, till the two great volumes of his memoirs could be completed and given to the world, that his family might not be left dependent. Early in June, 1885, as he was failing rapidly, he was taken to Mt. McGregor, near Saratoga, where a cottage had been offered him by Mr. Joseph W. Drexel. He worked now more heroically than ever, till the last page was written, with the words: "The war has made us a nation of great power and intelligence. We have but little to do to preserve peace, happiness, and prosperity at home, and the respect of other nations. Our experience ought to teach us the necessity of the first; our power secures the latter.

"I feel that we are on the eve of a new era, when there is to be great harmony between the Federal and Confederate. I cannot stay to be a living witness to the correctness of this prophecy; but I feel it within me that it is to be so. The universally kind feeling expressed for me at a time when it was supposed that each day would prove my last seemed to me the beginning of the answer to 'Let us have peace.'"

Night and day the nation watched for tidings from the bedside of the dying hero. At last, in July, when he knew that the end was near, he wrote an affectionate letter to the Julia Dent whom he had loved in his early manhood, and put it in his pocket, that she might read it after all was over. "Look after our dear children, and direct them in the paths of rectitude. It would distress me far more to think that one of them could depart from an honorable, upright, and virtuous life, than it would to know that they were prostrated on a bed of sickness from which they were never to arise alive. They have never given us any cause for alarm on their account, and I earnestly pray they never will.

"With these few injunctions and the knowledge I have of your love and affection, and of the dutiful affection of all our children, I bid you a final farewell, until we meet in another, and, I trust, a better world. You will find this on my person after my demise." Blessed home affection, that brightens all the journey, and makes human nature well-nigh divine!

On July 23, 1885, a few minutes before eight o'clock in the morning, the end came. In the midst of his children, Colonel Frederick, Ulysses, Jesse, and Nellie Grant-Sartoris, and his grandchildren, his wife bending over him, he sank to rest. In every city and town in the land there was genuine sorrow. Letters of sympathy came from all parts of the world. Before the body was put in its purple casket, the eldest son placed a plain gold ring upon the little finger of the right hand, the gift years before of his wife, but which had grown too large for the emaciated finger in life. In his pocket was placed a tiny package containing a lock of Mrs. Grant's hair, in a good-bye letter. Sweet and beautiful thought, to bury with our dead something which belongs to a loved one, that they may not sleep entirely alone!

"We shall wake, and remember, and understand." Let the world laugh at sentiment outwardly—the hearts of those who laugh are often hungering for affection!

The body, dressed in citizen's clothes, without military, was laid in the casket. Then, in the little cottage on the mountain-top, Dr. Newman, his pastor, gave a beautiful address, from the words, "Well done, thou good and faithful servant; enter thou into the joy of thy Lord." "His was the genius of common-sense, enabling him to contemplate all things in their true relations, judging what is true, useful, proper, expedient, and to adopt the best means to accomplish the largest ends. From this came his seriousness, thoughtfulness, penetration, discernment, firmness, enthusiasm, triumph.... Temperate without austerity; cautious without fear; brave without rashness; serious without melancholy, he was cheerful without frivolity. His constancy was not obstinacy; his adaptation was not fickleness. His hopefulness was not utopian. His love of justice was equalled only by his delight in compassion, and neither was sacrificed to the other.... The keenest, closest, broadest of all observers, he was the most silent of men. He lived within himself. His thought-life was most intense. His memory and his imagination were picture galleries of the world and libraries of treasured thought. He was a world to himself. His most intimate friends knew him only in part. He was fully and best known only to the wife of his bosom and the children of his loins. To them the man of iron will and nerve of steel was gentle, tender, and confiding, and to them he unfolded his beautiful religious life."

After the services, the body of the great soldier was placed upon the funeral car, and conveyed to Albany, where it lay in state at the Capitol. At midnight dirges were sung, while eager multitudes passed by looking upon the face of the dead. Arriving in New York, the casket was laid in the midst of exquisite flowers in the City Hall. On this very day memorial services were held in Westminster Abbey, Canon Farrar delivering an eloquent address.

During the first night at the City Hall, about fifteen thousand persons passed the coffin, and the next day ninety thousand; rich and poor, black and white; men, women, and little children. A man on crutches hobbled past the casket, bowed with grief. "Move on," said one of the guards of honor. "Yes," replied the old man, "as well as I can I will. I left this leg in the Wilderness." An aged woman wept as she said, "Oh! general, I gave you my husband, my sons, and my son's beautiful boys."

On August 8, General Grant was laid in his tomb at Riverside Park, on the Hudson River, a million people joining in the sad funeral ceremonies. The catafalque, with its black horses led by colored grooms, moved up the street, followed by a procession four miles long. When the tomb was reached, the casket, placed in a cedar covering, leaden lined, was again enclosed in a great steel casket, round like an immense boiler, weighing thirty-eight hundred pounds. The only touching memento left upon the coffin was a wreath of oak-leaves wrought together by his grandchild Julia, on his dying day, with the words, "To Grandpa." Guns were fired, and cannon reverberated through the valley, as the pall-bearers, Confederate and Union generals, turned their footsteps away from the resting-place of their great leader. It was fitting that North and South should unite in his burial. Here, too, will sometime be laid his wife, for before his death he exacted a promise from his oldest son: "Wherever I am buried, promise me that your mother shall be buried by my side." Already she has received over three hundred thousand dollars in royalty on the memoirs which he wrote in those last months of agony. Beautifully wrote Richard Watson Gilder:—

> "All's over now; here let our captain rest,—
> The conflict ended, past men's praise and blame;
> Here let him rest, alone with his great fame,—
> Here in the city's heart he loved the best,
> And where our sons his tomb may see
> To make them brave as he:—
>
> "As brave as he,—he on whose iron arm
> Our Greatest leaned, our gentlest and most wise,—
> Leaned when all other help seemed mocking lies,
> While this one soldier checked the tide of harm,
> And they together saved the State,
> And made it free and great."

JAMES A. GARFIELD

Not far from where I write is a tall gray stone monument, in the form of a circular tower, lined with various polished marbles, and exquisite stained-glass windows. It stands on a hill-top in the centre of three acres of green lawn, looking out upon blue Lake Erie and the busy city of Cleveland, Ohio.

Within this tower rests the body of one whom the nation honors, and will honor in all time to come; one who was nurtured in the wilderness that he might have a sweet, natural boyhood; who studied in the school of poverty that he might sympathize with the sons of toil; who grew to an ideal manhood, that other American boys might learn the lessons of a grand life, and profit by them.

In the little town of Orange, Ohio, James Abram Garfield was born, November 19, 1831. The home into which he came was a log cabin, twenty by thirty feet, made of unhewn logs, laid one upon another, to the height of twelve feet or more, the space between the logs being filled with clay or mud. Three other children were in this home in the forest already; Mehetabel, Thomas, and Mary.

Abram, the father, descended from Revolutionary ancestors, was a strong-bodied, strong-brained man, who moved from Worcester, Otsego County, New York, to test his fortune in the wilderness. In his boyhood, he had played with Eliza Ballou, descended from Maturin Ballou, a Huguenot, from France. She also at fourteen moved with her family from New Hampshire, into the Ohio wilderness. Abram was more attracted to Ohio for that reason. They renewed the affection of their childhood, and were married February 3, 1821, settling first in Newburg, near Cleveland, and later buying eighty acres in Orange, at two dollars an acre. Here their four children were born, seven miles from any other cabin.

When the boy James was eighteen months old, a shadow settled over the home in the woods. A fire broke out in the forest, threatening to sweep away the Garfield cabin. For two hours one hot July day the father fought the flames, took a severe cold, and died suddenly, saying to his wife, "I have planted four saplings in these woods; I must now leave them to your care." He had kept his precious ones from being homeless, only to leave them fatherless. Who would have thought then that one of these saplings would grow into a mighty tree, admired by all the world?

In a corner of the wheat-field, in a plain box, the young husband was buried. What should the mother do with her helpless

195

flock? "Give them away," said some of the relatives, or "bind them out in far-away homes."

"No," said the brave mother, and put her woman's hands to heavy work. She helped her boy Thomas, then nine years old, to split rails and fence in the wheat-field. She corded the wool of her sheep, wove the cloth, and made garments for her children. She sold enough land to pay off the mortgage, because she could not bear to be in debt, and then she and Mehetabel and Thomas ploughed and planted, and waited in faith and hope till the harvest came. When the food grew meagre she sang to her helpful children, and looked ever toward brighter days. And such days usually come to those who look for them.

It was not enough to widow Garfield that her children were decently clothed and fed in this isolated home. They must be educated; but how? A log school-house was finally erected, she wisely giving a corner of her farm for the site. The scholars sat on split logs for benches, and learned to read and write and spell as best they could from their ordinary teaching. James was now nearly three, and went and sat all day on the hard benches with the rest.

But a school-house was not sufficient for these New England pioneers; they must have a church building where they could worship. Mrs. Garfield loved her Bible, and had taught her children daily, so that James even knew its stories by heart, and many of its chapters. A church was therefore organized in the log school-house, and now they could work happily, year after year, wondering perchance what the future would bring.

James began to show great fondness for reading. As he lay on the cabin floor, by the big fireplace, he read by its light his "English Reader," "Robinson Crusoe" again and again, and, later, when he was twelve, "Josephus," and "Goodrich's History of the United States." He had worked on the farm for years; now he must earn some money for his mother by work for the neighbors. He had helped his brother Thomas in enlarging the house, and was sure that he could be a carpenter.

Going to a Mr. Trent, he asked for work.

"There is a pile of boards that I want planed," said the man, "and I will pay you one cent a board for planing."

James began at once, and at the end of a long day, to the amazement of Mr. Trent, he had planed one hundred boards, each over twelve feet long, and proudly carried home one dollar to his mother. After this he helped to build a barn and a shed for a potashery establishment for leeching ashes. The manufacturer of the "black-salts" seemed to take a fancy to the lad, and offered him work at nine dollars a month and his board, which James accepted.

In the evenings he studied arithmetic and read books about the sea. This arrangement might have continued for some time had not the daughter of the salt-maker remarked one evening to her beau, as they sat in the room where James was reading, "I should think it was time for hired servants to be abed."

James had not realized how the presence of a third party is apt to restrain the confidential conversation of lovers. He was hurt and angered by the words, and the next day gave up his work, and went home to his mother, to receive her sympathy and find employment elsewhere. Doubtless he was more careful, all his life, from this circumstance, lest he wound the feelings of others.

Soon after this he heard that his uncle in Newburg was hiring wood-choppers. He immediately went to see him, and agreed to cut one hundred cords of wood, at twenty-five cents a cord. It was a man's work, but the boy of sixteen determined to do as much as a man. Each day he cut two cords, and at last carried twenty-five dollars to his mother; a small fortune, it seemed to the earnest boy.

While he chopped wood he looked out wistfully upon Lake Erie, recalled the sea stories which he had read, and longed more than ever to become a sailor. The Orange woods were growing too cramped for him. He was restless and eager for a broader life. It was the unrest of ambition, which voiced itself twenty years later in an address at Washington, D. C., to young men. "Occasion cannot make spurs, young men. If you expect to wear spurs, you must win them. If you wish to use them, you must buckle them to your own heels before you go into the fight. Any success you may achieve is not worth the having unless you fight for it. Whatever you win in life you must conquer by your own efforts; and then it is yours—a part of yourself.... Let not poverty stand as an obstacle in your way. Poverty is uncomfortable, as I can testify; but nine times out of ten the best thing that can happen to a young man is to be tossed overboard, and compelled to sink or swim for himself. In all my acquaintance I have never known one to be drowned who was worth saving.... To a young man who has in himself the magnificent possibilities of life, it is not fitting that he should be permanently commanded; he should be a commander. You must not continue to be employed; you must be an employer. You must be promoted from the ranks to a command. There is something, young men, that you can command; go and find it, and command it. You can at least command a horse and dray, can be generalissimo of them and may carve out a fortune with them."

Mrs. Garfield, with her mother's heart, deprecated a life at sea for her boy, and tried to dissuade him. Through the summer he worked in the hay-field, and then, the sea-fever returning, his mother wisely suggested that he seek employment on Lake Erie and see if he liked the life.

With his clothing wrapped in a bundle, he walked seventeen miles to Cleveland, with glowing visions of being a sailor. Reaching the wharf, he went on board a schooner, and asked for work. A drunken captain met him with oaths, and ordered him off the boat. The first phase of sea life had been different from what he had read in the books, and he turned away somewhat disheartened.

However, he soon met a cousin, who gave him the opportunity of driving mules for a canal boat. To walk beside slow mules was somewhat prosaic, as compared with climbing masts in a storm, but he accepted the position, receiving ten dollars a month and his board. Says William M. Thayer, in his "From Log-Cabin to the White House": "James appeared to possess a singular affinity for the water. He fell into the water fourteen times during the two or three months he served on the canal boat. It was not because he was so clumsy that he could not keep right side up, nor because he did not understand the business; rather, we think, it arose from his thorough devotion to his work. He gave more attention to the labor in hand than he did to his own safety. He was one who never thought of himself when he was serving another. He thought only of what he had in hand to do. His application was intense, and his perseverance royal."

After a few weeks he contracted fever and ague, and went home to be cared for by his mother, through nearly five months of illness. The sea-fever had somewhat abated. Could he not go to school again? urged the mother. Thomas and she could give him seventeen dollars; not much, to be sure, for some people, but much for the widow and her son.

At last he decided to go to Geauga Seminary, at Chester; a decision which took him to the presidential chair. March 5, 1849, when he was eighteen, James and his cousins started on foot for Chester, carrying their housekeeping utensils, plates, knives and forks, kettle, and the like; for they must board themselves. A small room was hired for a pittance, four boys rooming together.

The seventeen dollars soon melted away, and James found work in a carpenter's shop, where he labored nights and mornings, and every Saturday. Though especially fond of athletic games, he had no time for these. The school library contained one hundred and fifty volumes; a perfect mine of knowledge it seemed to the youth from Orange. He read eagerly biography and history; joined the debating society, where, despite his awkward manners and poor clothes, his eloquence soon attracted attention; went home to see his mother at the end of the first term, happy and courageous, and returned with ninepence in his pocket, to renew the struggle for an education. The first Sunday, at church, he put this ninepence into the contribution box, probably feeling no poorer than before.

While at Chester, the early teaching of his mother bore fruit, in his becoming a Christian, and joining the sect called "Disciples." "Of course," said Garfield, years later, "that settled canal, and lake, and sea, and everything." A new life had begun—a life devoted to the highest endeavor.

Each winter, while at Chester, he taught a district school, winning the love of the pupils by his enthusiasm and warm heart, and inciting them to study from his love of books. He played with them as though a boy like themselves, as he was, in reality, and yet demanded and received perfect obedience. He "boarded around," as was the custom, and thus learned more concerning both parents and pupils than was always desirable, probably; but in every house he tried to stimulate all to increased intelligence.

During his last term at the seminary, he met a graduate of a New England college, who urged that he also attend college; told how often men had worked their way through successfully, and had come to prominence. Young Garfield at once began to study Latin and Greek, and at twenty years of age presented himself at Hiram College, Ohio, a small institution at that time, which had been started by the "Disciples." He sought the principal, and asked to ring the bell and sweep the floors to help pay his expenses. He took a room with four other students, not a wise plan, except for one who has will enough to study whether his companions work or play, and rose at five in the morning, to ring his bell.

A lady who attended the college thus writes of him: "I can see him even now, standing in the morning with his hand on the bell-rope, ready to give the signal calling teachers and scholars to engage in the duties of the day. As we passed by, entering the school-room, he had a cheerful word for every one. He was probably the most popular person in the institution. He was always good-natured, fond of conversation, and very entertaining. He was witty and quick at repartee, but his jokes, though brilliant and sparkling, were always harmless, and he never would willingly hurt another's feelings.

"Afterward, he became an assistant teacher, and while pursuing his classical studies, preparatory to his college course, he taught the English branches. He was a most entertaining teacher,—ready with illustrations, and possessing in a marked degree the power of exciting the interest of the scholars, and afterward making clear to them the lessons. In the arithmetic class there were ninety pupils, and I cannot remember a time when there was any flagging in the interest. There were never any cases of unruly conduct, or a disposition to shirk. With scholars who were slow of comprehension, or to whom recitations were a burden on account of their modest or retiring dispositions, he was specially attentive, and by encouraging words and gentle assistance would manage to put all at their ease, and awaken in them a confidence in themselves.... He was a constant attendant at the regular meetings for prayer, and his vigorous exhortations and apt remarks upon the Bible-lessons were impressive and interesting. There was a cordiality in his disposition which won quickly the favor and esteem of others. He had a happy habit of shaking hands, and would give a hearty grip which betokened a kind-hearted feeling for all....

"One of his gifts was that of mezzotint drawing, and he gave instruction in this branch. I was one of his pupils in this, and have now the picture of a cross upon which he did some shading and put on the finishing touches. Upon the margin is written, in the hand of the noted teacher, his own name and his pupil's. There are also two other drawings, one of a large European bird on the bough of a tree, and the other a church-yard scene in winter, done by him at that time. In those days the faculty and pupils were wont to call him 'the second Webster,' and the remark was common, 'He will fill the White House yet.' In the Lyceum, he early took rank far above the others as a speaker and debater.

"During the month of June the entire school went in carriages to their annual grove meeting at Randolph, some twenty-five miles away. On this trip he was the life of the party, occasionally bursting out in an eloquent strain at the sight of a bird or a trailing vine, or a venerable giant of the forest. He would repeat poetry by the hour, having a very retentive memory."

The college library contained about two thousand volumes, and here Garfield read systematically and topically, a habit which continued through life, and made him master of every subject which he touched. Tennyson's poetry became, like the Bible, his daily study.

Mr. J. M. Bundy, in his Life of Garfield, said, years later, "His house at Washington is a workshop, in which the tools are always kept within immediate reach. Although books overrun his house from top to bottom, his library contains the working material on which he mainly depends. And the amount of material is enormous. Large numbers of scrap-books that have been accumulating for over twenty years in number and value—made up with an eye to what either is or may become useful, which would render the collection of priceless value to the library of any first-class newspaper establishment—are so perfectly arranged and indexed that their owner, with his all-retentive memory, can turn in a moment to the facts that may be needed for almost any conceivable emergency in debate. These are supplemented by diaries that preserve Garfield's multifarious, political, scientific, literary, and religious inquiries, studies, and readings. And, to make the machinery of rapid work complete, he has a large box, containing sixty-three different drawers, each properly labelled, in which he places newspaper cuttings, documents, and slips of paper, and from which he can pull out what he wants as easily as an organist can play on the stops of his instrument."

In Hiram College he formed an intellectual friendship with a fellow-student to whose inspiring help he testified gratefully to the end of his life; Miss Almeda A. Booth, eight years his senior, a brilliant and noble woman, pledged to "virgin widowhood" by the death of the young man to whom she was promised in marriage. Twenty years later, Garfield said, in a memorial address at Hiram College, "On my own behalf I take this occasion to say that for her generous and powerful aid, so often and so efficiently rendered, for her quick and never failing sympathy, and for her intelligent, unselfish, and unswerving friendship, I owe her a debt of gratitude and affection for the payment of which the longest term of life would have been too short.... I remember that she and I were members of the class that began Xenophon's 'Anabasis' in the fall of 1852. Near the close of that term I also began to teach in the Eclectic College, and, thereafter, like her, could keep up my studies only outside of my own class hours. In mathematics and the physical sciences I was far behind her; but we were nearly at the same place in Greek and Latin, each having studied them about three terms. She had made her home at President Hayden's almost from the first; and I became a member of his family at the beginning of the winter term of 1852-53. Thereafter, for nearly two years, she and I studied together, and recited in the same classes (frequently without other associates) till we had nearly completed the classical course....

"During the fall of 1853 she read one hundred pages of Herodotus, and about the same of Livy. During that term, also, Professors Dunshee and Hull, Miss Booth, and I met at her room two evenings of each week to make a joint translation of the Book of Romans. Professor Dunshee contributed his studies of the German commentators De Wette and Tholuck; and each of the translators made some special study for each meeting. How nearly we completed the translation I do not remember; but I do remember that the contributions and criticisms of Miss Booth were remarkable for suggestiveness and sound judgment. Our work was more thorough than rapid, for I find this entry in my diary for December

15, 1853: 'Translation Society sat three hours at Miss Booth's room, and agreed upon the translation of nine verses.'

"During the winter term of 1853-54 she continued to read Livy, and also the whole of Demosthenes 'On the Crown.' During the spring term of 1854 she read the 'Germania' and 'Agricola' of Tacitus and a portion of Hesiod."

To Garfield she was another Margaret Fuller. "I venture to assert that in native powers of mind, in thoroughness and breadth of scholarship, in womanly sweetness of spirit, and in the quantity and quality of effective, unselfish work done, she has not been excelled by any American woman.... I can name twenty or thirty books which will forever be doubly precious to me because they were read and discussed in company with her.... She was always ready to aid any friend with her best efforts. When I was in the hurry of preparing for a debate with Mr. Denton, in 1858, she read not less than eight or ten volumes, and made admirable notes for me on those points which related to the topics of discussion. In the autumn of 1859 she read a large portion of Blackstone's 'Commentaries,' and enjoyed with keenest relish the strength of the author's thought and the beauty of his style. From the rich stores of her knowledge she gave with unselfish generosity. The foremost students had no mannish pride that made them hesitate to ask her assistance and counsel. In preparing their orations and debates they eagerly sought her suggestions and criticisms....

"It is quite probable that John Stuart Mill has exaggerated the extent to which his own mind and works were influenced by Harriet Mill. I should reject his opinion on that subject, as a delusion, did I not know from my own experience, as well as that of hundreds of Hiram students, how great a power Miss Booth exercised over the culture and opinions of her friends."

The influence of such a woman upon an intellectual young man can scarcely be estimated, or over-estimated. The world is richer and nobler for such women. Garfield never forgot her influence. The year he died, he said at a Williams College banquet held in Cleveland, January 10, 1881: "I am glad to say, reverently, in the presence of the many ladies here to-night, that I owe to a woman, who has long since been asleep, perhaps a higher debt intellectually than I owe to any one else. After that comes my debt to Williams College."

He used to say, "Give me a log hut with only a simple bench, Mark Hopkins on one end and I on the other, and you may have all the buildings, apparatus, and libraries without him."

After two years at Hiram College, Garfield decided to enter some eastern college, and wrote to Yale, Brown, and Williams. Their replies are shown in his letter to a friend at this time. "Their answers are now before me. All tell me I can graduate in two years. They are all brief business notes; but President Hopkins concludes with this sentence: 'If you come here, we shall be glad to do what we can for you.' Other things being so nearly equal, this sentence, which seems to be a kind of friendly grasp of the hand, has settled the question for me. I shall start for Williams next week." A kind sentence gave to Williams a distinguished honor for all coming years.

Garfield had not only paid his way while at Hiram, but he had saved three hundred and fifty dollars for his course at Williams. Here he earned money, as he had at Hiram, by teaching, and borrowed a few hundreds from Dr. J. P. Robinson of Cleveland, Ohio, offering a life insurance policy as security.

In college, says Dr. Hopkins, "as General Garfield was broad in his scholarship, so was he in his sympathies. No one thought of him as a recluse or as bookish. Not given to athletic sports, he was fond of them. His mind was open to the impression of natural scenery, and, as his constitution was vigorous, he knew well the fine points on the mountains around us. He was also social in his disposition, both giving and inspiring confidence. So true is this of his intercourse with the officers of the college, as well as with others, that he was never even suspected of anything low or trickish.... General Garfield gave himself to study with a zest and delight wholly unknown to those who find in it a routine. A religious man and a man of principle, he pursued of his own accord the ends proposed by the institution. He was prompt, frank, manly, social, in his tendencies; combining active exercise with habits of study, and thus did for himself what it is the object of a college to enable every young man to do,—he made himself a MAN."

When Garfield was at Williams, the slavery question had become the exciting topic of the day. Preston Brooks' attack on Charles Sumner had aroused the indignation of the students, who called a meeting, at which Garfield made an eloquent and powerful speech. At his graduation in 1856, when he was twenty-five, he delivered the metaphysical oration, the highest honor awarded. He now returned to Hiram College, having been appointed professor of Greek and Latin. At once he began his work with zest. He said later: "I have taken more solid comfort in the thing itself, and received more moral recompense and stimulus in after life from capturing young men for an education than from anything else in the world.

"As I look back over my life thus far, I think of nothing that so fills me with pleasure as the planning of these sieges, the revolving in my mind of plans for scaling the walls of the fortress; of gaining access to the inner soul-life, and at last seeing the besieged party won to a fuller appreciation of himself, to a higher conception of life and of the part he is to bear in it. The principal guards which I have found it necessary to overcome in gaining these victories are the parents or guardians of the young men themselves. I particularly remember two such instances of capturing young men from their parents. Both of those boys are to-day educators, of wide reputation,—one president of a college, the other high in the ranks of graded-school managers. Neither, in my opinion, would to-day have been above the commonest walks of life unless I, or some one else, had captured him. There is a period in every young man's life when a very small thing will turn him one way or the other. He is distrustful of himself, and uncertain as to what he should do. His parents are poor, perhaps, and argue that he has more education than they ever obtained, and that it is enough. These parents are sometimes a little too anxious in regard to what their boys are going to do when they get through with their college course. They talk to the young man too much, and I have noticed that the boy who will make the best man is sometimes most ready to doubt himself. I always remember the turning period in my own life, and pity a young man at this stage from the bottom of my heart. One of the young men I refer to came to me on the closing day of the spring term, and bade me good-by at my study. I noticed that he awkwardly lingered after I expected him to go, and had turned to my writing again.

"'I suppose you will be back again in the fall, Henry,' I said, to fill in the vacuum. He did not answer, and, turning toward him, I noticed that his eyes were filled with tears, and that his countenance was undergoing contortions of pain. He at length managed to stammer out, 'No, I am not coming back to Hiram any more. Father says I have got education enough, and that he needs me to work on the farm; that education don't help along a farmer any.'

"'Is your father here?' I asked, almost as much affected by the statement as the boy himself. He was a peculiarly bright boy,—one of those strong, awkward, bashful, blond, large-headed fellows, such as make men. He was not a prodigy by any means; but he knew what work meant, and, when he had won a thing by true endeavor, he knew its value.

"'Yes; father is here, and is taking my things home for good,' said the boy, more affected than ever.

"'Well, don't feel badly,' I said. 'Please tell him Mr. Garfield would like to see him at his study, before he leaves the village. Don't tell him that it is about you, but simply that I want to see him.' In the course of half an hour the old gentleman, a robust specimen of a

Western Reserve Yankee, came into the room and awkwardly sat down. I knew something of the man before, and I thought I knew how to begin. I shot right at the bull's-eye immediately.

"'So you have come up to take Henry home with you, have you?' The old gentleman answered, 'Yes.' 'I sent for you because I wanted to have a little talk with you about Henry's future. He is coming back again in the fall, I hope?'

"'Wal, I think not. I don't reckon I can afford to send him any more. He's got eddication enough for a farmer already, and I notice that when they git too much they sorter git lazy. Yer eddicated farmers are humbugs. Henry's got so far 'long now that he'd rather hev his head in a book than be workin'. He don't take no interest in the stock nor in the farm improvements. Everybody else is dependent in this world on the farmer, and I think that we've got too many eddicated fellows setting around now for the farmers to support.'

"'I am sorry to hear you talk so,' I said; 'for really I consider Henry one of the brightest and most faithful students I have ever had. I have taken a very deep interest in him. What I wanted to say to you was, that the matter of educating him has largely been a constant outgo thus far, but, if he is permitted to come next fall term, he will be far enough advanced so that he can teach school in the winter, and begin to help himself and you along. He can earn very little on the farm in the winter, and he can get very good wages teaching. How does that strike you?'

"The idea was a new and good one to him. He simply remarked, 'Do you really think he can teach next winter?'

"'I should think so, certainly,' I replied. 'But, if he cannot do so then, he can in a short time, anyhow.'

"'Wal, I will think on it. He wants to come back bad enough, and I guess I'll have to let him. I never thought of it that way afore.'

"I knew I was safe. It was the financial question that troubled the old gentleman, and I knew that would be overcome when Henry got to teaching, and could earn his money himself. He would then be so far along, too, that he could fight his own battles. He came all right the next fall, and, after finishing at Hiram, graduated at an eastern college."

One secret of Garfield's success in teaching was his deep interest in the young. He said, "I feel a profounder reverence for a boy than for a man. I never meet a ragged boy of the street without feeling that I may owe him a salute, for I know not what possibilities may be buttoned up under his shabby coat. When I meet you in the full flush of mature life, I see nearly all there is of you; but among these boys are the great men of the future, the heroes of the next

205

generation, the philosophers, the statesmen, the philanthropists, the great reformers and moulders of the next age. Therefore, I say, there is a peculiar charm to me in the exhibitions of young people engaged in the business of an education."

He made himself a student with his students. He said: "I shall give you a series of lectures upon history, beginning next week. I do this not alone to assist you; the preparation for the lectures will compel me to study history."

He was always a worker. "When I get into a place that I can easily fill, I always feel like shoving out of it into one that requires of me more exertion."

His active mind was not content with teaching. He delivered lectures in the neighboring towns on geology, illustrated by charts of his own making; upon "Walter Scott;" Carlyle's "Frederick the Great;" the "Character of the German People;" government, and the topics of the times. He preached almost every Sabbath in some Disciple church. A year after his return from Williams he was promoted to the presidency of Hiram College.

In 1858, when he was twenty-seven, he married Lucretia Rudolph, whom he had known at Geauga Seminary, and who was his pupil in Latin and Greek at Hiram. He had been engaged to her four years previously, when he entered Williams, she being a year his junior. She was his companion in study, as well as domestic life, and helped him onward in his great career.

This same year, 1858, he entered his name as a student at law, with a Cleveland firm, carrying on his studies at home, and fitted himself for the bar in the usual time devoted by those who have no other work in hand.

The following year, having taken an active part in the Republican campaign for John C. Fremont for the presidency, Garfield was chosen State senator. The same year Williams College invited him to deliver the master's oration on Commencement day. On the journey thither, he visited Quebec, taking with his wife their first pleasure trip. Only eight years before this he was ringing the bell at Hiram. Promotion had come rapidly, but deservedly.

In the Legislature he naturally took a prominent part. Lincoln had been elected and had issued his call for seventy-five thousand men. Garfield, in an eloquent speech, moved, "That Ohio contribute twenty thousand men, and three million dollars, as the quota of the State." The motion was enthusiastically carried.

Governor Dennison appointed Garfield colonel of the Forty-second Ohio Regiment, and he left the Senate for the battlefield, nearly one hundred Hiram students enlisting under him. At once he began to study military tactics in earnest. He organized a school among the officers, and kept the men at drill till they were efficient in the art of war. January 10, 1862, he fought the battle of Middle Creek, with eleven hundred men, driving General Marshall out of Eastern Kentucky, with five thousand men. The battle raged for five hours, sometimes a desperate hand-to-hand fight. General Buell said in his official report of Garfield and his regiment: "They have overcome formidable difficulties in the character of the country, the condition of the roads, and the inclemency of the season, and, without artillery, have in several engagements, terminating in the battle of Middle Creek, driven the enemy from his intrenched positions and forced him back into the mountains, with the loss of a large amount of baggage and stores, and many of his men killed and captured. These services have called into action the highest qualities of a soldier—fortitude, perseverance, and courage." After this battle, President Lincoln made Garfield a brigadier-general.

Says Mr. Bundy: "Having cleared out Humphrey Marshall's forces, Garfield moved his command to Piketon, one hundred and twenty miles above the mouth of the Big Sandy, from which place he covered the whole region about with expeditions, breaking up rebel camps and perfecting his work. Finally, in that poor and wretched country, his supplies gave out, and, as usual, taking care of the most important matter himself, he went to the Ohio River for supplies, got them, seized a steamer, and loaded it. But there was an unprecedented freshet, navigation was very perilous, and no captain or pilot could be induced to take charge of the boat. Garfield at once availed himself of his canal-boat experience, took charge of the boat, stood at the helm for forty out of forty-eight hours, piloted the steamer through an untried channel full of dangerous eddies and wild currents, and saved his command from starvation."

Later, Garfield became chief of General Rosecrans' staff, was in the dreadful battle of Chickamauga, and was made major-general "for gallant and meritorious services" in that battle. Rosecrans said: "All my staff merited my warm approbation for ability, zeal, and devotion to duty; but I am sure they will not consider it invidious if I especially mention Brigadier-General Garfield, ever active, prudent, and sagacious. I feel much indebted to him for both counsel and assistance in the administration of this army. He possesses the energy and the instinct of a great commander."

In the summer of 1862 the Nineteenth Congressional District of Ohio elected Garfield to Congress. He hesitated about leaving the army, but, being urged by his friends that it was his duty to serve his country in the House of Representatives, he took his seat December, 1863. Among such men as Colfax, Washburn, Conkling, Allison, and others, he at once took an honorable position. He was made chairman of military affairs, then of banking and currency, of appropriations, and other committees.

On the slavery question he had always been outspoken. He said, on the constitutional amendment abolishing slavery: "All along the coast of our political sea these victims of slavery lie like stranded wrecks broken on the headlands of freedom. How lately did its advocates, with impious boldness, maintain it as God's own; to be venerated and cherished as divine! It was another and higher form of civilization. It was the holy evangel of America dispensing its mercies to a benighted race, and destined to bear countless blessings to the wilderness of the West. In its mad arrogance it lifted its hand to strike down the fabric of the Union, and since that fatal day it has been 'a fugitive and a vagabond in the earth.' Like the spirit that Jesus cast out, it has, since then, been 'seeking rest and finding none.' It has sought in all the corners of the republic to find some hiding-place in which to shelter itself from the death it so richly deserves. It sought an asylum in the untrodden territories of the West, but with a whip of scorpions indignant freemen drove it thence. I do not believe that a loyal man can now be found who would consent that it should again enter them. It has no hope of harbor there. It found no protection or favor in the hearts or consciences of the freemen of the republic, and has fled for its last hope of safety behind the shield of the Constitution. We propose to follow it there, and drive it thence, as Satan was exiled from heaven.... To me it is a matter of great surprise that gentlemen on the other side should wish to delay the death of slavery. I can only account for it on the ground of long continued familiarity and friendship.... Has she not betrayed and slain men enough? Are they not strewn over a thousand battle-fields? Is not this Moloch already gorged with the bloody feast? Its best friends know that its final hour is fast approaching. The avenging gods are on its track. Their feet are not now, as of old, shod with wool, nor slow and stately stepping, but winged like Mercury's to bear the swift message of vengeance. No human power can avert the final catastrophe."

On the currency he spoke repeatedly and earnestly. He carefully studied English financial history, and mastered the French and German languages that he might study their works on political economy and finance. Says Captain F. H. Mason, late of the Forty-second Ohio Regiment, in his sketch of Garfield, "In May, 1868, when the country was rapidly drifting into a hopeless confusion of ideas on financial subjects, and when several prominent statesmen had come forward with specious plans for creating 'absolute money' by putting the government stamp upon bank notes, and for paying off with this false currency the bonds which the nation had solemnly agreed to pay in gold, General Garfield stood up almost single-handed and faced the current with a speech which any statesman of this century might be proud to have written on his monument. It embraced twenty-three distinct but concurrent topics, and occupied in delivering an entire day's session of the House."

"For my own part," he said, "my course is taken. In view of all the facts of our situation, of all the terrible experiences of the past, both at home and abroad, and of the united testimony of the wisest and bravest statesmen who have lived and labored during the past century, it is my firm conviction that any considerable increase of the volume of our inconvertible paper money will shatter public credit, will paralyze public industry, and oppress the poor; and that the gradual restoration of our ancient standard of value will lead us by the safest and surest paths to national prosperity and the steady pursuits of peace."

Again he said: "I for one am not willing that my name shall be linked to the fate of a paper currency. I believe that any party which commits itself to paper money will go down amid the general disaster, covered with the curses of a ruined people.

"Mr. Speaker, I remember that on the monument of Queen Elizabeth, where her glories were recited and her honors summed up, among the last and the highest recorded as the climax of her honors was this: that she had restored the money of her kingdom to its just value. And when this House shall have done its work, when it shall have brought back values to their proper standard, it will deserve a monument."

On the tariff question, General Garfield took the side of protection, yet was no extremist. His oft reiterated belief was, "As an abstract theory, the doctrine of free trade seems to be universally true, but as a question of practicability, under a government like ours, the protective system seems to be indispensable."

He said in Congress: "We have seen that one extreme school of economists would place the price of all manufactured articles in the hands of foreign producers by rendering it impossible for our manufacturers to compete with them; while the other extreme school, by making it impossible for the foreigner to sell his competing wares in our market, would give the people no immediate check upon the prices which our manufacturers might fix for their products. I disagree with both these extremes. I hold that a properly adjusted competition between home and foreign products is the best gauge by which to regulate international trade. Duties should be so high that our manufacturers can fairly compete with the foreign product, but not so high as to enable them to drive out the foreign article, enjoy a monopoly of the trade, and regulate the price as they please. This is my doctrine of protection. If Congress pursues this line of policy steadily, we shall, year by year, approach more nearly to the basis of free trade, because we shall be more nearly able to compete with other nations on equal terms. I am for a protection which leads to ultimate free trade. I am for that free trade which can only be achieved through a reasonable protection.... If all the kingdoms of the world should become the kingdom of the Prince of Peace, then I admit that universal free trade ought to prevail. But that blessed era is yet too remote to be made the basis of the practical legislation of to-day. We are not yet members of 'the parliament of man, the federation of the world.' For the present, the world is divided into separate nationalities; and that other divine command still applies to our situation, 'He that provideth not for his own household has denied the faith, and is worse than an infidel,' and until that latter era arrives patriotism must supply the place of universal brotherhood."

Again he said: "Those arts that enable our nation to rise in the scale of civilization bring their blessings to all, and patriotic citizens will cheerfully bear a fair share of the burden necessary to make their country great and self-sustaining. I will defend a tariff that is national in its aims, that protects and sustains those interests without which the nation cannot become great and self-sustaining.... So important, in my view, is the ability of the nation to manufacture all these articles necessary to arm, equip, and clothe our people, that if it could not be secured in any other way I would vote to pay money out of the federal treasury to maintain government iron and steel, woollen and cotton mills, at whatever cost. Were we to neglect these great interests and depend upon other nations, in what a condition of helplessness would we find ourselves when we should be again involved in war with the very nations on whom we were depending to furnish us these supplies? The system adopted by our fathers is wiser, for it so encourages the great national industries as to make it possible at all times for our people to equip themselves for war, and at the same time increase their intelligence and skill so as to make them better fitted for all the duties of citizenship in war and in peace. We provide for the common defence by a system which promotes the general welfare.... I believe that we ought to seek that point of stable equilibrium somewhere between a prohibitory tariff on the one hand and a tariff that gives no protection on the other. What is that point of stable equilibrium? In my judgment, it is this; a rate so high that foreign producers cannot flood our markets and break down our home manufacturers, but not so high as to keep them altogether out, enabling our manufacturers to combine and raise the prices, nor so high as to stimulate an unnatural and unhealthy growth of manufactures.

"In other words, I would have the duty so adjusted that every great American industry can fairly live and make fair profits, and yet so low that, if our manufacturers attempted to put up prices unreasonably, the competition from abroad would come in and bring down prices to a fair rate."

On special occasions, such as his eulogies on Lincoln and General Thomas, and on Decoration Day at Arlington Heights, Garfield was very eloquent. At the latter place, he said: "If silence is ever golden, it must be here, beside the graves of fifteen thousand men, whose lives were more significant than speech, and whose death was a poem the music of which can never be sung. With words, we make promises, plight faith, praise virtue. Promises may not be kept; plighted faith may be broken; and vaunted virtue may be only the cunning mask of vice. We do not know one promise these men made, one pledge they gave, one word they spoke; but we do know they summed up and perfected, by one supreme act, the highest virtues of men and citizens. For love of country they accepted death, and thus resolved all doubts, and made immortal their patriotism and their virtue.

"For the noblest man that lives there still remains a conflict. He must still withstand the assaults of time and fortune; must still be assailed with temptations before which lofty natures have fallen. But with these, the conflict ended, the victory was won, when death stamped on them the great seal of heroic character, and closed a record which years can never blot."

Professor B. A. Hinsdale, the intimate friend of Garfield, says, in his "Hiram College Memorial," "General Garfield's readiness on all occasions has often been remarked. Probably some have attributed this readiness to the inspiration of genius. The explanation lies partly in his genius, but much more in his indefatigable work. He treasured up knowledge of all kinds. 'You never know,' he would say, 'how soon you will need it.' Then he forecasted occasions, and got ready to meet them. One hot day in July, 1876, he brought to his Washington house an old copy of The Congressional Globe. Questioned, he said, 'I have been told, confidentially, that Mr. Lamar is going to make a speech in the House on general politics, to influence the presidential canvass. If he does, I shall reply to him. Mr. Lamar was a member of the House before the war; and I am going to read some of his old speeches, and get into his mind.' Mr. Lamar made his speech August 2, and Mr. Garfield replied August 4. Men expressed surprise at the fulness and completeness of the reply, delivered on such short notice. But to one knowing his habits of mind, especially to one who had the aforesaid conversation with him, the whole matter was as light as day. His genius was emphatically the genius of preparation."

Both in Congress and in the army Garfield gave a portion of each day to the classics, especially to his favorite, Horace. He was always an omnivorous reader.

In 1880, he was elected United States senator. After the election he said, "During the twenty years that I have been in public life, almost eighteen of it in the Congress of the United States, I have tried to do one thing. Whether I was mistaken or otherwise, it has been the plan of my life to follow my convictions, at whatever personal cost to myself. I have represented for many years a district in Congress whose approbation I greatly desired; but, though it may seem, perhaps, a little egotistical to say it, I yet desired still more the approbation of one person, and his name was Garfield. He is the only man that I am compelled to sleep with, and eat with, and live with, and die with; and if I could not have his approbation I should have had bad companionship."

All these years the home life had been helpful and beautiful. Of his seven children, two were sleeping in the Hiram church-yard. Five, Harry, James, Mollie, Irvin, and Abram, made the Washington home a place of cheer in winter, and the summer home, at Mentor, Ohio, a few miles from Hiram, a place of rest and pleasure. Here Garfield, beloved by his neighbors, ploughed and sewed and reaped, as when a boy. His mother lived in his family, happy in his success.

When the national Republican convention met in June, 1880, at Chicago, the names of several presidential candidates came before the people,—Grant, Blaine, and others. Garfield nominated John Sherman, of Ohio, in a chaste and eloquent speech. He said: "I have witnessed the extraordinary scenes of this convention with deep solicitude. No emotion touches my heart more quickly than a sentiment in honor of a great and noble character; but, as I sat on these seats and witnessed these demonstrations, it seemed to me you were a human ocean in a tempest.

"I have seen the sea lashed into fury and tossed into spray, and its grandeur moves the soul of the dullest man; but I remember that it is not the billows but the calm level of the sea from which all heights and depths are measured. When the storm has passed and the hour of calm settles on the ocean, when the sunlight bathes its smooth surface, then the astronomer and surveyor takes the level from which he measures all terrestrial heights and depths.

"Gentlemen of the convention, your present temper may not mark the healthful pulse of our people. When our enthusiasm has passed, when the emotions of this hour have subsided, we shall find that calm level of public opinion, below the storm, from which the thoughts of a mighty people are to be measured, and by which their final action will be determined. Not here in this brilliant circle, where fifteen thousand men and women are assembled, is the destiny of the Republican party to be decreed. Not here, where I see the enthusiastic faces of seven hundred and fifty-six delegates, waiting to cast their votes into the urn and determine the choice of the republic, but by four million Republican firesides, where the thoughtful voters, with wives and children about them, with the calm thoughts inspired by love of home and country, with the history of the past, the hopes of the future, and reverence for the great men who have adorned and blessed our nation in days gone by burning in their hearts,—there God prepares the verdict which will determine the wisdom of our work to-night. Not in Chicago, in the heat of June, but at the ballot-boxes of the republic, in the quiet of November, after the silence of deliberate judgment, will this question be settled."

The thousands were at fever-heat hour after hour, in their intense excitement. After thirty-four ineffectual ballots, on the thirty-fifth, fifty votes were given for Garfield. The tide had turned at last. The delegates of State after State gathered around the man from Ohio, holding their flags over him, while the bands played, "Rally round the flag, boys," and fifteen thousand people shouted their thanksgiving for the happy choice. Outside the great hall, cannons were fired, and the crowded streets sent up their cheers. From that moment Garfield belonged to the nation, and was its idol.

On March 4, 1881, in the presence of a hundred thousand people, the boy born in the Orange wilderness was inaugurated President of the United States. None of us who were present will ever forget the beauty of his address from the steps of the national Capitol, or the kiss given to white-haired mother and devoted wife at the close. Afterward, the great procession, three hours in passing a given point, was reviewed by President Garfield from a stand erected in front of the White House.

Four months after this scene, on July 2, 1881, the nation was thrilled with sorrow. As General Garfield and his Secretary of State, James G. Blaine, arm in arm, were entering the Baltimore & Potomac Railroad depot, two pistol shots were fired; one passing through Garfield's coat-sleeve, the other into his body. He fell heavily to the floor, and was borne to the White House. The assassin was Charles Guiteau, a half-crazed aspirant for office, entirely unknown to the President. The man was hanged.

Through four long months the nation prayed, and hoped, and agonized for the life of its beloved President. Gifts poured in from every part of the Union, but gifts were of no avail. On September 5, Garfield was carried to Elberon, Long Branch, New Jersey, where, in the Francklyn Cottage, he seemed to revive as he looked out upon the sea, the sea he had longed for in his boyhood. The nation took heart. But two weeks later, at thirty-five minutes past ten, on the evening of September 19, the anniversary of the battle of Chickamauga, the President passed from an unconscious state to the consciousness of immortality. At ten minutes past ten he had said to General Swaim, who was standing beside him, as he put his hand upon his heart, "I have great pain here."

The whole world sympathized with America in her great sorrow. Queen Victoria telegraphed to Mrs. Garfield: "Words cannot express the deep sympathy I feel with you at this terrible moment. May God support and comfort you, as he alone can."

On September 21, the body of the President was taken to Washington. At the Princeton Station, three hundred students from the college, with uncovered heads, strewed the track and covered the funeral car with flowers. At the Capitol, where he had so recently listened to the cheers of the people at his inauguration, one hundred thousand passed in silence before his open coffin. The casket was covered with flowers; one wreath bearing a card from England's queen, with the words: "Queen Victoria, to the memory of the late President Garfield, an expression of her sorrow and sympathy with Mrs. Garfield and the American nation."

The body was borne to Cleveland, the whole train of cars being draped in black. Fifty thousand persons assembled at the station, and followed the casket to a catafalque on the public square. During the Sabbath, an almost countless throng passed beside the beloved dead. On Monday, September 26, through beautiful Euclid Avenue, the body was borne six miles, to its final resting-place. Every house was draped in mourning. Streets were arched with exquisite flowers on a background of black. One city alone, Cincinnati, sent two carloads of flowers. Among the many floral designs was a ladder of white immortelles, with eleven rounds, bearing the words: "Chester," "Hiram," "Williams," "Ohio Senate," "Colonel," "General," "Congress," "United States Senate," "President," "Martyr."

After appropriate exercises, the sermon being preached by Rev. Isaac Errett, D.D., of Cincinnati, according to a promise made years before, the casket, followed by a procession five miles long, was carried to the cemetery. It was estimated that a quarter of a million people were gathered along the streets; not idle sight-seers, but men and women who loved the boy, and revered the man who had come to distinguished honor in their midst.

Not only in Cleveland were memorial services held. The Archbishop of Canterbury spoke touching words in London. In Liverpool, in Manchester, in Glasgow, and hundreds of other cities, public services were held. Messages of condolence were sent from many of the crowned heads of Europe.

Under the white stone monument in Lake View Cemetery, the statesman has been laid to rest. For centuries the tomb will tell to the thousands upon thousands who visit it the story of struggle and success; of work, of hope, of courage, of devotion to duty. Like Abraham Lincoln, Garfield was born in a log cabin, battled with poverty, was honest, great-hearted, a lover of America, and, like him, a martyr to the republic. To the world both deaths seemed unbearable calamities, but nations, like individuals, are chastened by sorrow, and learn great lessons through great trials. "Now we know in part; but then shall we know even as also we are known."

www.ingramcontent.com/pod-product-compliance
Lightning Source LLC
LaVergne TN
LVHW030632080426
835511LV00020B/3442